Melissa Graham was born in Sunderland, in the north of England, and grew up only yards from a railway line. Along with half of County Durham, she claims to be a direct descendant of George Stephenson, the Father of Railways.

In 1988 she ventured south to read French and Spanish at Cambridge University. Subsequent travels have taken her rather further afield and have included large tracts of Europe, Southern Africa, South East Asia and North America.

Researching this guide in Canada she travelled from the Atlantic to the Pacific and north to Hudson Bay covering 15km by dog sled, 25km on foot, 35km by car, 45km by bus and 11,326km by rail.

Trans-Canada Rail Guide
First edition 1996
Reprinted with amendments 1997

Publisher
Trailblazer Publications
The Old Manse, Tower Rd, Hindhead, Surrey, GU26 6SU, UK
Fax (+44) 01428-607571
E-mail: trailblazer@compuserve.com

British Library Cataloguing in Publication Data
A catalogue record for this book is available from the British Library

ISBN 1-873756-05-4

Editor: Patricia Major
Typesetting: Bryn Thomas and Anna Jacomb-Hood
Index: Jane Thomas

Printed and bound by Technographic Design & Print Ltd, Colchester, Essex, UK

TRANS-CANADA RAIL GUIDE

MELISSA GRAHAM

TRAILBLAZER PUBLICATIONS

Acknowledgements

This project would not have been possible without the support and assistance of numerous people. Among these I am particularly indebted to Malcolm Andrews and Louise Beauchamp of VIA Rail, and to Sue Armstrong, Dave Atherton and Andrew Hitchins of Leisurail. Thanks also to Carol Goddard of the Canadian High Commission; to John Bolton of the Visit Canada Centre for his encyclopaedic knowledge of the country; to Ruth Roberts of British Columbia House and to Jane Whigham and Paul Roberts of Air Canada.

Over in Canada, I'm grateful to the many people who helped me along the way, especially: Kathy Murphy of the Nova Scotia Department of Tourism; the staff at the Delta Barrington (Halifax); Glen Hamilton of VIA Rail (Halifax); Caroline Samson and Jan Schöning of the Château Frontenac (Quebec); Richard Séguin of the Office du Tourisme de Québec; Pierre Tougas and Christine St-Pierre of the Greater Montreal Convention and Tourism Bureau; John Hamilton of the Metropolitan Toronto Visitors' Association; Meryl Baron and Tom Smith of the Royal York Hotel; Collette Fontaine of Travel Manitoba and Sandra Malcomson of Tourism Winnipeg; the staff at the Sheraton Winnipeg; Lorena Tyschuk of Edmonton Tourism; Tammy Phillips of CPR Hotels and Resorts in Vancouver, Tom Ryan of Tourism BC and the staff at the Coast Hotel in Prince Rupert; for permission to use the photograph on the cover: VIA Rail, and for permission to use the photograph opposite p64: Rocky Mountaineer Railtours. Extra special thanks go to Barbara Maclean in Edmonton and to Michael Maclean in Vancouver for their warm hospitality.

Back in the UK, I'm particularly grateful to Bryn Thomas for the hard work put into turning my manuscript into a book. Thanks also to Patricia Major for editing the text, Anna Jacomb-Hood for typesetting and Jane Thomas for compiling the index. A large debt is owed to Charlie Ball for a spontaneous phone call in the small hours of the morning (and to Dominic S-J for answering it). And also to Martin Storey for all the gear (how many beers do I owe you?). Finally, enormous thanks to Richard for his unflagging enthusiasm and support and to my family for all their encouragement.

A request

The author and publisher have tried to ensure that this guide is as accurate and up-to-date as possible. However things change: prices rise, rail services are extended or cut back, hotels open and close. If you notice any omissions or changes that should be included in the next edition of this book, please write to Melissa Graham at Trailblazer Publications (address on p2). A free copy of the next edition will be sent to persons making a significant contribution.

Front cover: VIA Rail's service between Toronto and Vancouver, known as *The Canadian*, is operated three times a week in both directions.

CONTENTS

INTRODUCTION

The overwhelming thing about Canada is its sheer size. How can one train ride in a single country take three whole days and three whole nights? And you've still got further to go. No other mode of transport conveys such an acute sense of Canada's vastness, of its beautiful, desolate, wide-open spaces. Endless stretches of track take you through a wilderness scarcely touched by man. You can travel for hours without seeing a road or a house, or indeed any sign of habitation – it's an incredible, almost haunting, experience. Back in 1872 an early traveller wrote a book about Canada's interior called *The Great Lone Land*. It captured the North American imagination and became an instant best-seller. Today, much of Canada is still a 'great lone land' that continues to fire the imagination of the modern traveller; the huge iron artery stretching across the continent is truly the best way to cross it.

It is also the reason why this massive country exists at all. When the 'Dominion of Canada' was created in 1867 it was no more than a set of loosely connected colonies with no sense of unity or nationhood. It was, moreover, under a very real threat of being swallowed up by its powerful southern neighbour. The railroad was the single most important reason why this never happened: it gave the new country its life-blood and bound the provinces together into a transcontinental nation. When the last spike was driven in on 7 November 1885 it paved the way for rapid expansion, mass immigration and economic boom. Urban development ran parallel to the tracks and the stops along the line became the backbone of a new nation – which makes a rail trip today a fascinating journey into this young country's history.

What you'll probably remember about the trip more than anything, though, is the dazzling scenery you travel through. In 1885 the General Manager of the Canadian Pacific Railway Company realised that travellers would flock from all corners of the world to ride through such magnificent landscape. 'If we cannot export the scenery,' he declared, 'we shall have to import the tourists!' And tourists have quite joyfully been imported ever since. Imagine the snow-capped peaks towering right over the tracks; the sweeping panoramas of lakes, waterfalls and glaciers gliding past you. Better still, imagine looking out of the window onto a jade-green lake to find yourself staring at a moose. The whole thing takes your breath away.

On top of all this, a rail ride across Canada is a supremely relaxing experience, a rare joy in today's climate of rapid communications and jet-travel. In the words of Robert Louis Stevenson 'the train disturbs so little the scenery through which it takes us, that our heart becomes full of the placidity and stillness of the country.' Nowhere is this more true than in Canada.

PART 1: PLANNING YOUR TRIP

Routes and costs

Travel a thousand miles up a great river; more than another thousand miles along great lakes; a thousand miles across rolling prairies; and another thousand through woods and over the great ranges of mountains, and you have travelled from Ocean to Ocean. Rev Grant, *Ocean to Ocean*

ROUTE OPTIONS

Canada's transcontinental through service runs three times a week between Toronto and Vancouver. You can take connecting trains to extend or alter your route in several ways. For a start, if you want to make it a truly transcontinental journey from coast to coast, you can begin or end it in Halifax on the Atlantic. Alternatively you can make Montreal or Quebec City the eastern terminus of your trip. Another option is to start or end in Prince Rupert on the Pacific instead of Vancouver; this is very popular with travellers who want to combine their rail trip with the Inside Passage ferry ride between Prince Rupert and Vancouver Island.

Once you've chosen your route, the next thing to decide is which direction to do it in. You see the same scenery whichever way you go since scheduling by VIA (the national passenger rail network) has east-bound and westbound trains travelling through the same stretches of the journey at night. That said, there's no doubt that the approach to the Rocky Mountains is far more dramatic from the prairies than from the Pacific. Furthermore, if you're interested in charting Canada's history on your rail trip, travelling from east to west follows the direction of railway development and settlement across the country. It's worth noting, howev-er, that westbound trains get booked up far earlier than eastbound trains.

Routes at a glance
- **Ocean**: Halifax to Montreal (p139)
- **Corridor**: Montreal to Toronto (p147)
- **Canadian**: Toronto to Vancouver (p151)
- **Skeena**: Jasper to Prince Rupert (p168)
- **Rocky Mountaineer**: privately run daylight-only train ride between Vancouver and Banff or Jasper (p177)
- **Hudson Bay**: Winnipeg to Churchill (p185)

BREAKING YOUR JOURNEY

Few people want to spend their entire holiday sitting on a train; fortunately, the railway takes you through some superb cities where you can break up your journey. Some of the best, notably **Vancouver**, **Toronto** and **Montreal**, are conveniently located at the beginning or end of a line, so spending time there is no problem as far as your ticket's concerned. There are, however, some restrictions on stopping off on a through ticket: only one break is allowed on the Canadian. If I had to recommend a single stopover en route it would be in **Jasper**, simply because the Rocky Mountains are so spectacular it would be a sin not to spend some time walking (or at least strolling) around them. If you want to make more than one break on the Canadian you need to buy separate tickets, which works out a bit more expensive. If you're happy to do this, then **Winnipeg** is a good place to stop off, not least because it's right in the middle of the journey and you're likely to be in serious need of a leg-stretch at this point. On the Skeena and the Corridor only Coach class passengers can break their journey on a through ticket but all passengers can make unlimited stopovers on the Hudson Bay and the Ocean. If you're travelling on the latter, you should definitely try to stop off at **Quebec City**; it's one of the most beautiful cities in Canada.

COSTS

Overall costs

The overall costs of a rail trip across Canada will vary enormously, depending mainly on when you go, how many nights you spend off the train (and the kind of accommodation you chose to stay in), the length of your rail journey, the type of ticket you buy and how you get to Canada.

Rail tickets from Toronto to Vancouver range from $305 (for a low season super saver) to $1216 (for a private bedroom in high season). The cheapest ticket from Halifax to Vancouver is $383 (using the Canrail Pass); the most expensive is $1502. When you add the cost of accommodation to these prices, it can sometimes work out cheaper to get a package deal, particularly if you plan to stay in upmarket accommodation. Packages start at £1175 for a 10-day trip from Toronto to Vancouver including flights from the UK, up to £3197 for a luxury 16-day trip from Halifax to Vancouver (including flights). If you're getting your own flights, there are some good charter deals from London: from £290 flying into Toronto and out of Vancouver; from £320 into Halifax and out of Vancouver. Equivalent Apex scheduled flights are around the £530 mark.

> **Prices in this book**
> Note that all prices are given in Canadian dollars, unless otherwise indicated. The current exchange rate is C$1 to US$0.70 or £0.45.

Hotel costs

Prices are nearly always per room rather than per person, with doubles only a couple of dollars or so more expensive than singles. This makes travelling in a pair extremely good value but lone travellers can end up feeling rather badly done by. Bear in mind that room rates are always quoted before taxes are added on (an extra 12%-14% – see p46).

Upmarket hotels tend to offer exceptionally good value compared to their European counterparts, with rooms going from around $120 – just $60 (£30) each if there are two of you. Note that it's cheaper to stay in these places at weekends, since weekday 'rack rates' are designed with business travellers in mind. Also, when you're quoted a room price, always ask if there are any 'specials' going, particularly during low or mid-season.

Typical **mid-range accommodation** will give you a double with a private bathroom for around $60-70, though prices can go down to $45 and up to $80 or more depending on location, the number of frills thrown in and the general state of the place.

Budget travellers can count on paying about $16 for a youth hostel bed in the smaller cities, and about $22 in the bigger places.

Room rates

Unless otherwise stated, the rates given in this book are for high season double rooms, before tax. Prices in most hotels drop significantly in low season (around November to April).

Rail tickets and fares

You can buy either a **coach class** ticket or a **sleeper ticket** (known as Silver & Blue class on the Canadian). Sleeping accommodation comes as a **section** (upper or lower birth), a **roomette** (for one person) or a **bedroom** (for two people). See p61 for a description of each type.

• **Discounts** There's a 10% discount on all fares for seniors (60 and over), youths (12 to 24) and students over 24 (with ID). For children aged 2-11 there's a 50% discount in Coach class and 25% in VIA 1. Children under 2 travel free (when not occupying a seat)

• **Canrail Pass** This gives twelve days of Coach class travel throughout the VIA national network within a 30-day period. Extra days can be bought, up to a maximum of three, and in some cases passengers can upgrade to sleeper class. Prices are as follows:

	High season (1 June-15 Oct)		Low season*	
	Basic pass	extra day	Basic pass	extra day
Adult	$540	$48	$369	$31
Concessions	$486	$43	$332	$28
			* 16 October to 31 May	

• **Fares** The fares for routes covered in this guide are given below. See previous page for information on discounts.

The Canadian: Silver & Blue (Sleeper)

Toronto to:	Peak (15 May-15 Oct)		Off-peak (rest of year)		Super Saver (rest of year)*	
	Section§	R/B†	Section§	R/B†	Section§	R/B†
Winnipeg	$483	$720	$363	$542	$289	$432
Edmonton	$626	$875	$470	$657	$376	$525
Jasper	$698	$973	$524	$731	$418	$583
Vancouver	$907	$1301	$681	$976	$545	$781
Edmonton to:						
Vancouver	$435	$672	$326	$504	$261	$403
Jasper to:						
Vancouver	$358	$580	$270	$435	$215	$348

* Super Saver tickets must be bought at least seven days in advance.
§ Supplement for lower berths: $50-100.   † R=Roomette; B=Bedroom

The Canadian: Coach class

Toronto to:	Peak (15 May-15 Oct)* Coach	Off-peak (rest of year)* Coach	Super Saver*† Coach
Winnipeg	$241	$181	$144
Edmonton	$362	$271	$217
Jasper	$412	$309	$247
Vancouver	$503	$377	$302
Edmonton to:			
Vancouver	$198	$148	$118
Jasper to:			
Vancouver	$142	$107	$85

† Dates as for off-peak but must be bought at least seven days in advance.

The Ocean – Halifax to Montreal

	Peak*		Super Saver**	
	Coach	Section†	Coach	Section†
Halifax to Montreal	$151	$199	$91	$119

* Peak: 01 July to 08 September, and for sleepers also 19 December to 05 January
** Super Saver: 09 September to 30 June (sleepers as for peak between 19 December and 05 January); tickets must be purchased at least seven days in advance.
† Supplement for lower berths: $20-30. Roomettes and bedrooms also available.

The Skeena – Jasper to Prince Rupert

The Skeena now operates as a two-day, daylight only service. The train stops overnight at Prince George, where you must arrange your own accommodation. First class tickets (all meals included) cost $160 from Jasper to Prince George, $275 for the whole two-day trip from Jasper to Prince Rupert.

VIA's Web site
You can now check out schedules, fares and special offers on **http://www.viarail.ca**. Ticket booking started in 1997 with a discount for tickets booked via the site.

The Hudson Bay – Winnipeg to Churchill

	Peak*		Super Saver**	
	Coach	Section†	Coach	Section†
Winnipeg to Churchill	$186	$261	$112	$157

* Peak: 15 May to 15 October for sleepers only.
** Super Saver: tickets must be purchased at least seven days in advance; for sleepers booked between 15 May and 15 October peak fare applies.
† Supplement for lower berths: $20-30. Roomettes and bedrooms also available.

The Corridor – Montreal to Toronto

	Peak*		Off-peak**
	Coach	VIA 1	Coach
Montreal to Toronto	$87	$129	$52

* Peak: all Fridays and Sundays (except student and youth fares); plus all statutory holidays.
** Off-peak: tickets for all other days when bought at least five days in advance.

The Rocky Mountaineer

Route	Service	Regular: June to Sep		Value: May & Oct	
		Single	Double†	Single	Double†
Vancouver to Banff/Jasper	Signature	$630	$575	$530	$475
Vancouver to Calgary	Signature	$690	$635	$590	$535
Vancouver to Banff	Gold Leaf	$1130	$1075	$1030	$975
Vancouver to Calgary	Gold Leaf	$1230	$1175	$1130	$1075

† Price per person sharing in a double

> **Rocky Mountaineer Railtours Web site**
> Visit the Web site at **http://www.rkymtnrail.com** for the latest prices and schedules.

When to go

Corny as it sounds, Canada is beautiful in every season. Autumn is a tourist attraction in itself as it turns the country's forests into a glorious blaze of reds and golds. In winter the snow-covered landscapes are dazzling but best experienced from the comfort of the train; you have to be pretty hardy to cope with sight-seeing in sub-zero temperatures. Canadians, like hedgehogs, tend to hibernate in these cold months, so city centres can be depressingly empty. Spring is lovely in Canada (as spring usually is anywhere) with May temperatures averaging 13-15°C/55-59°F in most cities. The warmest, driest and sunniest months are July and August when temperatures reach about 22°C/72°F in places on the line.

Of course, there's more than the weather to take into account in deciding when to go. An important consideration is the cost of the trip: rail fares and hotel rates are considerably cheaper out of tourist season (generally considered to be May to October). It's also a lot easier to get train reservations in the quieter months whereas peak period sleeper tickets should be booked about five to six months in advance. Something else to bear in mind is the number of fellow tourists you can expect to be surrounded by on your visit: July and August are very, very busy so if you're going to Canada for its tranquillity and big empty spaces, give these months a miss.

Making a booking

WITH A TOUR OR ON YOUR OWN?

Canada is one of the easiest and most hassle-free countries in the world to travel in, and arranging a trans-Canada rail trip is an extremely uncomplicated process. Simply choose the dates you want to travel, make the reservations with a VIA agent, then book your flights. Once you're in Canada there's no shortage of accommodation. In light of this, it hardly seems worth taking a package tour, particularly as you can decide exactly how much time you want to spend where if you organise it yourself, whereas this decision will usually be taken for you on a tour. Moreover, independent travel invariably works out cheaper if you plan to stay in mid-range or budget accommodation.

Where tours really come into their own is if you want to stay in upmarket hotels. Many tour operators put you in luxurious establishments such as the Canadian Pacific hotels; they make huge block bookings which means a) they get big discounts so you end up paying less than if you booked the accommodation yourself, and b) if you turn up at these hotels trying to book a room, there's often nothing left as the tour companies have booked everything going. Escorted tours take most decision-making and the responsibility of getting from A to B out of your hands, which can be a good or a bad thing depending on what you're after. Bear in mind, though, that the pace of many tours is often considerably more gruelling than that of independent travel, as you will be whisked off on countless sight-seeing trips in between your days on the train.

VIA RAIL SALES AGENTS

VIA Rail has a number of general sales agents dotted around the world. These act as VIA's representatives: they answer rail enquiries, send out timetables and make reservations for you. You buy your tickets from them in local currency. This is extremely convenient and saves you making transatlantic payments in Canadian dollars. Many of them also act as agents for Rocky Mountaineer Railtours, who operate the Rocky Mountaineer train, (see p64).

MAKING A BOOKING IN BRITAIN

Reserving your rail tickets

VIA's UK sales agent is **Leisurail** (☎ 01733-335599) PO Box 113, Peterborough, Cambridgeshire PE3 8HY. The staff are helpful and competent; booking through them is very straightforward. They also do bookings for the Rocky Mountaineer.

Getting to Canada

If you're organising your rail reservations yourself you'll need to sort out your flights as well. The obvious choice is **Air Canada** (☎ 0990-247226) at 7-8 Conduit St, London W1R 9TG, as they have more flights to more places in Canada than any other airline and are the only one to offer non-stop scheduled flights to Halifax from London. Like many airlines, they offer 'open jaw' tickets which allow you to fly into one point and out of another; the fare is calculated by halving the cost of a return to each destination and adding them together. Their prices aren't as high as you might expect: Super Saver returns from London to Halifax, Toronto and Montreal start at £319 (£479 in the summer); to Winnipeg, Edmonton and Vancouver they go from £419 (or from £579 in the summer). This means you could fly into Halifax, Toronto or Montreal and out of Vancouver for as little as £369, excellent value for a scheduled transatlantic flight.

You might also want to consider getting a cheap ticket from a charter airline. **First Choice Flights** (☎ 0161-745 7000) is one of the few airlines offering direct charter flights from London to Halifax; tickets are available May to October and cost from £269 to £369. Returns to Toronto are £219 to £359, and to Vancouver they're £369 to £489. **Globespan** (☎ 0131-441 2900) also has charter flights to Halifax but only between July and September – fares are between £249 and £369. They have some good deals to Toronto (returns from £199 to £339) and to Vancouver (£299 to £479). **Bluebird Express** (☎ 01444-235678) has charter flights to Toronto (£239 to £359) and to Vancouver (£299 to £489).

Booking a package tour

Most package tours including a trans-Canada rail trip are fully escorted (all those listed below are escorted unless otherwise stated). Most combine a VIA rail trip with a ride on the Rocky Mountaineer (see p64); a common itinerary is Toronto to Jasper with VIA, Jasper to Banff by motor coach then Banff to Vancouver on the Rocky Mountaineer (or the same in reverse). NB: the Rocky Mountaineer is abbreviated to RM below.

• **Media Travel** (☎ 01784-434434) Lawrence House, 45A High St, Egham, Surrey TW20 9DP. Their 10-day 'Trans-Canadian' tour is one of the few packages to use VIA services all the way from Toronto to Vancouver. It's outstanding value, with prices starting at £1175 and going up to £1440. You can even get 15% off these prices if you book early enough.

• **Thomas Cook** (☎ 01733-330111) PO Box 36, Thorpe Wood, Peterborough, Cambs PE3 6SB. A range of escorted and independent rail tours through Canada; their 16-day 'Trans-Canadian' tour takes you from Vancouver to Toronto on the Canadian, then on to Ottawa and Montreal by coach. Prices range from £1295 to £1695. The 17-day 'Rocky Mountain Ranger' combines the Skeena from Jasper to Prince Rupert with a cruise down the Inside Passage and costs £1545-£1795. There's also an 11-day Rocky Mountaineer tour (Jasper to Vancouver); prices start at £1095 and go up to £1460.

• **Vacation Canada** (☎ 0141-332 1511) Cambridge House, 8 Cambridge St, Glasgow G2 3DZ. One of the few companies to offer unescorted tours, one of which incorporates a cruise up the Inside Passage with a rail ride on the Skeena (Prince Rupert to Jasper), followed by a coach trip to Toronto; 15 days from £1785.

• **Page & Moy** (☎ 0116-252 4433) 136-140 London Rd, Leicester, Leics LE2 1EN. Toronto to Jasper on the Canadian, Banff to Vancouver on the RM; 16 days from £1395 to £1595.

• **NAR UK** (☎ 01753-855031) America House, 1 Bolton Rd, Windsor, Berks SL4 3JW. Combined coach and rail trip from Vancouver to Toronto; 10 days from $1906 to $2427 (excluding flights).

• **All Canada** (☎ 01502-585825) 90 High St, Lowestoft, Suffolk NR32 1XN. The Canadian from Toronto to Edmonton, then coach from Calgary to Vancouver; 16 days from £1101 to £1426 (excluding flights).

• **Bales Tours** (☎ 01306-885991) Bales House, Junction Rd, Dorking, Surrey, RH4 3HB. Bales Tours have a fifteen-day 'Canadian Pacific' which is one of the most luxurious tours available with all off-train accommodation in Canadian Pacific hotels, including the famous Banff Springs Hotel and Jasper Park Lodge. Vancouver to Banff is on the Rocky Mountaineer, and Jasper to Toronto on the Canadian. The package also includes an optional rail extension to Halifax. Prices start at £1999 (or £2298 including Halifax), going up to £2898 (or £3197 including Halifax).

• **Travel Pack Canada** (☎ 0161-707 4404). Clarendon House, Clarendon Rd, Eccles, Greater Manchester M30 9AL. Another luxury tour using Canadian Pacific accommodation. You travel on The Canadian from Toronto to Jasper, then the RM from Banff to Vancouver; 13 days from £2575 to £2955.

MAKING A BOOKING IN CONTINENTAL EUROPE

From Austria
• **Gateway Touristic** (☎ 243 85570) A-3400 Klosterneuberg, Buchberggasse 34. Sales agent for RMR.
• **Air Canada** (☎ 515 5537) IBUSZ, Krugerstr 4, 1010 Vienna. Returns from Vienna to Toronto – low season: AS10,410; high season: AS13,560.
• **Okista** (☎ 401 480) Turkenstrasse 6, 1090 Vienna. Low-cost flights.

From Belgium
• **Air Canada** (☎ 02-513 9150) België Aviasales BD Maurice Lemonnier 131/6 1000 Brussels. Returns to Toronto from Brussels – low season:BF 27,890; high season: BF36,410.
• **Connections** (☎ 02-512 5060) Zuidstraat 19-21 rue du Midi, Brussels. Low cost flights.

From Denmark
• **Benns Rejser** (☎ 9742 5000) Hovedkontor Norregade 51, Holstevro 7500. Sales agent for RMR.
• **Air Canada** (☎ 3311 4555) Suite 2356, Vester Farimagsgade 1, 2 DK-1606, Copenhagen. Returns from Copenhagen to Toronto – low season: K5100; high season: K6100.
• **Kilroy Travels** (☎ 3311 0044) Skindergade 28, 1159 Copenhagen K. Low-cost flights.

From Finland
• **Finam Tours** (☎ 0622 1132) Linankata 3, Helsinki 00160. Sales agent for RMR; package tours.
• **Kilroy Travels** (☎ 0680 7811/13) Kaivokatu 10 D, Helsinki 00100. Low-cost flights.
• **Finland Travel Bureau** (☎ 018261) Keskuskatu 5, Helsinki 00100. Package tours.

From France
• **Express Conseil** (☎ 44 77 88 00) 5 rue du Louvre, Paris 75001. Sales agent for VIA.
• **Canadien National** (☎ 47 42 76 50) 1 rue Scribe, Paris 75009. Sales agent for RMR.
• **Air Canada** (☎ 44 50 20 20) 10 rue de la Paix, Paris 75002. Returns from Paris to Toronto – low season: FF5040; high season: FF5695.
• **Usit Voyages** (☎ 42 44 14 00) 12 rue Vivienne, Paris 75002. Low-cost flights.
• **Via Voyages** (☎ 40 82 50 50) 43 rue de Dunkerque, Paris 75010. Package tours.
• **Pacific Holidays** (☎ 45 41 52 58) 34 ave du Général Leclerc, Paris 75041. Package tours.

From Germany

• **Canada Reise Dienst** (☎ 04102-51167) Rathausplatz 2, 22926 Ahrensburg, Hamburg. Sales agent for VIA and RMR.

• **Air Canada** (☎ 030-882 5879) Kurfürstendamm 209, 10719 Berlin. Returns from Berlin to Toronto – low season: DM999; high season: DM1399.

• **Team Reisen** (☎ 780 0000) Hauptstrasse 9, 10827 Berlin. Low-cost flights.

• **Reisebüro Helios** (☎ 860 0050) GmbH, Uhlandstrasse 73, 10717 Berlin. Package tours.

• **Thomas Cook** (☎ 378 087) Reisebüro Caravelle, GmbH, Friedrichstrasse 42a, 40217 Düsseldorf. Package tours.

From Hungary

• **Air Canada** (☎ 118 6536) Ferenciek Tere 10, Budapest. Returns from Budapest to Toronto – low season: HF93,950; high season: HF114,830.

• **Ibusz Hungarian Travel Co** (☎ 118 6466) Vigadó Utca 6, H-1051 Budapest. Package tours.

From Northern Ireland and Eire

• **Usit** (☎ 324073) Fountain Centre, College St, Belfast BT1 6ET. Discount flights.

• **Air Canada** Returns from Dublin to Toronto – low season: IR£459; high season: IR£599. Returns from Belfast to Toronto – low season: UK£436; high season UK£596. Note that Air Canada does not have an office in Dublin, and flights go via the UK.

• **Usit** (☎ 679 8833) 19/21 Aston Quay, O'Connell Bridge, Dublin 2. Discount flights.

• **Thomas Cook Overseas Ltd** (☎ 677 7422) 51 Grafton St, Dublin 2. Package tours.

• **J Barter Travel Group** (☎ 274261) 92 Patrick St, Cork. Package tours.

From Italy

• **Gastaldi Tours** (☎ 2-668 121) Viale Restelli 5/A, 20124 Milan. Sales agent for VIA; package tours.

• **Air Canada** (☎ 2-295 23943), c/o Azimut, Viale Regina Giovanna N8, Milan. Returns from Rome to Toronto – low season: L1,454,000; high season: L1,739,000.

• **CTS** (☎ 6-467 9291) Via Genova 16, 00184 Rome. Low-cost flights.

• **Sestante CIT** (☎ 592 3058) Viale Città d'Europa 807, 00144 Rome. Package tours.

From the Netherlands

• **Incento BV** (☎ 02159-48586) Stationsplein 1, PO Box 457, 1400 Al Bussum. Sales agent for VIA and RMR.

• **Air Canada** (☎ 020-604 1489) Amsterdam. Returns from Amsterdam to Toronto – low season: Dfl1400; high season: Dfl1951.
• **NBBS Reizen** (☎ 624 0989) Rokin 38, Amsterdam. Low-cost flights.

From Norway
• **Nordmanns-Reiser** (☎ 233 4530) Radjusgt 23b, Oslo 1. Sales agent for RMR.
• **Kilroy Travels** (☎ 4201 20) Nedre Slottsgate 23, 0157 Oslo 1. Low-cost flights.

From Sweden
• **Tour Canada of Sweden** (☎ 23-20681) Box 5012 S-79105 Falun. Sales agent for VIA; package tours.
• **Kilroy Travels** (☎ 8-23 4515) Kungsgatan 4, 103 87 Stockholm. Low-cost flights.

From Switzerland
• **Touring Club Suisse** (☎ 22-737 1313) rue Pierre Fatio 9, 1211 Geneva 3. Sales agent for VIA and RMR.
• **Air Canada** (☎ 22-731 4980) 1-3 rue Chantepoulet, Geneva. Returns from Geneva to Toronto – low season: SF1265; high season: SF1632.
• **SSR-Reisen** (☎ 297 1111) Leonhardstrasse 10, 8001 Zurich. Low-cost flights.

MAKING A BOOKING IN NORTH AMERICA
From Canada
• **VIA Rail Canada Inc** (☎ 514-871-1331) 2 Place Ville-Marie, Montreal, Quebec, H3B 2C9 (Via's headquarters). You can phone for information or reservations on the following toll-free numbers – Newfoundland: ☎ 1-800-561-3926; Prince Edward Island: ☎ 1-800-561-3952; Nova Scotia: ☎ 1-800-561-3952; New Brunswick: ☎ 1-800-561-3952; Quebec: ☎ 1-800-361-5390; Ontario: ☎ 1-800-361-1235; from everywhere else in Canada: ☎ 1-800-561-8630.
• **Rocky Mountaineer Railtours** (☎ 604-606-7245) Pacific Central Railway Station. You can call them toll-free on ☎ 1-800-665-7245 from anywhere in Canada or the US, or fax the reservations department on 604-606-7250.
• **Air Canada** There are toll-free numbers for every province: Newfoundland: ☎ 1-800-563-3940; Prince Edward Island: ☎ 1-800-268-7240; Nova Scotia: ☎ 1-800-565-3940; New Brunswick: ☎ 1-800-565-3940; Quebec: ☎ 1-800-361-8620; Ontario: ☎ 1-800-268-7240; Manitoba: ☎ 1-800-542-8940; Saskatchewan: ☎ 1-800-665-0520; Alberta: ☎ 1-800-332-1080; British Columbia: ☎ 1-800-663-3721; Yukon & NWT: ☎ 1-800-663-9100.

• **Travel Cuts** (☎ 416-979-2406) 187 College St, Toronto, Ontario M5T 1P7. Low-cost flights. Their other branch is in Vancouver (☎ 604-681-9136) 602 W Hastings no 501, Vancouver, BC V6B 1P2.
• **Marlin Travel** (☎ 416-979-9300) Eaton Centre, 218 Yonge St, Toronto. Their Vancouver branch (☎ 604-689-3333) is at 1654 Robson St – they have a range of rail package tours.

From the USA
VIA doesn't have a sales agency in America, since you can make reservations at most travel agents. Following are organisations you can get in touch with about getting to Canada, and some package tour operators:
• **Destination Unlimited** (☎ 415-573-8788) PO Box 4806, 236 Shearwater Isle, Foster City, California. Sales agent for RMR.
• **Mallia & Associates** (☎ 617-340-6292) 52 Bayview St, North Weymouth, Maryland. Sales agent for RMR.
• **Air Canada** (☎ 800-776-3000) 300 N State St, Room 1100, Marina City Office Bldg, Chicago, IL. Flights from all over the US to all over Canada. From New York to Toronto the year round return fare is: US$189; from Los Angeles to Toronto it's US$352.
• **Council Travel** (☎ 212-661-1450) 205 E 42nd St, New York, NY. Cut price student and youth flights; many more branches.
• **STA Travel** (☎ 212-986-9470) 17 E 45th St, Suite 805, New York, NY. Low-cost flights; other offices in San Francisco, LA and Boston.
• **Amtrak** (☎ 1-800-872-7245). Direct rail connections with VIA: New York to Montreal or Toronto (via Niagara Falls); Chicago or Detroit to Toronto; Seattle to Vancouver.
• **Maupintours** (☎ 913-843-1211) 1515 St Andrew's Dr, Lawrence, Kansas 66046. Package tours.
• **Four Winds Travel** (☎ 212-777-0261) 175 5th Ave, New York, NY 10010. Package tours.

From Mexico
• **Grandes Viajes** (☎ 5-682-3397) 2 A Cda de Concepcion, Beistegui No 24, Col del Valle, 03100 DF. Sales agent for VIA; package tours.
• **Continental Airlines** (☎ 280-3434) Andres Bello 45 18 Piso, Col. Chapultepec Polanco, Mexico City 11560. Returns to Toronto from Mexico City – low season: US$399; high season: US$425.
• **Setej Mexico** (☎ 211-0743) Hamburgo 305, Col Juarez, 06600 Mexico City. Low-cost flights.

MAKING A BOOKING IN AUSTRALASIA
From Australia
• **Walshes World** (☎ 02-232 7499) 92 Pitt St, GPO Box 51, Sydney, NSW 200. VIA and RMR sales agent.

• **United Airlines** (☎ 237 8888) 5th Floor, 10 Barrack St, Sydney 2000. Returns to Toronto from Sydney or Melbourne – low season: AS$2079; high season: AS$2472.
• **STA Travel** (☎ 02-519-9866) 1a Lee St, Railway Square, Sydney 2000. Discount flights.
• **Thomas Cook Ltd** (☎ 229 6611) 175 Pitt St, Sydney. Package tours.

From New Zealand
• **Walshes World** (☎ 09-379 3708) 87 Queen St 2nd Floor, Auckland 1. VIA and RMR sales agent.
• **United Airlines** (☎ 307 9500) 7 City Rd, Auckland. Returns to Toronto from Auckland – low season: NA$2369; high season: NZ$2519. From Wellington – low season: NZ$2511; high season: NZ$2661.
• **STA Travel** (☎ 09-309 0458) 64 High St, Auckland. Low-cost flights.
• **Thomas Cook (NZ) Ltd** (☎ 849 2071) Shop 250A, St Luke's Sq, Auckland. Package tours.

MAKING A BOOKING IN SOUTH AFRICA

• **Bill Paterson Ltd** (☎ 403 4445) 10th Floor Noswal Hall, PO Box 31061, Braamfontein 2017, Johannesburg. Sales agent for RMR.
• **Air Canada** (☎ 880 8931) PO Box 52701, Saxonwold 2132, Johannesburg. Returns to Toronto from Johannesburg – low season: R4690); high season: R5290. From Cape Town – low season: R5510; high season: R6110.
• **ITN** (☎ 21-685 1808) Leslie Social Science Building, University of Capetown, Rondebosch 7700. Low-cost flights.
• **Oriole Travel** (☎ 838 6541) 4th floor, Ten Sixty Six, 35 Pritchard St, Johannesburg. Package tours.
• **Rennies Travel** (☎ 252 370) 10th floor, Southern Life Centre, 8 Riebeek St, Cape Town. Package tours.

MAKING A BOOKING IN ASIA

From Japan
• **Japan Travel Bureau Inc** (☎ 03-3284 7376) 1-6-4 Marunouchi, Chiyoda-ku, Tokyo 100. Sales agent for VIA.
• **Great Canadian Railtour Japan** (☎ 03-3575 4183) 5th Floor, Kashikei Bldg, 19-3-2 chome Shimbashi, Minato-ku, Tokyo 105. Sales agent for RMR.
• **Air Canada** (☎ 03-3586 3891) 2-3-3 chome, Akasaka, Minato-ku, Tokyo. Returns to Toronto from Tokyo – low season: ¥179,000; high season: ¥282,000.
• **Council Travel** (☎ 03-3581 5517) Sanno Grand Building, Room 102, 14-2 Nagata-cho 2-chome, Chiyoda-ku, Tokyo 100. Low-cost flights.

• **Thomas Cook Ltd** (☎ 03-3254 4945) Ascend Kanda Bldg, 10 Tomiyama-cho, Kanda, Chiyoda-ku, Tokyo 100. Package tours.

From Hong Kong
• **Japan Travel Bureau** (☎ 2734 9288) Room 1305-1309, New East Ocean Centre, 9 Science Museum Rd, Tsimshatsui east, Kowloon. Sales agent for VIA.
• **Air Canada** (☎ 2522 1001) Room 1002-3 Wheelock House, 20 Pedder St Central. Returns to Toronto from Hong Kong – low season: HK$18,270; high season: HK$20,950.
• **Sincerity Travel** (☎ 2730 0888) Suite 408-413 World Finance Centre, Sth Tower, Harbour City, 17-19 Canton Rd, Tsimshatsui, Kowloon. Low-cost flights.
• **Thomas Cook Travel Service** (☎ 2853 9888) 18th Floor, Vicwood Plaza, 199 Des Voeux Road, Central, Hong Kong. Package tours.

From Taiwan
• **World Express Inc** (☎ 2-503 3030) 4Fl, 90 Chien Kuo N Rd, Section 2, Taipei. Sales agent for VIA.
• **Ken Shin Travel Services** (☎ 2-503 3302) 11Fl, No 9 Section 3 Nanking E Rd, Taipei. Sales agent for RMR.
• **Air Canada** (☎ 02-507 8133) 8F, No 61 Nanking E Rd, Section 3, Taipei. Returns to Toronto from Taipei – low season: NT$83,495; high season NT$91,563.
• **SEN Travel** (☎ 591-8228) 7-1F Section 2, 162 Chung Shan North Road, Taipei. Low-cost flights.
• **China Travel Service** (☎ 395 5123) 6/7 Floor, No 16, Sec 2 Jen-Ai-Road, Taipei 100. Package tours.

Visas and health precautions

Visas
Visitors from the UK and Ireland don't need a visa to get into Canada, just a full passport. Nor are visas required by citizens of Australia, Austria, Belgium, Chile, Denmark, Finland, France, Germany, Greece, Hungary, Iceland, Israel, Italy, Japan, Luxembourg, Malaysia, Malta, Mexico, Monaco, the Netherlands, New Zealand, Norway, Saudi Arabia, Singapore, Slovenia, South Korea, Spain, Sweden, Switzerland, United States and Zimbabwe.

   In addition, citizens of most Commonwealth countries or British dependent territories do not need a visa. Check with your nearest Canadian Embassy or High Commission.

If you do need a visa you should contact the Immigration section of a Canadian Embassy or High Commission and ask for a visa application form. This must then be submitted in English or French. You also have to pay a visa processing fee – $55 for single entry, or $85 for multiple entry. Visas are valid for six months.

Health precautions

Since there is absolutely nothing to inoculate yourself against in Canada, the only health precaution you need to worry about is medical insurance. It's vital that you arrange this before your trip as medical treatment in Canada is extremely expensive. Most all-round travel insurances contain comprehensive medical cover – popular companies in the UK include **Columbus** (☎ 0171-375 0011), **Endsleigh** (☎ 0171-436 4451) and **STA Travel** (☎ 0171-937 9971).

What to take

Clothes

If you're going in winter, warm clothing is absolutely essential and should include a heavy coat, a hat, gloves and generous supplies of thermal underwear. You should also take a pair of warm, water resistant boots ('moon boots' are perfect, though the fashion-conscious among you may draw the line here).

For the rest of the year, the weather is more or less comparable to that in the UK, though if you're taking the train up to Prince Rupert in spring or autumn, or Churchill at any time of the year, be sure to pack the hat, gloves and thermals.

One of the most important things to get right is footwear. Sight-seeing is tiring business and shouldn't be attempted in anything other than a pair of very comfortable shoes. Special walking shoes may be your best bet, as these can double up for walking in the Rockies if you plan to get off at Jasper.

Medical supplies

You won't have any trouble at all getting hold of medical kit in Canada, so only the most basic supplies need to be included in your luggage (paracetamol, antiseptic cream and plasters should be enough).

Money

Travellers' cheques are always a bit of a hassle so I would recommend getting most of your cash out of automated teller machines at banks, as and when you need it, using your debit card (see p40 for more on this). It would be unwise, however, to rely on the card as your sole means of obtaining money, just in case it's stolen. In this case, travellers' cheques are an invaluable backup; even if they're stolen you can claim back their value very easily, provided you've kept the numbers in a safe place.

Background reading

Trees and lakes are all very well but they can get a bit tedious in large doses. Reading of some sort is essential on the train and is all the more interesting if it's relevant to your journey. Here are a few suggestions:

• *Scenic Rail Guide to Western Canada* and *Scenic Rail Guide to Central & Atlantic Canada* by Bill Coo. Collectively the bible of Canadian rail guides, written by a man who worked on the lines for over thirty years. Used to be given away free on the Canadian, but now out of print. Copies are like gold dust, but you could try Halifax and Montreal railway stations.

• *Van Horne's Road* by Omer Lavallée. Detailed and exhaustively researched book chronicling the construction of the Canadian Pacific Railway – by the man who set up the Canadian Pacific Archives. Lots of wonderful old black and white photos.

• *The National Dream* and *The Last Spike* by Pierre Berton. Eminently readable best-sellers on the trials, tribulations and dramas involved in building the first transcontinental railway across Canada (turned into a mini-series a few years ago). They're published together in an abridged version called *The Great Railway*, widely available throughout Canada.

• *Railways of Canada* by Jim Lotz and Keith McKenzie. Colourful and readable hardback book, sold in major bookshops (like Coles) throughout the country.

• *All Aboard* by David Mitchell. Big glossy paperback focusing on rail travel through the Rocky Mountains. Well written (by BC historian) and with some excellent colour photography; available at Dulthie's in Vancouver (919 Robson St) or onboard the Rocky Mountaineer.

The following are out of print, but should be available in libraries:

• *Ocean to Ocean* by Rev George M Grant. The author accompanied Sandford Fleming, head of the Canadian Pacific Survey, on his mammoth expedition across Canada in 1872. The book is a chronicle of the journey, and a fascinating insight into Canada before the railway.

• *The Great Lone Land* by Capt W F Butler. The impressions of a young soldier as he journeys into the depths of Canada's North-West, at the time of the Riel rebellion. The book was a best-seller in its time.

• *The Queen's Highway* by Stuart Cumberland. Lively account of the railway journey from Port Moody to Halifax, by one of the CPR's first passengers.

For a more general spread of background material, you might like to try some of the following titles:

• *Oh Canada! Oh Quebec!* by Mordecai Richler. An incisive and witty send-up of some of the excesses of Quebec's independence movement.

• *The Betrayal of Canada* by Mel Hurtig. Typical Canadian anxiety about the state of the nation by one of the country's best known writers.

• *The Will of a Nation: Awakening the Canadian Spirit* by George Radwanski and Julia Luttrell. More Canadian self-enquiry and meditation on the national identity.

• *A Short History of Canada* by Desmond Morton. Sensible and highly readable history book.

• *The Battle for Room Service* by Mark Lawson. Reflections of a British journalist as he travels through the 'world's safest places,' including Vancouver, Winnipeg, Toronto and Montreal. Cynical, scathing and hilarious.

• *The Edge* by Dick Francis. Dastardly doings on a private, luxury train as it crosses Canada – some good landscape descriptions amongst the intrigue and suspense. Don't read it if you're travelling alone.

• *The Republic of Love* by Carol Shields. A superb comic romance by one of Canada's best contemporary novelists, set in the unlikely location of Winnipeg.

• *Cat's Eye* by Margaret Atwood. Excellent, sensitive novel about a painter who returns to Toronto to find it – and herself – indelibly changed.

• *Maria Chapdelaine* by Louis Hémon. Enduring best-seller written in 1913 about a young girl's life in the backwoods of northern Quebec. It veers towards sentimentality, but nonetheless paints a vivid picture of the uncompromising harshness of frontier life.

• *The Shipping News* by E Annie Proulx. Pulitzer prize-winning novel set in a remote village on the Newfoundland coast. Apart from being a wonderful read it gives you an insight into the incredible regional diversity within Canada.

If you want to equip yourself with more **guidebooks**, there are dozens to choose from. *The Rough Guide to Canada* is packed with useful information on the whole country, and contains some quirky and entertaining asides. There's also *Canada - a travel survival kit* from Lonely Planet. *Baedeker's Canada* is a good reference source, and has glossy colour pictures on just about every other page. Probably the best books are the Fodor range. As well as *Fodor's Canada* there are numerous in-depth guides to various parts of the country, including *The Upper Great Lakes region*, *Canada's Atlantic Provinces*, *the Rockies*, *Montreal & Quebec City* and *Toronto* – all of them full of good practical information.

If you're continuing your rail travel south over the border, *USA by Rail* by John Pitt (Bradt Publications/Globe Pequot) is recommended.

PART 2: CANADA

Facts about the country

GEOGRAPHICAL BACKGROUND

Great stretches of wilderness, so that its frontier is a circumference rather than a boundary; a country with huge rivers and islands that most natives have never seen, a country that has made a nation out of the stops on two of the world's longest railway lines. Northrop Frye *Sudia Varia*, 1957

Canada is the second largest country in the world, covering a vast 9,970,610 square km (almost four million square miles). It's flanked by the Atlantic on the east and the Pacific on the west, with some 6000km in between. Its southern boundary is the US border, which follows the 49th parallel from the Pacific to the Great Lakes, then loops all over the place between Lake Ontario and the Atlantic. To the north Canada stretches all the way up to Ellesmere Island in the Arctic Ocean, 4400 km away from Toronto. In the northwest is the other US/Canada border, separating the Yukon and British Columbia from Alaska.

This colossal area is divided into ten provinces and two territories: Newfoundland, Nova Scotia, Prince Edward Island, New Brunswick, Quebec, Ontario, Manitoba, Saskatchewan, Alberta, British Columbia, Northwest Territories and Yukon Territory.

Climate

In 1881 a British periodical called *Truth* described Canada as 'frostbound for seven or eight months in the year....[and] as forbidding a country as any on the face of the earth', a familiar but slightly unfair stereotype that persists to this day. Okay, so it does get a bit chilly in winter (everywhere except the west coast has average January temperatures well below freezing point and continuous snow cover) but the populated stretch along the south has very good springs and summers. A typical July on the prairies, for instance, is dry and hot (usually mid-20°sC/70°sF) while an average summer in Quebec and Ontario will be warm and humid. West coast summers tend to be temperate rather than hot, but winters here are the mildest in the country thanks to the influence of the warm Pacific Ocean (Vancouver's average January temperature is 3°C/37°F, compared to Winnipeg's -20°C/-4°F).

Moving further north, the 'frost-bound' label is somewhat more justified, indeed much of the upper two thirds of the country is continuously affected by *permafrost* (ground remaining at or below 0°C/32°F for at least two years). The only train taking you into this frozen region is the Hudson Bay to Churchill, where winter temperatures regularly drop to minus 30°C (minus 22°F).

Transport and communications

As might be expected of a country of this size and economic ranking, Canada's transport infrastructure is extensive and efficient. The majority of internal communications run east-west, such as the Trans-Canada Highway connecting St Johns (NF) to Vancouver – the longest national highway in the world at 7821km. Rail remains an important means of transporting freight (principally bulk commodities like grain, lumber and coal, often carried in 'unit trains' of 100 or more cars) but it has been overtaken by the motor car and the aeroplane as the chief transporters of people around the country. Shipping provides another important means of freight transportation, both from ocean ports like Vancouver and Halifax, and along the Great Lakes/St Lawrence Seaway system.

Landscape zones: flora and fauna

The main landscape zones you'll travel through on your trans-Canada rail journey are as follows:

• **St Lawrence Lowlands** Spreading across the northern shores of the Great Lakes and east along the St Lawrence River towards the Atlantic Ocean, this is the most densely populated area of Canada. The high degree of urbanisation and industrialisation in this region is interrupted by large areas given over to agriculture and forestry, mainly mixed conifers (eg red spruce and pines) and various deciduous trees (especially red and sugar maple). In autumn the blazing red foliage of these trees is spectacular and draws thousands of tourists each year.

• **Canadian Shield** This is Canada's dominant geographic feature, stretching in a massive band from Hudson Bay down to the Great Lakes and east into Labrador. It spreads over 4.5 million square km, much of it covered by Precambrian rock (570-1100 million years old). The erosive effects of glaciation over the last million years have scoured the Shield's surface leaving a striking landscape of bare rock and countless lakes, rivers and streams. Much of the Shield is covered by coniferous **boreal forest** (millions of spruce, larch and pine, plus some poplar and aspen).

The Great Lakes
Lakes Superior, Michigan, Huron, Erie and Ontario are known collectively as the Great Lakes. Together they make up the largest body of fresh water in the world, with a total area of over 246,000 square km. Apart from Lake Michigan, which lies entirely within the United States, they are located on the border between Canada and America. The largest is Lake Superior; it is 563km long, 257km wide and reaches a depth of 406m. It is the largest freshwater lake in the world.

• **Tundra** Travellers aboard the Hudson Bay will find themselves (as they approach Churchill) in the most barren and inhospitable part of the country covered by rail track. Tundra is a region of permafrost and bitter cold where vegetation is stunted and sparse. The few trees that can survive here (mainly birch) rarely grow higher than a metre and most of the earth is covered by lichens, shrubs and mosses, though the most beautiful wild flowers spring up for a few weeks in summer. Wildlife, on the other hand, is plentiful, though most of it is well camouflaged: arctic fox, arctic ptarmigan, white squirrels and caribou are all local inhabitants.

• **The prairies** The vast expanse of land between the Shield and the Rockies is part of the Interior Plains which spans the whole length of Canada from the US border up to the Arctic coast. The famous part of the plains is the southern fertile belt, known universally as 'the prairies'. This is where Canada's wheat is produced, an average of 25 billion tonnes of it each year. It's known for its prodigious flatness, especially in Saskatchewan; the Alberta prairies are a little more undulating. The area was once home to enormous numbers of bison: an estimated 50-60 million roamed the plains in 1800 but had been hunted almost to extinction by 1885. These days you'll probably see little more than crops and grain elevators as you pass through.

• **Western Cordillera** The western mountains are part of the massive 14,000km-long chain that spans the length of the continent from Tierra del Fuego right up to Alaska. In Canada they're made up of several ranges, the most famous and most easterly being the **Rockies**. West of these is the Columbia system (the Purcell, Selkirk and Monashee ranges) followed by the Coast Mountains. The Rockies are your best bet out of the entire route for spotting wildlife (see below). In spring and summer

---

Wildlife from the train

You know it's out there but it's doing its damnedest to hide from you. Still, the vigilant observer should be rewarded with a couple of sightings – here's a rough guide to what to look out for and where:

• **Ocean** Tantramar Marshes near Amherst: Canada geese, marsh hawks, black ducks, blue-winged teal; around Mont-Joli: moose and deer.

• **Canadian** Whiteshell Provincial Park (around Rice Lake): black bear, deer, moose, coyotes and beavers; Wainwright: peregrine falcons (breeding ground nearby); near Viking: elk, coyote, ruffed grouse; Wabamun Lake (near Edmonton): moose, beaver, white-tailed deer; Rocky Mountains: grizzly and black bear, moose, elk, caribou; mountain goats, bighorn sheep; Coast Mountains: osprey, bald eagles, bears.

• **Skeena** Rocky Mountains: (see above); Endako to Smithers: moose; Pacific bears; Skeena Valley: many bald eagles.

• **Hudson Bay** Wildcat Hills Wilderness Area near Hudson Bay (SK): bear, lynx, wolves, deer; Cormorant Lake, near The Pas: geese, teal, crow-ducks, other waterfowl; approaching Churchill: arctic ptarmigan, snow geese, arctic fox, caribou.

• **Rocky Mountaineer** (see Rocky Mountains and Coast Mountains above).

you'll also be treated to a profusion of wild flowers with beautiful names like Indian Paintbrush and Glacier Lily. As you move into central BC the terrain becomes arid, and is sparsely covered by low shrubs such as sagebrush and prickly pear. Much of the coastal range, in contrast, is covered by luxuriant green fur trees, particularly towards Prince Rupert, with its dripping rain forest, cliffs, mosses and fjords. These mountains are home to numerous bald eagles; sightings are almost guaranteed.

HISTORICAL OUTLINE

Of the two wild men which we took in our former voyage, it was told us that this was part of the Southerne coaste & that there was an island, on the Southerly parte of which is the way to goe from Honguedo (where the year before we had taken them) to Canada, and that two days journey from the sayd Cape and Island began the Kingdome of Saguenay, on the North Shore extending toward Canada. Jacques Cartier, *Second Voyage* (1535-36)

First nations

The first inhabitants of what we now call Canada arrived from Asia between 12 and 20,000 years ago, having crossed the land bridge connecting Siberia to North America. A second wave of migration from Asia occurred around 3000 BC. These people spread themselves around the continent, adapting and developing according to the different environments they settled in. By the time the European explorers 'discovered' Canada, it was populated by a range of distinct peoples with differing languages, belief systems, lifestyles and traditions. The tribes scattered between the Yukon and the Atlantic led a hunting-gathering existence and fell into two language groups: Athapaskan and Algonquin. To the south were the agricultural based communities of the Iroquois. Far north were the Innu who had adapted to life in the harsh conditions of the Arctic tundra. Tragically, all native peoples were rapidly depleted with the arrival of European diseases which they weren't immune to.

French colonisation

Early visitors to Canada's Atlantic coast included the Vikings around 1000 AD, John Cabot in 1497 and scores of European fishermen soon after. It wasn't until the beginning of the 17th century that a permanent European settlement got going when Samuel de Champlain, following the course down the St Lawrence River taken by Jacques Cartier 70 years earlier, set up a small colony in 1608 at what is now Quebec City. It was a great success and another settlement was founded at present-day Montreal in 1642. The French presence gradually spread throughout the region and in 1663 New France was officially declared a royal colony.

The Hudson's Bay Company

New France was the source of a vast supply of furs which fed the insatiable demands of European fashion, and it wasn't long before France's

arch rival, Britain, decided to muscle in on the action and corner a share
of the profits of this new land for itself. In 1670 the Hudson's Bay
Company was set up to exploit the wealth of fur-trading possibilities
around Hudson Bay. Charles II claimed thousands of miles of land around
the bay and granted this to the Company; they named it Rupert's Land,
after the King's cousin, Prince Rupert, who was instrumental in creating
the company. Trading posts were erected throughout the area and intense
rivalry developed between the HBC and the French traders, which would
continue for the next century, often spilling over into violence.

New France becomes British

Meanwhile, Britain's involvement in Canada was not limited to the fur
trade: renewed efforts were being made to drive the French out of their
Atlantic settlements in Acadia, which the British had renamed Nova
Scotia. In 1713 the Treaty of Utrecht gave Britain what it wanted and the
French were forced to hand over their mainland Maritime territories. Still
not satisfied, Britain pushed for control of the remaining French strong-
holds, notably Quebec with its prime position on the St Lawrence River.
In 1759 the conflict came to a dramatic head when the British attacked
Quebec City, scaling the Heights of Abraham in the night, and defeating
the French in the famous battle on the Plains of Abraham. By now France
was ready to wash its hands of the troublesome North American colonies
and in 1763 it officially ceded all of New France to Britain.

The division of Quebec

In contrast to the treatment meted out to the Acadians who were forcibly
deported in the 1750s, the Quebec Act of 1774 safeguarded the rights of
the French Canadians to speak their own language, practise Catholicism,
hold civil appointments and keep their seigneurial land-owning system.
However, they soon found themselves deluged with 10,000 Loyalist settlers (following the American War of Independence) who clearly did not
expect to be governed according to the French system. In an attempt to
get round this problem, the province of Quebec was divided into Upper
Canada and Lower Canada in 1791. This way the French speakers, concentrated in Lower Canada, could remain separate from the English-
speaking Protestants in Upper Canada with each side controlling their
own local affairs.

The 1837 rebellions

In practice the French Canadians were increasingly discriminated against
and the ensuing tide of resentment resulted in a violent but short-lived
rebellion in 1837 led by Louis-Joseph Papineau. Upper Canadians had
their own political grievances, too, expressed in a more scaled down and
equally abortive rebellion led by William Lyon Mackenzie in the same
year. The British government's response was to reunite the two provinces

in 1840, forming the single province of Canada which would be granted greater powers of self government. It was hoped that this would bring the French Canadians into line and curb their demands for self-rule. As time would show, it was to do nothing of the sort.

Confederation

Britain's North American colonies got bigger and bigger as immigration stepped up in the 1840s. Many politicians recognised that the separate provinces would be economically and politically stronger if they were to unite – and strength was an all important issue given the aggressive annexationist tendencies of the United States. At the same time, Britain was ready to give the colonies more autonomy: it was wearying of the huge cost of defending them for virtually no returns. So, after a big Confederation campaign and a few years of debate, the dominion of Canada came into existence on 1 July 1867 when the British North America Act became law. It consisted of the former colonies of New Brunswick, Nova Scotia and Canada (subsequently divided into Ontario and Quebec). These were shortly joined by Manitoba (1870), British Columbia (1871), Prince Edward Island (1873).

Forging a nation

Canada's first Prime Minister was the Conservative leader, Sir John A Macdonald, a man blessed with both pragmatism and vision. Realising that the links binding the provinces together were extremely tenuous, he set about strengthening the nation by expanding its territory and filling it with people. One of the major bedrocks of this policy was the creation of a transcontinental railroad which would physically join the provinces from east to west and transport a flow of goods, trade and immigrants across Canada. Accordingly, the first act of his government was to purchase from the Hudson's Bay Company the vast expanse of land between

O Kanata!

It is ironic that the name of the second largest country in the world is derived from a word meaning 'village'. Cartier, in 1535, was directed to 'kanata' by a couple of Huron-Iroquois youths. They were referring to the village of Stadacona (where Quebec was later founded) but Cartier applied the word to the whole area subject to the rule of Donnacona, the chief of the village. The name somehow stuck and gradually came to be used for the region around the St Lawrence, and then for all of New France, but its boundaries were always vague and never officially delineated by the ruling French.

When the British took over New France they temporarily abandoned the name of Canada and called their new territory the Province of Quebec. The name was revived in 1791 when Quebec was divided into Upper Canada and Lower Canada, which were joined together again in 1841 as the single Province of Canada. Finally, when Nova Scotia, New Brunswick and Canada united in Confederation in 1867 they became 'One Dominion under the name of Canada'.

Ontario and British Columbia (still known as Rupert's Land) where settlers would be sent out to populate the southern, fertile stretch. This was not without its complications...

The first Riel rebellion

Rupert's Land had been almost, but not completely, unpopulated. At the meeting of the Red and Assiniboine Rivers (the site of present-day Winnipeg) was the small and isolated Red River Colony, made up principally of the Métis people (mixed French and Indian). When the government dispatched colonists and officials to 'settle' the area in 1870, the Métis, stirred up and organised by the passionate Louis Riel, staged a violent protest. Riel issued a series of demands to the Canadian government based on the creation of a French and English-speaking province with the provision of French-speaking schools. The government complied and the province of Manitoba was created but Riel was forced to flee to America following the execution of a Canadian by the Métis.

The second Riel rebellion

Fifteen years later, tensions between the Métis and the Canadian government broke out into a second rebellion. This time the Métis were supported by the Cree and Plains Natives whose lands had been encroached on by speculators and farmers. Louis Riel was whisked back from America (where he had been experiencing prolonged bouts of mental illness) to lead the rebellion, which he threw himself into with fervour. The uprising was crushed by Canadian troops, hastily transported to the scene by the almost completed railway, and Riel was captured and sentenced to death for high treason, even though he was clearly mentally unfit at the time. Riel was hanged in November, 1885 – immortalised for the French Canadians as a symbolic victim of brutal Protestant oppression.

Prosperity

It was prosperity, and not confrontation or drama, that characterised Canada's entry into the 20th century. Certainly the following decades were to bring their problems, such as the paralysing Depression of the 30s. On the whole, however, the nation followed a pattern of growth and success. New provinces were incorporated (Alberta and Saskatchewan in 1905); immigrants flooded in and the wheat empire of the prairies boomed. Meanwhile, successive Canadian governments (dominated first by the Conservatives and then by the Liberals after 1921) began to steer Canada along a more independent path, gradually severing all constitutional ties with Britain. In more recent decades, a series of prestigious

---

(Opposite): Animals such as the eagle, the raven and the beaver are often used as symbols of spirits in the carving of totem poles. This example is part of an impressive group standing in Vancouver's Stanley Park.

projects such as the Trans-Canada Highway and the St Lawrence Seaway fostered a growing sense of nationhood, and in 1965 Canada finally adopted its own flag – the red maple leaf. This new-found national pride was further boosted by the hosting of major international events such as Expo '67 and the 1976 Olympic Games. However, national harmony was disrupted as French Canadian discontentment took on a louder voice in the 60s and 70s.

THE QUEBEC ISSUE

Political awakening

French Canadians had been subjected to a multitude of social and economic injustices ever since the British had taken over New France in 1763. Incredibly, it wasn't until the 1960s that their needs and grievances were given a coherent political voice by Quebec's provincial government, under the Liberal premier, Jean Lesage. In response, a Royal Commission was set up in 1963 to investigate the situation. It concluded that Francophones earned less, had a lower standard of living and were less likely to advance economically and socially than their Anglophone counterparts. It also warned that the situation was heading towards a national crisis. The crisis duly exploded in 1970 when the militant separatist group, the Front de Libération du Québec (FLQ), embarked on a wave of terrorism culminating in the kidnapping and murder of a Quebec politician, leaving the country in a state of shock.

Parti Québecois in power

Meanwhile the nationalist wing of the Liberal Party in Quebec had broken away to form the Parti Québecois (PQ) under René Lévesque. In 1976 the PQ won provincial elections and Lévesque became Quebec's premier. The party turned Quebec into an officially monolingual province with a series of controversial language laws that triggered an exodus of thousands of Anglophones from Montreal. However, it failed to achieve its goal of independence when 60% of Quebec voters rejected the mild form of separation ('sovereignty-association') proposed by the 1980 referendum.

The 1995 referendum

In 1990 the Bloc Québecois was formed to represent Quebec's cause at a federal level. It was phenomenally successful, gaining the highest number of votes after the Liberal Party in the 1993 federal elections, making the Bloc Québecois the official government opposition. In 1995, fifteen

---

(**Opposite**): Grain elevators like this one at Wainwright, Alberta, tower over the rail track all the way across the prairies. It has been said that they are the only indigenous form of Canadian architecture.

years after the original referendum, a new sovereignty referendum was called in Quebec, considerably more radical than the first. Under the charismatic leadership of Lucien Bouchard, the separatist movement gained massive momentum and Quebec seemed to be spinning inexorably towards independence. In the event, the separatists were defeated by just one per cent of the vote, leaving the issue far from resolved.

> **DJ dupes the Queen**
> A few days before the referendum, a Montreal disc jockey phoned Buckingham Palace claiming to be the Canadian Prime Minister – and was obligingly put through to Her Majesty. 'Ah Prime Minister!' she exclaimed, and went on to chat about the referendum, her family and even her plans for Halloween to the delight of thousands of listeners tuned in to CKOI FM's 'Drive In' show, where the call was broadcast live. This wasn't the first time the mischievous DJ, Pierre Brassard, had pulled this kind of stunt: in April that year he had even managed to get the Pope on air.

ECONOMY

Voltaire somewhat underestimated Canada's potential when he dismissed it as 'several acres of snow' in 1759. In fact, it boasts one of the world's richest bases of natural resources including huge mineral deposits (potash, zinc, nickel, iron, copper and gold), generous supplies of coal, oil and gas and phenomenal quantities of trees. Almost half the country is covered in forests, providing pulp for the paper industry, as well as timber for the construction industry. In addition, the western prairies are among the world's biggest grain producers, and Canada's great provisions of water (what isn't covered by trees seems to be covered by lakes and rivers) is the source of a massive supply of hydroelectric power.

All this has been carefully and efficiently exploited to make Canada one of the richest countries in the world. It has developed a highly successful industrial and manufacturing sector: major industries include vehicle manufacturing, logging, pulp & paper and fish processing. Its most important trading partner is the US, which receives 75% of Canadian exports and provides 60% of Canada's imports, though Mexico looks set to play a larger role in Canada's economy now that NAFTA (North American Free Trade Agreement) is in operation. Most Canadians enjoy a very good standard of living, but unemployment remains high at over 10%.

THE PEOPLE

Canada's population of 27 million people is concentrated in a thin east-west strip in the south of the country – indeed 90% of all Canadians live within 150km of the US border. This pattern of settlement follows the path taken by the transcontinental railways and, much later, by the Trans-

Canada Highway. The climate is considerably milder here than in the more northerly parts of Canada, and the land is more suitable for farming. The most densely populated provinces are Quebec and Ontario which are home to about 62% of Canadians. Even in the most populated areas of these provinces there are a mere 60 people to each square km – compared to a miserable 230 per square km in the UK.

The immigrants

Immigration has necessarily played a key role in boosting Canada's population and economy. Today, Canada's biggest ethnic group is of British origin (almost 50%) followed by that of French origin (about 27%). First the need to populate the prairies, and then the shortage of a post-war work force resulted in an influx of non French/British immigrants – mainly Germans, Italians, Finns, Ukrainians and Poles. Today, about 20% of Canadians are of non French/British European extract. Canada's immigration policies have often been characterised by racial discrimination; for example Chinese and Japanese were virtually banned from settling in the country between 1885 and 1940. Since the 1970s, however, immigration policies have become increasingly liberal and Asians have constituted a high proportion of the annual 100,000 or so people settling in Canada over recent years.

The native peoples

At the time of early European contact, Canada had an indigenous population of up to two million people. Today there are just 600,000 aboriginals in Canada – a tiny 2% of the population. These consist of about 30,000 Inuit (until recently known as Eskimos) and 360,000 'status Indians' (the remainder being 'non-status' Indians who have either abandoned their status rights or are of mixed blood). The decline of these people is the saddest story of modern Canada. First their numbers are ravaged with the arrival of Western diseases such as TB; then they are manoeuvred into a state of near-dependency on the fur traders and their European goods; finally they are forced off their land by British colonists and shunted into inadequate, isolated reservations where they witness a complete breakdown of the lifestyle that has served their people for thousands of years. For many native communities, the legacy of modern Canada has been high unemployment, alcoholism and depression.

On a more positive note, the Assembly of First Nations (AFN) has been formed to provide native peoples with political and legal representation. In 1992 the AFN scored a huge victory by negotiating a settlement for the Inuit land claim: in 1999 Nanavut (in the Northwest Territories) will become a separate territory to be governed by native Canadians. This will be the first time in modern Canadian history that natives will be responsible for local government.

GOVERNMENT

Canada is a federal state with democratic parliamentary representation. It is also a constitutional monarchy (yes, the Queen is still the official head of state). The way it works is that each of the provinces have their own government with their own premiers and their own legislative bodies. They're in charge of things like taxes, social welfare, education, transport and general administration. Then there's the federal government, in charge of everything else. Executive power is in the hands of the Prime Minister and his or her cabinet. Legislative power rests with the Canadian Parliament in Ottawa, consisting of the House of Commons (elected) and the Senate (appointed by the Prime Minister).

Since Confederation in 1867, central power has swung between the Conservatives and the Liberals with few major differences between the two. The other main party is the New Democratic Party (mildly socialist). The current Prime Minister is Jean Chrétien of the Liberal Party, with the next elections due in 1998.

EDUCATION AND SOCIAL WELFARE

Canada spends a higher percentage of its GDP on education (over 7%) than any other country in the world. It has a universal, free and compulsory school system: all children are required to attend elementary and secondary schools from the age of six to about sixteen. Education is the responsibility of the provinces, not the federal government, which results in distinct differences across the country. Newfoundland, for example, has an exclusively denominational school system, whereas BC's is totally nondenominational. Controversial issues have included the provision of minority language teaching (eg for Francophones outside Quebec, for Anglophones inside Quebec and for the children of immigrant groups) and the often ill-conceived programmes for the education of native children. There are 69 public universities in Canada and over 200 other post-secondary institutions.

Canadians are proud of their social welfare system, which provides free medical care, old age pensions, family allowance and unemployment insurance. The costs of these programmes are shared by the federal and provincial governments, and Canadians can generally take advantage of them whether they're in their own province or an outside province.

RELIGION

Religious mythology and ceremony were highly developed among the native peoples before the arrival of the bible-brandishing Europeans. Beliefs and practices often differed from tribe to tribe, but some were shared by many groups such as the myth of the Earth Diver in which the

Transformer plunges into the ancient waters and gathers the mud from which he moulds the earth. Another common myth told of the mischievous Trickster who steals fire, light, water and food and sets them all lose to create a chaotic world.

Catholicism was, of course, imported by the French as soon as they arrived. Indeed the Catholic Church provided the foundations for the society of New France, and continued to be a dominant power in Quebec until recent decades. British settlers, on the other hand, were Protestant and set about populating the country with more of their ilk. The resulting pattern continues today: over 90% of Quebeckers are Catholic, while Protestantism (of various flavours) dominates all the other provinces. All in all, about 90% of Canadians claim to be Christian. These include significant numbers of Orthodox Christians, particularly in the prairie provinces. The remaining 10% are made up principally of Jews, Muslims, Sikhs, Hindus and Buddhists, large numbers of whom are centred in or around Toronto.

Practical information for the visitor

DOCUMENTS

Americans aren't officially required to show a passport when crossing the border (just solid ID), though it's very much preferred. For everyone else, a full passport is mandatory – a visitor's passport will not be accepted. You must also be able to provide evidence that you will be leaving the country within three months (eg a return or onward air ticket). Travellers' cheques and a copy of your travel insurance policy should also be at the top of your document checklist, and if you plan to rent a car remember, of course, to bring your driver's licence. Other useful ID includes student or OAP cards which will get you substantial reductions at most museums and tourist attractions.

ARRIVING IN CANADA

Before you touch down (or when you arrive at the border if you're coming overland) travellers who don't need a visa (see p22) will be given a waiver form to complete then hand in at passport control. If you do need a visa you'll have to line up in a separate queue at passport control and show your visa documentation. If you're travelling alone, and/or are staying for more than a few weeks and/or have a vaguely shifty look about you, be prepared to answer a long list of searching questions from a Port of Entry examining officer about your travel plans/job back home/childhood holidays in Brighton. If you're travelling as a couple or family, especially if you've got a couple of kids in tow, you should be spared the detective work.

Customs

Import allowances are: 200 cigarettes and 50 cigars; 400gms tobacco; 1.4 litres of spirits or 8.5 litres of beer (for persons aged 18 or over in Alberta, Manitoba and Quebec, 19 elsewhere in Canada) and gifts worth up to $60 each. Any food, plants and animals among your luggage must be declared to customs.

HOTELS

Canada is well supplied with hotels and most of them are of a high standard. Many of the **upmarket hotels** are enormous and luxurious establishments, boasting grand lobbies, sumptuous dining rooms and state of the art gym and pool facilities. Among the best – and certainly the most appropriate for the trans-Canada railway traveller – are the old Canadian Pacific railway hotels, many of them built to accommodate wealthy tourists travelling across the country at the turn of the century.

Mid-range hotels are usually clean, well-equipped and comfortable. They fall into two broad categories: the large and faceless (usually with good facilities which nearly always include private bathroom, TV and phone) and the smaller inn or guesthouse type of place ranging from the very elegant to the distinctly shoddy. It is these smaller places that have the most character, particularly in the numerous converted Victorian or Georgian homes in eastern Canada, but some of them can be a little spartan.

The most popular base for **budget travellers** seems to be the Hostelling International youth hostels. On the whole their standards are excellent (small dorms, cafeterias, laundry rooms, plenty of hot showers) though this is reflected in their prices. Hostels in general (YMCA, YWCA, university digs etc) are much cleaner and more pleasant than the really cheap 'hotels' you'll find adjoined to some of the less salubrious downtown bars, many of which are rowdy doss-houses left over from the days when alcohol could be served only in places that had rooms to let.

LOCAL TRANSPORT

Local transport in Canadian cities is exactly how you'd expect it to be: wide-ranging and frequent, clean, safe and efficient. In many remote areas, however, it is non-existent, so if jumping off the train at a trappers' flag stop in northern Ontario takes your fancy, don't expect to be greeted by a shuttle bus.

Taxis

These are numerous in all cities, and even small towns have their fair share of them. Fares are comparable to those in Europe. Note that it's customary to give cab drivers a tip of about 10-15%.

Subway

There are subway systems in Montreal and Toronto. Both are clean, safe and always busy but since there are relatively few lines it's often as quick to walk or take the bus if you just want to get around the downtown core.

Buses

Bus travel is far better than taking the subway as you can see where you're going and get a better idea of the city's geography. Buses are the mainstay of local transport in Canada with extensive routes in every city. You'll be able to get a route map at the local tourist office; alternatively you can ring the local transport information line – for the number, see the Transport section of the relevant city guide in this book. One irritating thing about buses is that you need the exact change (which you deposit in a plastic box in front of the driver) to travel on them. There's usually a flat fare of about $1.50 or so.

Internal flights

Canada's cities are spaced out over thousands of miles, which makes flying the quickest and most convenient way of getting between them. Accordingly, the country's internal flight network is highly developed and heavily patronised. The main carriers are Air Canada and Canadian Airlines, serving hundreds of places in the country, including some of the most remote outposts such as Inuvik on the Arctic Coast. Internal flights are cheaper if you book them from outside Canada (you don't have to pay tax), and if you plan to take more than one enquire about air passes.

Ferries

Canada has plenty of busy local ferry services such as those from Halifax to Dartmouth, Lévis to Quebec City, Vancouver to Victoria, and from Newfoundland, Prince Edward Island and Cape Breton Island to the mainland. New Brunswick operates toll free ferries across the Saint John and Kennebecasis rivers as part of the highway system. The most popular ferry service among tourists is probably the spectacular 15-hour ride up the Inside Passage from Vancouver Island to Prince Rupert.

Car rental

Renting a car in Canada is expensive (at least $400 a week). As well as your driver's licence it helps to have a major credit card, especially if you're under 25. People under the age of 21 aren't normally eligible to rent cars. Note also that International Driving Permits aren't valid without a supporting national driver's licence.

ELECTRICITY

This is 110 volts AC. Sockets take two-pin continental-type plugs or adapters. Be sure to buy the adapter before you get to Canada as they're very difficult to get hold of once you're there as, understandably, most stores sell the other type of adapter, for Canadians travelling to Britain.

TIME

Canada has six standard time zones which are between $3\frac{1}{2}$ and 8 hours behind GMT as follows:

- Newfoundland Time $\quad$ -3$\frac{1}{2}$ hrs
- Atlantic Time $\quad$ -4 hrs
- Eastern Time $\quad$ -5 hrs
- Central Time $\quad$ -6 hrs
- Mountain Time $\quad$ -7 hrs
- Pacific Time $\quad$ -8 hrs

On the first Sunday in April the clocks are put forward an hour into Daylight Saving Time, which lasts until the last Sunday in October. This does not take place in most of Saskatchewan. Train timetables always show local time, and indicate when the transition into a new time zone is made.

MONEY

Currency

Canada has a decimal currency system: 1 dollar is divided into 100 cents. Coins come in 1, 5, 10, 25 and 50 cent denominations, as well as the $1 coin referred to by Canadians as a 'loonie' after the bird on one side. Notes come in $2, $5, $10, $50, $100, $500 and $1000 bills.

The Canadian dollar has been very weak against the US dollar for the last few years which is one of the reasons why American tourists are flocking to Canada. The current exchange rate is C$1.45 to US$1. You get C$2.2 for £1.

Withdrawing cash

By far the easiest way to get your Canadian currency is to withdraw cash from an automated teller machine at a bank, of which there are dozens in all Canadian cities, using your ordinary debit card. The amount you withdraw is then automatically debited from your account back home. Most debit cards can be used worldwide at teller machines displaying either a Cirrus, Visa or Access/Mastercard symbol; all major Canadian banks accept one of these, eg the Royal Bank of Canada takes Visa and the National Bank of Canada takes Mastercard. The advantages are obvious: most teller machines operate 24 hours a day, seven days a week, so you don't have to worry about bank closing times. Note, however, that many banks add a 1.5% handling fee to the amount you withdraw; check with your branch before you go.

Travellers' cheques
The traditional way to get your dollars is of course to take travellers' cheques. Some banks don't change these (and if they do you usually have to pay a commission) but many restaurants, hotels and shops will accept small-denomination American Express or Visa cheques as cash.

Credit cards
All major cards – eg Visa, Access/Mastercard, American Express, Diners – are accepted throughout Canada and are a very useful backup. No extra charges are made when you use the card to pay for goods and services, but if you use it to get a cash advance you are normally charged a 1.5% handling fee.

Banking hours
Standard banking hours are 10am-3pm, Monday to Friday but more and more banks are staying open much later during the week and on Saturday mornings as well.

Tipping
Tipping, usually around 15% of the bill, is practically obligatory in restaurants; some establishments even fill in the tip box for you on your credit card slip. It is also standard practice to tip bartenders, taxi drivers, hotel porters and doormen.

POST AND TELECOMMUNICATIONS

Post services
Post offices are open 8am-5pm or 9am-6pm Monday to Friday; some big offices also open on Saturday mornings. Many drug stores have post office counters inside (look for the Canada Post sign on the window) and you can buy stamps from countless newsagents, general stores, hotels or stamp machines. It currently costs 88 cents to send a post card overseas; prepaid aerograms are also 88 cents. The service is very reliable and speedy: it takes about five days for a letter to get from Toronto to London (London, England, that is, not London, Ontario).

Making phone calls
In the country that was once home to Alexander Bell, attempting to make an international phone call can be an incredibly frustrating experience. The problem lies in the fact that many public phones accept nothing bigger than a 25 cent coin which means you need hundreds of the things just to get connected. After dialling the number you'll hear an automatic mes-

sage telling you how much it will cost to get through. You then traipse off
to beg the nearest drug store to change all your loonies into quarters,
come back, redial, listen to the message again, start shovelling coins in
frantically, get them all in then....watch the machine spit them out because
you've overloaded it with coins!

The only way to get round this is by buying a **phone card** (usually for
$10 or $20) which you can use to pay for calls made from coin-operated
phones by keying in a pin number. It's still unnecessarily complicated but
at least it doesn't involve coins. The problem is, hardly anywhere sells the
cards; the only place you can be sure of getting hold of one is in youth
hostels. Alternatively look out for one of the smart new phones (mainly
in Montreal and Toronto) that let you pay for your call by swiping your
credit card through. Although this is a bit dangerous in that you can stay
on for ages, oblivious to the time, it still seems to be the cheapest way to
pay for the call and is certainly the easiest.

Useful telephone codes

☎ Nova Scotia	902		☎ Manitoba	204
☎ Quebec City (& around)	418		☎ Saskatchewan	306
☎ Montreal (& around)	514		☎ Alberta	403
☎ Toronto (& around)	416		☎ British Columbia	604

NEWSPAPERS

The most widely read broadsheet is the *Globe and Mail* – it has good
nationwide and some foreign news coverage, and is the only paper circu-
lated right across the country. Many cities have their own quality newspaper (eg the *Toronto Star*, the *Vancouver Sun*) as well as a selection of
tabloids. Canada's answer to *Time* magazine is *Maclean's* which is available throughout the country.

HOLIDAYS

As well as national holidays, which apply throughout Canada, there are a
number of provincial holidays. In both cases banks, offices, schools and
some shops are closed, though restaurants and tourist attractions usually
remain open.

National holidays
• New Year's Day
• Good Friday
• Easter Monday
• Victoria Day: Monday before 25 May
• Canada Day: 1 July
• Labour Day: first Monday in September

- Thanksgiving: second Monday in October
- Remembrance Day: 11 November
- Christmas Day
- Boxing Day

Provincial holidays

- **Alberta** – Heritage Day: first Monday in August
- **British Columbia** – British Columbia Day: first Monday in August
- **New Brunswick** – New Brunswick Day: first Monday in August
- **Newfoundland and Labrador** – St Patrick's Day: 17 March or Monday before; St George's Day: 23 April or Monday before; Discovery Day: Monday nearest to 25 June; Memorial Day: Monday nearest to 1 July; Orangeman's Day: Monday nearest to 10 July
- **Manitoba, NWT, Ontario, Saskatchewan** – Civic Holiday: first Monday in August
- **Quebec** – St-Jean Baptiste Day: Monday before 24 June
- **Yukon** – Discovery Day: third Monday in August

FESTIVALS

The Canadians take their festivals very seriously and great numbers of these events take place throughout the year, right across the country. The great diversity and frequent bizarreness of their themes reflect the contrasts contained within Canada. Interesting examples include the Trappers' Festival in The Pas, MN (February), the Indian Festival in Chilliwack, BC (June), the Potato Festival in Grand Falls, NB (July), the Trout Festival at Flin Flon, MN (July), the National Ukrainian Festival in Dauphin, MN (August) and the Whoop Up and Rodeo Festival in Lethbridge, AB (August).

The major festivals of interest to the trans-Canada rail traveller are the Montreal International Jazz Festival (June/July), the Carnival de Québec in Quebec City (February), the Festival d'Eté in Quebec City (July) and Caribana, the Caribbean carnival in Toronto (August). These and other festivals are listed in the relevant city guides in this book.

FOOD

Canada holds few gastronomic surprises. The most prolific food outlets you'll come across are the standard Western fast food chains (McDonald's, Burger King, Kentucky Fried Chicken, Pizza Hut and the countless spin-offs) crammed into 'food halls' in shopping malls and lining main streets. Added to these are the typical North American diners and countless bagel stores.

This is not to say that you can't eat well in Canada. On the contrary, if you can afford to give the cheapies a miss you'll find plenty of good quality upmarket restaurants in most cities. Typical trans-Canada fare seems to be grilled meat (especially beef steak, pork fillet, chicken breast) accompanied by vegetables and fries, but there are some notable regional specialities. The Maritimes, for instance, are famous for their excellent fish, particularly their lobster, salmon, oysters and scallops. Then there's the province of Quebec, where the generally superb food owes far more to Gallic than to North American influences. At the same time, the choice in most big cities is considerably enlivened by a wide range of ethnic restaurants, typically Italian, Greek, Vietnamese, Chinese and Japanese.

DRINKS

Non alcoholic

The nation's favourite non-alcoholic drink is coffee, which is invariably the freshly-ground variety, served with milk or cream. Canadians drink a lot of it and empty cups are nearly always refilled at no extra charge. Tea, on the other hand, is not their speciality. British travellers may well be shocked by the manner in which this is prepared: instead of pouring the boiling water *over* the tea or tea bag (essential for a good brew), they simply fetch you a pot of vaguely hot water with a tea bag lying limply by the side. Their milk shakes, on the other hand, are a credit to the country.

Alcoholic

The most popular alcoholic drink is beer. Most of it is brewed by Labatt's or Molson and tends to be on the light and fizzy side. Another favourite is whisky – as well as importing foreign labels, Canada brews its own stuff. A good and seriously strong Canadian malt whisky is Yukon Jack, while popular rye whiskies are Canadian Club and Seagram's. Believe it or not, Canada also has its own wine, produced from grapes grown in southern Ontario and BC. In a good year it's surprisingly drinkable, but the quality is unpredictable and most tourists stick to the foreign imports.

WHAT TO DO IN THE EVENING

While many of Canada's smaller towns offer little more than a seedy, rough-edged bar by way of evening entertainment, there's usually no shortage of options in the big cities.

Drinking takes place in numerous establishments including English-style pubs, super-trendy bars, mellow 'lounges' (sit-around-chat-and-relax kind of places) and hundreds of bog-standard dimly lit taverns. A lot of these places serve food, too, and some have regular **live music** slots (lots of folk, rock and indie – with the quality ranging from good to dire-and jazz, usually the safest bet).

If **dancing** is what you're after, the best place for this is Montreal which boasts hundreds of nightclubs catering to all ages and tastes. This activity is less widely pursued in the other cities, apart from in the prairies where the extraordinary country and western 'line dancing' is undergoing a massive revival.

If this sounds a bit too energetic, there's always the **movies** – Canadian cities have plenty of cinemas showing all the mainstream American output, which is screened there ages before it reaches the UK. You'll usually find a couple of local art-house cinemas as well, or cinemas showing mainly Canadian releases.

Theatre is particularly well represented in Toronto which claims to be the third biggest theatre city in the English-speaking world after London and New York. Certainly there's lots to choose from, ranging from Andrew Lloyd-Webber to Shakespeare to new Canadian talent such as the excellent Brad Fraser, winner of the 1994 London Evening Standard award for the most promising new playwright.

Ballet (from classical to contemporary) is widely performed not only in Montreal, Toronto and Vancouver but also in Winnipeg whose Royal Winnipeg Ballet is internationally respected. **Classical music** and **opera** enthusiasts should find enough to keep them happy among companies such as the Montreal Symphony Orchestra, the Canadian Opera Company (Toronto) and Vancouver Opera. Moreover all this high-brow cultural entertainment is very good value (much cheaper than in London) with tickets ranging from about $15-$40.

Finally, if none of this takes your fancy you can always join the best part of Canada's youth and simply sit around with a bunch of mates in a shopping mall.

SHOPPING

Shopping in Canada is, on the whole, no different from shopping in the US. Most of it takes place in malls, of which there are thousands spread across the country. The advantage of these is that they protect shoppers from Canada's fierce winter weather. On the down side, they're often oppressively crowded and the absence of natural light makes them a bit depressing. The big department stores are Eaton's and The Bay (part of the original Hudson's Bay Company), which you'll find in every city. Most shops are open 9am-6pm, or later in the bigger cities.

Souvenirs

Prints of Inuit paintings (originals are very expensive) and Inuit soapstone carvings are popular with tourists and Canadians alike. Indian crafts are also undergoing a revival; you'll find some beautiful and reasonably priced goodies for sale, such as beaded moccasins and handwoven sweaters. Look out for the cooperative stores owned and run by natives themselves so you can be sure that the profits are all going back to the people who produced the goods. Moving west, local specialities include stetson hats and cowboy boots (obligatory if you're thinking of taking up line dancing). Finally, wherever you go in Canada you'll come across zillions of bottles of maple syrup.

TAXES

When you first arrive in Canada you'll be amazed at how cheap everything seems until you go and buy something and watch the price shoot up by about 14% at the checkout. This is because most things you pay for including food, drink and accommodation are subject to a 7% Goods and Services Tax (GST). In addition, all provinces except Alberta, NWT and the Yukon levy a 5-7% Provincial Sales Tax (PST) on goods, restaurant bills and sometimes hotel bills.

You can claim a rebate for GST you paid for goods subsequently taken out of Canada, and for some accommodation **but you must keep all of your receipts**. You can also reclaim PST on goods bought in Newfoundland, Nova Scotia, Quebec and Manitoba. Booklets containing a claim form and details on conditions and restrictions are available in tourist offices and many stores and hotels.

CRIME

Canada justifiably has a reputation for being one of the safest countries in the world to travel in. That said, crime against tourists isn't unheard of. Use your common sense: don't stray into the rougher neighbourhoods waving a map about; don't wander around alone late at night, women in particular; keep your important tickets and documents in a money belt, preferably with a belt-style strap rather than a quick release catch. Also, be careful about where you leave your luggage: if you're staying in a hostel leave valuables in a locker and remember that even the most expensive, security-conscious hotels aren't invulnerable to petty thieves.

PART 3: TRANS-CANADA RAILWAY

Building the first trans-Canada railway

What tempted the people of Canada to undertake so gigantic a work as the Canadian Pacific Railway? The difficulties in the way were great, unprecedented, unknown... We were under the inspiration of a national idea, and went forward. We were determined to be something more than a fortuitous collection of provinces. The Century (1885)

The story of Canada's first transcontinental railway has a plot as thick as a Jeffrey Archer novel. The only thing missing is sexual intrigue; everything else is there: corporate greed, political skulduggery, brave men, bankruptcy, war, danger, death, glory... It's a story that has gripped Canadians for more than a century spawning countless books, an epic poem and, of course, the inevitable TV mini-series.

Canada's ongoing preoccupation with the railway is due not only to the drama surrounding its construction but also to the crucial role it played in shaping Canadian history. For the CPR did more than build a railway, it built a nation. 'It can be argued,' reads a display in Winnipeg's Union Station, 'that November 7th 1885 – the day on which the last spike was driven on the CPR line at Craigellachie – is a more appropriate day from which to date the existence of Canada than July 1st, 1867.' Rather a tall claim for a railroad. But to understand this railroad's significance it is necessary to abandon one's concept of modern Canada and take a look at the young dominion of the 1860s and 70s.

CANADA BEFORE THE RAILWAY

The infant country

Canada officially became a country when Queen Victoria signed the British North America Act on 1 July 1867 but in no way did it resemble the country we know today. The new 'dominion' was basically a disparate collection of eastern colonial provinces with no real sense of unity or nationhood. It covered a relatively small chunk of a vast territory, for the most part uninhabited. British Columbia, which remained under the jurisdiction of Great Britain, lay 3000 miles west of Ottawa, beyond the Rocky Mountains. Stretching east from the Rockies were the immense prairies, still controlled by the Hudson's Bay Company – barren and empty save the little Red River settlement where Winnipeg now stands.

Fear of the Yankees

To make matters worse, Canada lay in the shadow of a large, intimidating neighbour. The United States boasted an ever growing population of 40 million, an alarming number of people next to Canada's scanty three and a half million. Moreover, America had been pursuing an aggressive policy of expansion and annexation for a number of years.

'That the U.S. are bound finally to absorb all the world and the rest of mankind,' declared a San Francisco newspaper in 1869, 'every well-regulated American is prepared to admit. When the fever is on our people do not seem to know when and where to stop, but keep on swallowing, so long as there is anything in reach.' Canada, understandably, felt threatened.

Some twenty years earlier America had effortlessly absorbed Texas and California. Then, in 1867, it purchased Alaska from the Russians for $7.2 million. Any fool could see that the Americans now had their eye on British Columbia and the Northwest – natural extensions of California and Minnesota. Indeed, for these isolated communities, America was their closest link with the outside world; annexation would in many ways be logical and sensible. The future of Canada was by no means assured.

Macdonald reaches across the continent

Sir John A Macdonald, Canada's first Prime Minister, firmly believed that if Canada were to survive as a nation it would have to expand westwards and take control of British Columbia, the Pacific coast and the giant stretch of land in between. But this was easier said than done. How were these areas to be obtained and consolidated? How were settlers to be induced to move west with virtually no east-west transportation or communication? The answer came in the form of a demand put to the government by British Columbia as a condition of entering Confederation: a railway across Canada to the Pacific.

The railway is promised

The British Columbians got their way; the province joined Canada in 1871 and in return the government formally pledged to build the railway. The terms agreed were somewhat optimistic: it was guaranteed that construction of the line, which would take an all-Canadian route instead of cutting south of the Great Lakes through America, would begin within two years of union and that the railway would be completed within ten!

Macdonald rightly saw in this enterprise the key to the creation of a transcontinental nation. As well as securing Canada its sixth province, the railway would encourage immigration, carry thousands of settlers out west and open up trade with the Orient. But it wasn't going to be easy. The distances to cover were enormous, the expense would be colossal and the physical challenges of laying track across the mountains and the Precambrian Shield would be back-breaking. It took a man of

Macdonald's expansive vision not to balk at these difficulties. Others did indeed balk. The leader of the Opposition, Alexander Mackenzie, was almost apoplectic in his outrage at what he repeatedly denounced as 'an act of insane recklessness!'

The survey begins

The first gigantic step was to survey the land and determine the route. The government formed the Canadian Pacific Survey to do this work and placed it under the direction of Sandford Fleming. Thousands of miles of wild and inhospitable land had to be covered on foot, and the towering mountains had to be climbed again and again by men searching for passes the railway could go through. Over the next six years Fleming's team was to complete 46,000 miles of survey and thirty-eight men were to die in the process.

THE PACIFIC SCANDAL

Macdonald seeks a private company

Meanwhile Macdonald was searching for a suitable private company to build and operate the new railway. This way the government would avoid having to pay for it by increasing taxation. Two companies emerged in competition for the charter, one of them headed by the multi-millionaire, Sir Hugh Allan, and backed by a group of Americans. Macdonald stipulated that the two companies should merge and insisted on Allan disassociating himself from his American backers; it was imperative that this should be a Canadian enterprise. Everyone complied and the charter was granted in March 1873, with Allan appointed as president of the new company.

Sir Hugh's double dealing

All the while, however, Allan had been engaged in a series of complicated secret agreements. In the first instance he and his American partners, owners of the Northern Pacific Railway lines in America, had plotted to delay completion of the all-Canadian route while they pushed on with a connection from the main line down to their own lines in the US. Later, Allan entered into clandestine talks with the government regarding his role in the new company. Then, when it became clear that he must disentangle himself from the Americans if he were to succeed in his plans, he proceeded to wriggle out of his previous US pact. The Americans were furious with him and decided to blow Allan's cover and reveal a few incriminating details to the Opposition...

Scandal erupts: the government collapses

The Liberals seized upon this gift horse with zeal. More investigations unearthed even better ammunition. Not only could the government be charged with handing over the railway to a bunch of American schemers disguised as a Canadian company; it also emerged that Allan had advanced large amounts of cash to fund Macdonald's 1872 election campaign – presumably in return for the promise of the presidency of the company. Particularly indicting was a stolen telegram from Macdonald to Allan's lawyer: 'I must have another ten thousand; will be the last time of calling; do not fail me; answer today.' The Pacific Scandal, as it was known, filled all the newspapers and was on everyone's tongue. Finally, charged with corruption in parliament, Macdonald resigned on 6 November 1873 and the government was dissolved.

THE RAILWAY UNDER THE LIBERALS

The dream gets watered down

The newly elected Liberal government found itself lumbered with a project it had never supported in the first place. Moreover, Canada was suddenly entering a continental depression. Private investment shrivelled up so the government was forced to undertake the railway as a public works, handing out contracts for the construction of sections of track. The ambitious scheme was literally watered down as Mackenzie talked not of a single continuous track but of a land and water route. He planned to shorten the railway and use steam ships to cross the Great Lakes.

Slowly on

To avoid corruption, Mackenzie ruled that contracts should always be awarded to the lowest bidder. These men, however, were not always the most qualified or competent builders. The first section of track to be built was, in fact, a branch line going south from Winnipeg to the US border. Its construction was characterised by costly incompetence and blunder. Work progressed slowly – the Pacific Survey seemed to be dragging on forever – and it wasn't until June 1875 that construction began on the main line, the section linking Lake Superior and Winnipeg. It was becoming clear that the railway was languishing in the hands of the government.

OVER TO THE CPR

Macdonald back in power

It had been generally assumed that Macdonald's career had ended with the ruin and dishonour of the Pacific Scandal. But Canada was fed up with the Liberals and in the 1878 elections 'the Old Chief' was returned to power with a landslide victory. Once more he took up his old vision of transforming Canada into a strong transcontinental nation. This policy depended on completing the railway as quickly as possible. More government contracts were awarded for the 125-mile section between Yale and Kamloops, west of the Rockies; but Macdonald was on the lookout for a group of private capitalists to take over the venture. This time their credentials would have to be flawless.

The CPR is formed

Such a group presented itself in the form of the CPR Syndicate. Its key members were leading directors of the Bank of Montreal. They came with an impeccable reputation, considerable financial backing and experience in running a railroad (they had recently transformed a bankrupt line into a resounding financial success). They were clearly perfect for the job and, following lengthy negotiations with the government, the Canadian Pacific Railway Company was incorporated in February 1881, a decade after British Columbia had been promised the transcontinental line. Macdonald pledged a $25 million cash subsidy and 25 million acres of land to the new CPR, and agreed to turn over all the government contracted lines to the company once they were completed.

The task ahead

The CPR was faced with a mammoth task: a total of 1,900 miles of track remained to be laid. In the east, there was the formidable challenge of carving a way through the Canadian Shield north of the Great Lakes. In the prairies they had to lay 900 miles of track west of Winnipeg to the Rockies. In the west they had to take that track over or through the Rockies and the Selkirks to meet the government contracted line at Kamloops. The company hoped to forge ahead with this work as quickly as possible: the quicker the railway was completed, the quicker it could turn in a profit. The building season usually lasted only from April to November. The first season's work, however, was very disappointing – only 130 miles of track were laid. It became clear that some dynamic force was required to galvanise the operation and push it full steam ahead.

Enter Van Horne

This dynamic force was provided by William Cornelius Van Horne, a rising star in American railroad management. The appointment of Van Horne as General Manager of the CPR was possibly the most important decision the company ever made – he was soon to be ranked as one of the world's greatest railway men. He took the railway by the scruff of the neck, established control of the entire line himself and began work in February 1882 by declaring he'd have 500 miles of track laid by the end of the season.

Whirlwind construction across the prairies

The press and politicians openly scoffed at Van Horne's extravagant boast. But soon their jaws were hanging open at the breakneck speed of the track-laying west of Winnipeg. Men worked around the clock to push the track forward, and construction gobbled up a mountain of supplies. In the end, Van Horne's goal was not reached; he was thwarted by spring flooding. But by the end of the building season no less than 418 miles of track had been laid.

The next season, 1883, was to see the fastest construction rate of the entire project, with the record set in the month of July when 92.3 miles were laid under scorching temperatures.

By November the prairie section was completed. However, the track had been racing towards the mountains all summer with one crucial question remaining to be answered: which route was it going to take across them?

Problems with the route

Based on the results on the exhaustive Pacific Survey, Sandford Fleming had concluded that the best route west of Winnipeg would be north to Fort Edmonton, then over the Rockies through the Yellowhead Pass. When the CPR took over they rejected this decision in favour of a southerly route – partly to shorten the line, and partly because they realised it would be easier to control and profit from an area as yet unpopulated. The problem was that a suitable pass through the Rockies had yet to be established, and a pass through the Selkirks had not even been discovered.

The company dispatched Major A B ('Hells Bells') Rogers. It took him one and a half years of scouring the mountains to discover a pass through the Selkirks (still known as Rogers Pass) that the railway could take after crossing the Rockies via the Kicking Horse pass. Rogers himself had some doubts about the feasibility of this route and alternative passes were still being explored as the track was approaching the mountains from Winnipeg in 1883. It wasn't until autumn that year that the CPR confirmed, to Rogers' great relief, that his route would be adopted after all.

Meanwhile, the planned route across the Shield was also proving controversial. Although the government had always stipulated that the railway should take an all-Canadian route north of Lake Superior, some of the directors had believed that this would never be enforced given how much cheaper and easier it would be to connect the line with existing American tracks south of the lakes. When George Stephen, the CPR president, made it clear that he was determined to follow the all-Canadian route two of the directors resigned; they obviously felt that this plan was doomed to failure.

The track through the prairies had been straight and relatively easy to lay. Now the railway had to be forced across the two dreaded barriers: the Shield and the mountains. The challenges were to prove enormous.

DANGERS AND DIFFICULTIES

Muskeg, sinkholes and rock

Van Horne is said to have described the section north of Lake Superior as 'two hundred miles of engineering impossibilities'. Workmen had to blast their way through the granite of the Shield, often finding solid rock well below the level where earth had been expected. Track-layers also had to contend with the infamous muskeg and sinkholes, seemingly solid earth which would suddenly swallow up track under the weight of a train. One such sinkhole required fill to be dumped in it for three months before it could safely support trains.

Whisky peddlers

Life along the line in Ontario was frequently disrupted by the workmen's enthusiasm for liquor. A railway worker's life was particularly harsh and comfortless and, for many, whisky was the only diversion. They were easy targets for the illegal whisky merchants, and results were often colourful.

The problem became chronic in the summer of 1884 as this construction supervisor's report testifies: 'These whisky peddlers would get off in the woods near the supply roads – get the teamsters drunk, racing teams, breaking wagons; destroying property and supplies would follow. They would waylay men, get them drunk, rob them of everything of value and threaten the life of anyone who opposes the traffic...' These events took place in areas so remote that few policemen were available to halt the lawlessness.

The weather

All along the line the workers had to cope with the paralysing effects of the weather. In 1884 there was no winter break on the Ontario line. Track had to be laid in snow that was sometimes up to five feet deep and in temperatures occasionally as low as minus fifty. Freezing weather conditions were also a problem in the mountains. Track was laid between Blaeberry Creek and Donald in temperatures of minus thirty; then, when the warmer weather came, the rails expanded and it was found that the track was out of gauge.

Construction in the Selkirks took place under the continual threat of avalanches. James Ross, head of construction in the mountain division, wrote to Van Horne of the dangers: 'I find that the snow-slides on the Selkirks are much more serious than I anticipated, and I think are quite beyond your ideas of their magnitude and of the danger to the line.... at one point, ten slips came down within six days, piling the snow 50 feet deep and 1800 feet in length along the located line..... The great trouble we are labouring under at present is that the men are frightened. Seven have already been buried in different slides, though fortunately only two were killed...'

The CPR built numerous snowsheds to protect the railway's passage through the Selkirks (nonetheless, avalanches were to cause the deaths of two hundred people between 1885 and 1909, prompting the construction of the remarkable Connaught Tunnel).

Mountains, tunnels and bridges

Of course the biggest challenge facing the railway builders was the physical barrier of the mountains. Trains had to cross three major summits – Kicking Horse Pass, Rogers Pass and Eagle Pass – each presenting an engineering nightmare. Tunnels had to be blasted through rock, bridges built over precipitous gorges, track laid close to vertical drops. It took thousands of workers to get the line through the gruelling mountain division; the Kicking Horse pass alone required 12,000 men. Typical of the kind of construction that had to be built was the Mountain Creek bridge on the eastern slopes of the Selkirks; this amazing feat of engineering was 164 feet high and 1086 feet long, and contained two million board feet of timber.

On Andrew Onderdonk's section from Yale to Kamloops the difficulties of drilling tunnels through the Fraser Canyon was so great his men were able to advance the track no more than six feet a day. In some parts, the men had to be winched down to the track on ropes. Scores of men died on this treacherous route, some as a result of rockslides, many as a result of careless handling of explosives. The nearby hospital at Yale had to be enlarged to cope with all the injuries.

ON THE VERGE OF BANKRUPTCY

The money runs out

Despite these enormous difficulties, the track moved ever on. Then, in 1884, the CPR found itself in the midst of a severe financial crisis that threatened to throw the company into ruin even as completion of the line was in sight. The railway was swallowing up vast amounts of money. George Stephen, the CPR president, had been frantically trying to raise capital at home and in London, but the funds he secured were not sufficient to keep the operation going. The CPR's debt in January 1884 ran to $15 million and time was running out. In desperation he begged the government for a loan of $22.5 million.

Temporary relief

Macdonald knew he'd have a tough time getting this through parliament but he also knew that if the CPR went under so would the government. He forced his party to support the relief bill by threatening to resign if it was rejected. As parliament dragged out the issue in endless debate, the CPR was sinking fast. Stephen wrote to Macdonald: 'I do not, at the moment, see how we are going to get the money to keep the work going... If I find we cannot go on I suppose the only thing to do will be to put in a Receiver. If that must be done the quicker it is done the better.'

At the end of February the bill was passed and the money was loaned to the company. By the end of the year it was gone. The CPR had reached its darkest hour. Stephen and his cousin Smith, a fellow CPR director, had sunk their entire personal fortune into the company. There was no more money to be had. Wages were months in arrears all along the line and men were striking or rioting. There was virtually no chance of persuading parliament to loan yet more money. The CPR was done for.

The Northwest rebellion

Events suddenly took a dramatic turn in the spring of 1885 when the bloody Northwest Rebellion broke out in Manitoba. Van Horne ingeniously seized on this opportunity to demonstrate the importance of the railway to the government: he immediately offered to move troops out by train to crush the rebellion. The line was not yet finished; there were four gaps, totalling 86 miles, but by shifting the men across the gaps by sled or on foot Van Horne was able to get them to Winnipeg in a week. Just fifteen years earlier, during the first Northwest Rebellion, that same journey had taken three months. By the time the troops returned, the gaps had been closed and the section was completed.

The final loan

As summer approached the CPR's credit could stretch no further. Disaster seemed imminent, as this telegram from Van Horne to George Stephen indicates: 'Have no means of paying wages, pay car can't be sent out, and unless we get immediate relief we must stop. Please inform Premier and Finance Minister. Do not be surprised, or blame me, if an immediate and most serious catastrophe happens.' Once more a desperate Stephen begged Macdonald to bail out the company. He knew that they could quickly recoup the money once the line was completed and a through service was in operation; without a loan, however, the CPR faced bankruptcy even at this eleventh hour. Given the railway's crucial role in dealing with the recent rebellion, parliament could hardly fail to back the CPR. In July it passed another relief bill. This was the last time the CPR had to ask the government for a loan.

COMPLETION OF THE RAILWAY

The last spike

It took just a few more months to complete the line; all that was left to do was to close the gap between Onderdonk's tracks in the Gold Range and James Ross's in the Selkirks. The tracks met on 7 November 1885 in Eagle Pass at a spot named Craigellachie. The driving of the last spike was surely an emotional moment for all involved but it was a simple affair without pomp or ceremony. Van Horne declined to celebrate the occasion with the traditional golden last spike: 'The last spike will be just as good an iron one as there is between Montreal and Vancouver,' he said, 'and anyone who wants to see it driven will have to pay full fare.'

The spike was driven by Donald A Smith, the eldest member of the CPR Syndicate. His first blow bent the iron, the spike was quickly replaced with a new one, and Smith's second attempt was a success. The crowds cheered and demanded a speech of Van Horne. His response was typically succinct: 'All I can say is that the work has been done well in every way.'

EARLY RAILWAY SERVICE

Passenger service begins
The line had to be properly finished off and upgraded before a passenger service could be inaugurated. The CPR had extended the track to Montreal by taking over existing lines in eastern Canada and on 28 June 1886 the first regular passenger train, the 'Pacific Express', left Montreal at 20:00 hours. On 1 July it reached Winnipeg and on 4 July it reached Port Moody at 12:00 hours – exactly on time. This was the first scheduled trans-Canada rail trip and at the time the longest scheduled passenger train trip in the world. With the extension of the line from Port Moody to Vancouver in May 1887, the main line was 4675 km long.

The first travellers
Until 1899, transcontinental trains ran on a daily basis; the westbound train was known as the Pacific Express and the eastbound train as the Atlantic Express.

The carriages were extremely luxurious with all sleeping cars boasting bathtubs, an unheard of novelty in North America at the time. The dining cars served fine international cuisine and vintage wines, and were generally patronised by passengers travelling First Class. Coach passengers usually dined in the much cheaper Canadian Pacific restaurants located at division points along the line, while the train was being serviced or the locomotive was being changed. It was the popularity of these restaurants that gave birth to the famous Canadian Pacific hotels, still flourishing today.

As Macdonald had predicted, the railway carried droves of settlers out to the now accessible west. Special 'land seeker' tickets were offered at reduced rates to encourage people to go and investigate areas under development. By the end of the railway's first decade of operation it had changed the lives of thousands of Canadians and, in turn, had changed the face of Canada itself.

Into the 20th century: CNR & VIA Rail

Consult the annals of Canada for the past fifty years at random and whatever party may be in power, what do you find? The government is building a railway, buying a railway, selling a railway or blocking a railway. Paul Lamarche, Speech in Montreal, 1917

The CPR proved to be an enormous financial success. Not only did it operate a highly profitable railway service; it also established a national telegraph network, an express parcel service and branched out into steamships, hotels and real estate. Entrepreneurs clamoured to emulate the company's achievements and the early twentieth century saw a rapid and undisciplined growth in railway building, all of which finally led to the birth of the CPR's present-day competitor: the Canadian National Railways system.

TWO MORE TRANSCONTINENTAL LINES

The boom years of the first decade of the twentieth century brought thousands of settlers flooding out west to make their fortunes. It was felt that the country needed a second transcontinental line and two companies eagerly put themselves forward for the task. Somewhat recklessly, the Liberal government, in power under Wilfrid Laurier, gave charters to both companies: the Canadian Northern Railway and the Grand Trunk Pacific.

The Canadian Northern Railway

This young company operated a series of railway lines along the northern prairies. The entrepreneurial owners planned to extend the prairie route to the Pacific via the Yellowhead pass in the Rockies – Sandford Fleming's original choice for the first transcontinental. The line would go down to Kamloops where it would meet the tracks of the CPR. From there it would follow the course of the CPR down the Fraser Canyon, always on the opposite bank since there was room for only one track on one side. Building proceeded and the last spike was driven on 23 January 1915.

The Grand Trunk Pacific

The Grand Trunk was one of Canada's oldest railway companies with a well established network in eastern Canada. The epitome of prudence and circumspection, the Grand Trunk wasn't ordinarily given to taking risks but its new general manager, Charles Hays, was convinced that the company needed to expand westwards to capture a share of the Pacific market. His new line would also take a northern prairie route, taking the

Yellowhead pass through the Rockies. From here, however, it would part company with the Canadian Northern and travel northwest up to the new coastal town of Prince Rupert. This was the closest Canadian port to Asia, and Hays envisioned it as the port of the future, the key to the Grand Trunk's success. Sadly Hays was never to see the line reach this terminus. Following a trip to London to raise more funds for the project, he returned in April 1912 aboard the ill-fated *SS Titanic* and drowned with the sinking ship. Two years later in April 1914 the last spike was driven in the Grand Trunk Pacific railway.

Failure

Canada had overstretched itself. There was nowhere near enough traffic to sustain three transcontinental lines. A world-wide depression was having dire effects on the economy, which grew steadily worse with the outbreak of World War I. The two new lines were dead losses. And they weren't the only ones. Canada's railways had by now got completely out of hand – there were about two hundred companies operating a chaotic network of profitless lines. In 1916 a royal commission investigating the railway crisis concluded that the private companies should be taken over and reorganised by the government. This is exactly what happened in 1923 when all the railways, with the notable exception of the CPR, were combined to form the publicly owned Canadian National Railways (CNR) system.

THE CNR TAKES OVER

Railways overhauled

The CNR lost no time in trimming down, shaking up and integrating the sprawling rail lines it had inherited. As a result of innovative restructuring and tight management the chaos was eliminated and the CNR emerged as a highly efficient business. Like its competitor, the CPR, the

---

Canada's rail lines earned themselves a variety of nicknames over the years, some of them affectionate, some of them definitely not. A few of the most widely used are:
- **Atlantic, Quebec and Western**: All Queer and Wobbly
- **Canadian National Railways**: Certainly No Rush
- **Canadian Pacific Railway**: Can't Pay Rent; Can't Promise Returns; Chinese Pacific
- **Grand Trunk Pacific**: Get There Perhaps
- **Grand Trunk Railway**: The Big Suitcase, The Leaky Roof
- **Hudson Bay**: The Muskeg Special
- **Niagara, St Catharines and Toronto**: Naturally Slow and Tiresome; Never Starts on Time
- **Pacific Great Eastern**: Please Go Easy; Prince George Eventually; Past God's Endurance
- **Quebec, Montreal and Southern**: Quel Maudit Service

new railway system carried both passengers and freight across its transcontinental lines. It also followed the CPR's example by building a series of grand railway hotels in major cities along the line.

Decline in passenger travel

As the railways advanced further into the twentieth century the volume of passenger traffic steadily decreased, particularly after World War II. Motor cars were taking over as the primary mode of transport and highways were constructed right across the nation. Air travel, too, became increasingly affordable and cut travelling time down to the minimum.

In an effort to win back passengers, both railways launched faster, spruced up services in 1955: 'the Canadian' was introduced by the CPR and 'the Super Transcontinental' by the CNR. Nonetheless, the volume of passenger traffic remained low and the CPR decided to concentrate on its freight operations, leaving the CNR to handle the bulk of Canada's passenger service.

Formation of VIA Rail

The completion of the Trans-Canada Highway in 1962 dealt a crippling blow to rail traffic. By the 1970s the situation had become dire and in 1976 a government report concluded that passenger traffic was set to decrease even further. In response to this situation the government decided to discontinue non-essential rail services and place the remaining passenger lines in the hands of a new government-owned body: VIA Rail Canada. VIA would operate the passenger service, leasing CPR and CNR tracks while these companies focused on freight transportation.

Southern route abandoned

For some years VIA ran the Canadian across the southern and northern routes through the Rockies. In 1988 it introduced the Rocky Mountaineer, a daylight-only train ride through the mountains. However, the experiment proved a failure and a year after its launch the government decided to privatise this route. The Rocky Mountaineer was subsequently taken over by The Great Canadian Railtour Company Ltd who have succeeded in turning the route into a highly profitable tourist attraction.

Meanwhile the southern (and more historic) route via Calgary and Banff was abandoned by VIA Rail in 1989 leaving the northern route, via Edmonton and Jasper, as the only remaining transcontinental passenger line.

The future

Faced with ever shrinking government subsidies and the continual pressure to cut costs, a question mark hangs over the future of some of VIA's less profitable lines. You may hear rumours, for instance, about the supposedly imminent discontinuation of the Hudson Bay route to Churchill or the Skeena route to Prince Rupert. Even aboard the Canadian, fellow travellers may tell you they've heard the transcontinental line is soon to be terminated – and many people outside Canada think it's already stopped running! But behind the gossip no one knows for sure what the future holds for passenger rail service in Canada. One can only hope that what is truly a first class service over one of the most beautiful countries in the world will be able to withstand the onslaught of declining passenger traffic and cruise into the next century intact.

The lines today

If you take the train right across Canada you'll notice that different sections of the route use different types of train and offer slightly different services. By far the longest through train is VIA's flagship, the Canadian – the tri-weekly transcontinental between Toronto and Vancouver. The other routes covered by this book are the Ocean (Halifax to Montreal), the Corridor (Montreal to Toronto), the Hudson Bay (Winnipeg to Churchill), the Skeena (Jasper to Prince Rupert) and the privately-run Rocky Mountaineer (Vancouver to Jasper or Banff/Calgary).

THE CANADIAN

Renovation

The Canadian was first introduced by the CPR in 1955. At that time the streamlined, stainless steel trains, designed and built in America, were considered high-tech and ultra modern, representing the latest in railway technology. Thirty-seven years later VIA reinvented the Canadian, this time marketing its nostalgic appeal, elegant appearance and the luxurious comforts of old-style, long distance rail travel.

Before launching a new service aboard the Canadian, VIA carried out a massive renovation project on the 190 trains. Steam heating was converted to electric; new wiring and lighting were installed; air conditioning was introduced; showers were fitted in each sleeping car; ventilation was improved; mechanical components such as brakes and trucks were completely overhauled and the interiors were recarpeted and reupholstered throughout. The total cost of the project was over $200 million.

Coach or Silver & Blue

There are now two ways of travelling on the Canadian: in Coach class or in Silver & Blue. Coach class is the cheaper fare; you get reclining seats (where you sleep overnight) with pull down trays, overhead lights and leg rests. The seating seems to have been designed with your average basketball player in mind: the leg room is very generous

Silver & Blue is for passengers travelling in sleeping cars. It's much more luxurious than Coach class. This section has its own dome car and lounges, and passengers have exclusive use of the dining car.

Staff on the train

VIA's onboard staff are almost without exception helpful, efficient and friendly They also tend to be very knowledgeable about the train and the places it takes you through, particularly the older people who've clearly worked on the railway for many years. Don't feel shy about asking them questions – they're usually more than happy to talk about anything to do with the journey. During the peak season, however, the Canadian gets packed out and things can get rather hectic, which leaves the staff with little time to sit around and chat.

Boss of the train is the Conductor. The Conductor will usually introduce himself (I've yet to come across a female conductor) to Coach class passengers at the beginning of a trip and will explain the layout of the train, the facilities onboard and give a brief description of the highlights of the scenery or towns you'll pass through.

Next in line are the Service Managers and the Service Coordinators, the latter working mainly in the sleeping cars, where they'll see passengers to their seats and explain the facilities and service. The staff you'll meet most – whether in Coach or Silver & Blue – are the Service Attendants who generally run around making sure everything's okay. The staff are attentive in both sections of the trains but Silver & Blue passengers are particularly well looked after, with drinks and snacks brought to their seats as and when they please.

Sleeping accommodation

There are four types of sleeping accommodation available to Silver & Blue passengers:

• **Section** These are wide double seats facing each other which convert to bunk beds at night. It's an open section of the train and people will be wandering up and down the carriage all day on their way to the dome car or the dining car. You do get a bit of privacy at night time, however, when the bunks are enclosed by heavy curtains. There's always a toilet close by.

• **Roomette** These ingenious little one-person rooms contain a private loo (doubles up as a leg rest) and your own corner sink and mirror. You sleep on a pull out bed which slots into position on top of your seat and the toilet. If you need the loo in the night it can be a little tricky sliding back the bed to get to it quickly; it is advisable to practice this handy manoeuvre before going to sleep.

• **Bedroom** These private rooms contain two armchairs by day and pull down bunks by night. Unlike the roomettes and the sections, these beds lie along the width instead of the length of the train which apparently induces a pleasant rocking or cradling sensation as the train chugs along. The bedrooms are equipped with their own washbasin, fold out table and a private loo in an adjoining little room.

• **Drawing room** like the bedroom but for three people. The drawing rooms are the most spacious private compartments on the train.

Bathrooms
Each sleeping car has its own piping hot shower but these are not available to Coach class passengers, who have to make do with the wash basins. You might expect the Coach to get a bit whiffy by the third day but this rarely seems to be the case. The passengers seem happy to improvise with the basin – or else the air conditioning is extremely effective.

Eating and drinking
If you're travelling in Coach class you'll be feeding yourself at the Skyline Cafe which serves light snacks you can take back to your seats (sandwiches, crisps, and the ubiquitous Oh Henry bars) or warm meals you can eat at the tables (burgers, fries, pizza etc). Alcohol is served here, as well as in the Skyline Bar (always thick with smoke since it's the only place passengers are allowed to indulge their habit). You can't, however, take your booze back to your seat: you must drink it where you bought it.

Over in Silver & Blue the dining car is all yours with its crisp, linen tablecloths and at-your-seat service. You're given a choice of three sittings which are rarely on time in the busy summer months. All meals are included in the price of the ticket and the food is usually very good. Typical evening fare is soup, followed by salmon steak with potatoes and vegetables, followed by (invariably sickly) pastries or gateaux. Breakfast is hearty – usually toast, bacon and eggs, or pancakes with maple syrup – and lunch will be something like a burger, or fried chicken. The menu always includes vegetarian options. The dining car also has a good range of alcohol on sale which you'll be billed for at the end of your meal. Be warned that the dining car experience can be a little manic in the middle of peak season as the harassed staff work flat out to serve three sittings of three meals a day to hundreds of hungry people.

In Silver & Blue you can also help yourself to complimentary tea and coffee in the Park Car, or, get a Service Attendant to bring a cup to your seat.

The dome cars
The glass roofed, panoramic observation domes are probably the most famous feature of the Canadian. There's one in the sleeping car section and one in the Coach section, and seats are at a premium in both.

Passengers tend to treat the dome the way holiday makers treat pool-side sun loungers: they get there early, they stake their claim and they stay there. They do get hungry, though, so you can usually find a free seat at mealtimes and in the early morning or late evening. The best time to sit in the dome is at dawn. No one's around, the only sound is the movement of the train and Canada's vast, wide open space is at its most haunting.

Life on the train

If you're travelling in Coach class you'll doubtless find yourself sur-rounded by a young and cosmopolitan crowd. Fellow travellers are often backpacking or hostelling and there are a lot of Europeans on board in the summer months. Strangers strike up conversations quite easily and meet-ing new people is all part of the enjoyment of the trip. Between scanning the horizon for bears you can stretch your legs by wandering to and from the cafe, or hover around the dome car in the hope that someone will offer you their seat.

Silver & Blue passengers are a particularly convivial lot. The service is inevitably patronised by slightly older and wealthier travellers who all appear (when thrown together three times a day in the dining car) to get on extremely well. There is a shared preoccupation with nocturnal com-forts. Conversations at breakfast tend to focus on the previous night's sleep, and conversations at dinner on the impending night's sleep. Silver & Bluers may also pursue a social life in the bullet lounge or the mural lounge, where they can discuss the merits of the specially commissioned artwork on display. The original murals, painted by artists from the Group of Seven (p108), are now on show in a museum in Ottawa.

THE OTHER TRAINS

The Ocean

Between Halifax and Montreal you travel aboard the same stainless steel trains as the Canadian. Again, you can travel either in Coach class or in sleeping cars, known on the Ocean as Easterly class. Both services are pretty much the same as those offered by the Canadian with one notable exception: everyone is allowed to use the dining car, and every one has to pay for their meals. The train never gets as manically busy as the Canadian and the 19½ hour journey proceeds at a leisurely, relaxed pace.

The Corridor

Moving on from Montreal to Toronto you'll take the aptly titled Corridor route. The LRC trains (light, rapid and comfortable) operating along the Corridor carry the highest volume of passenger traffic in Canada. The trains are sleek, modern and very fast – downtown Montreal to downtown Toronto takes just four hours. The train offers First Class travel, known as VIA 1, or Coach class. VIA 1 is super luxurious: you get to sit in a posh lounge before boarding, delicious three course meals are served to you at your seat and you're plied with wine or liqueurs during and after each meal. Coach class has the usual roomy seats and the attendants periodically bring round refreshments for which you have to pay. The journey is more functional than recreational and you're not likely to walk around the train meeting people. It gets you from A to B good and fast, but it's probably the least memorable train ride you'll take in Canada.

The Skeena

Aboard the Skeena you're back to the pristine stainless steel trains of the Canadian. The Conductor proudly introduced me to his train as 'VIA's jewel' and it's certainly one of the best train rides through Canada. The services on board are exactly the same as those on the Canadian except that, as on the Ocean, everyone can use the dining car and everyone pays for meals. It's never as hectic as the Canadian, though, and dining in particular is an unhurried, highly pleasurable occasion, especially on the first evening as you travel through the Rocky Mountains in the sunset.

The Rocky Mountaineer

The Great Canadian Railtour Company Ltd took over the Rocky Mountaineer from VIA Rail in 1989. It's subsequently (and with some justification) dubbed itself 'the most spectacular train trip in the world' and turned the daylight-only two-day package into a roaring success.

There are two ways of travelling on the Rocky Mountaineer: Signature service or the newly launched Gold Leaf service. Gold Leaf passengers travel in a brand new, ultra luxurious dome car – and pay $400 extra for the privilege. The dome area seats 74 people who are assigned seating there for the whole of the journey. Downstairs there's an open air observation platform and a dining area which serves hot gourmet meals.

At either end of the dome car are the ordinary coaches where you'll be travelling if you're taking Signature service. These are nowhere near as stylish as VIA's stainless steel fleet and you might be disappointed by the absence of a dining car or observation dome if you've already taken the Canadian. But the Rocky Mountaineer makes up for these shortcomings in other ways, primarily with your Onboard Service Attendant. Each carriage has its own attendant who (ingenious recruitment policies ensure) will almost certainly be warm, outgoing and charismatic, inspiring instant devotion among the passengers. His or her duties include serving you breakfast, lunch, snacks and soft drinks at your seat (included in the price of the package) and providing you with commentary about the route. This is one of the highlights of the trip; the attendants have obvi-

(**Opposite**): The privately-owned Rocky Mountaineer winds its way along the Bow River Valley between Banff and Lake Louise. It is the only passenger train still using the original CPR route through the Rocky Mountains.

ously been required to learn large volumes of information by heart, as their knowledge of the history of the railway and the landscape you pass through is encyclopaedic. They also do a good line in amusing anecdotes and corny jokes. Our attendant told us the railway workers constructing the line from Kamloops to Revelstoke were so fed up with the local fare – moose for breakfast, moose for dinner, moose for tea – that they expressed their frustration in the name they chose for the next station we were to pass. It was Sicamous. One attendant is also known to switch out the lights and recite Shakespeare through the five-mile Spiral Tunnels.

The Rocky Mountaineer is essentially group travel and the service attendants encourage everyone to join in, getting people to look out for mile markers or shout out to the others if they see any wildlife. This makes for a highly enjoyable atmosphere, though the real draw is, of course, the magnificent scenery and the luxury of travelling through it all in daylight.

The Hudson Bay

The train that takes you on the one thousand mile journey up to Churchill has rather gone to seed. Operated by VIA, it's as old as the Canadian but lacks its elegance and expensive renovations. All the same it has a charm and character all of its own and travelling aboard the Hudson Bay is a magical railway experience.

For a start there'll be very few of you on the train unless you go in the middle of the polar bear season. This creates a special camaraderie among the passengers and by the second night you may well find yourself playing poker, drinking whisky, swapping spurious anecdotes, telling obscene jokes and singing Abba songs.

Life on the train gets particularly interesting north of The Pas as you're joined by Cree and Chepewyan natives, or wizened fishermen and trappers. For once you're travelling not only with fellow tourists or elderly Canadians but face to face with an entirely different culture.

The crew on the Hudson Bay is uniformly relaxed and friendly and, to tell the truth, a little on the eccentric side. This is no doubt due to the fact that most of them have been working this lonely line for many, many years. They know the route inside out, back to front and will happily tell you everything they know about the land you're travelling through. Best for this is Teddy Barylski (affectionately known as Trapper by his colleagues) who will point out all the osprey, geese, teal and ducks, and tell you the names of all the wild flowers, trees and lakes that you're passing.

(**Opposite**) **Top**: VIA's flagship, the Canadian, takes a rest at Jasper station. Note the famous observation dome in the centre. **Bottom**: The dining car staff snatch a minute to pose for a photo during a rare moment of calm between servings.

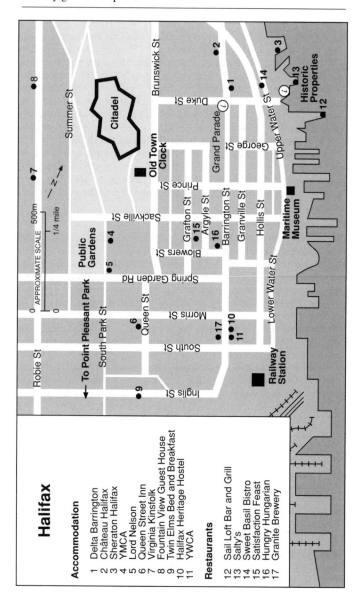

Halifax

Accommodation

1 Delta Barrington
2 Château Halifax
3 Sheraton Halifax
4 YMCA
5 Lord Nelson
6 Queen Street Inn
7 Virginia Kinsfolk
8 Fountain View Guest House
9 Twin Elms Bed and Breakfast
10 Halifax Heritage Hostel
11 YWCA

Restaurants

12 Sail Loft Bar and Grill
13 Salty's
14 Sweet Basil Bistro
15 Satisfaction Feast
16 Hungry Hungarian
17 Granite Brewery

PART 4: CITY GUIDES AND PLANS

Halifax

I am neither a prophet, nor the son of a prophet, yet...I believe than many in this room shall live to hear the whistle of the steam engine in the passes of the Rocky Mountains and to make the journey from Halifax to the Pacific in five or six days. Joseph Howe, Speech in Halifax, 15 May 1851

Halifax, the hub of the Maritime Provinces, is exactly as you'd expect it to be: bustling, lively streets clustered around the waterfront; brightly painted clapboard houses; fish markets; quay-side bars; the smell of salt in the air; old-fashioned charm. It's the capital of Nova Scotia and is located on the second largest natural harbour in the world. The downtown core is extremely compact and all the interesting parts are within easy walking distance of each other.

Being one of the older Canadian cities, Halifax has taken enormous care to preserve its colonial heritage and you'll see some fine old buildings dotted around the place. It does tend to overdo the history thing though, and just about every building over eighty years old seems to have a plaque on it. Halifax is an excellent starting point for a trip across Canada (it somehow feels like the proper place to begin) and it's well worth a couple of days' visit.

HISTORY

The Micmacs
The first people to live here were the Micmac Indians who named the settlement 'chebucto' meaning 'great long harbour'. Their fishing and hunting communities proliferated throughout the region until contact with European fishermen in the early sixteenth century exposed them to new diseases which seriously depleted their numbers. These fishermen came over to take advantage of the area's prodigious supplies of cod, discovered by John Cabot in 1497.

Britain and France vie for power
The French staked the first European claim to the area in 1605 when they founded Port Royal on the Bay of Fundy. Britain was keen to get in on the act and attempted to establish its own colony nearby. In 1621 the area occupied by the French, known as Acadie, was claimed for the British

Crown and renamed Nova Scotia ('New Scotland'). The rival claims dragged on until 1713 when the Treaty of Utrecht handed over the mainland Maritimes to Britain, forcing France to shift its power base to Louisbourg on Cape Breton Island.

Garrison town established

Britain continued to feel threatened by the French presence at Louisbourg, so in 1749 Edward Cornwallis was sent over with 2500 settlers to found a garrison town by the harbour to protect the New England colonies. They named it Halifax, after the second Earl of Halifax, and built a fort at the top of the town's hill.

The Royals in Halifax

For many years Halifax provided a home to the two wayward sons of King George III, who were practically kicked out of Britain by their frustrated father. The youngest, Prince Edward, future father of Queen Victoria, served as the commander of the Nova Scotia forces for six years. He was notorious for his obsession with discipline and punctuality. Modern-day Haligonians can still keep an eye on the time by the great clock tower standing on the hillside – a gift from Prince Edward to the city.

Halifax today

The city's importance as a military and naval base has continued well into the twentieth century. Halifax has also emerged as the industrial, commercial and educational centre of the Maritime Provinces, boasting one of Canada's busiest ports (ice-free all year) and no fewer than five universities. Its world standing is also rising, and it was chosen to host the 1995 G-7 summit meeting, an event which sent the city into an orgy of frenzied preparations and face-lift programmes. However, while Halifax has gone from strength to strength in recent decades, it suffered a horrific tragedy in the earlier part of this century – see page 73..

ARRIVING IN HALIFAX

By air

Flights into or out of Halifax touch down at Halifax International Airport, about 35km out of town. There are three ways of getting into town from the airport: on the Airbus, which costs $11 and stops off at all the major hotels in Halifax; by taxi for $33 a car or, for a couple of extra dollars, by limousine. The airbus runs between 6.30am and 10.45pm.

By rail

The train station is at the south end of Halifax, about a twenty-minute walk from downtown. The No 9 bus stops just outside the station and will take you into the city centre; it runs once every twenty or thirty minutes.

LOCAL TRANSPORT

Halifax is a very manageable size and the best way to get to most places is on foot. If you do need to go a little further afield, the bus network (Metro Transit) is very efficient. There's a flat fare of $1.25 per journey and you have to pay with the exact money.

Another good way of getting out of downtown, particularly for a jaunt to Point Pleasant Park, is by bike. These can be rented at Cyclepath at 5240 Blowers St. Rates are $15 a day and $25 a weekend.

ORIENTATION AND SERVICES

You can't get lost in Halifax. The city centre is situated on a hillside. At the top, you've got the **citadel**, at the bottom you've got the **waterfront** and in between are about six streets running parallel to the water's edge. Right in the centre of all this is the **Grand Parade**, the city's main square, home to the City Hall and St Paul's Church.

Tourist information

There are two tourist offices: one on the corner of Duke St and Barrington St (☎ 421-8736), open 9am-6pm from 1 June to 31 August, daily (and Monday to Friday for the rest of the year), and another, bigger one down by the waterfront in the Historic Properties (☎ 424-4247), open daily 9am-9pm mid-June to mid-September (and Monday to Friday 8.30am-4.30pm for the rest of year).

Money

All the main banks have several branches in Halifax, including the Royal Bank at 1785 Barrington St, the Bank of Montreal at 5151 George St and the Bank of Nova Scotia at 1709 Hollis St.

Consulates

Austria (☎ 429-8200) 710-1718 Argyle St
Belgium (☎ 423-6323) PO Box 1590 Stn M
Britain (☎ 423-8548) 1501-1959 Upper Water St
Denmark (☎ 429-5680) 1525 Birmingham St
Finland (☎ 420-1990) 1459 Hollis St
France (☎ 494-6804) 6234 Lawrence St
Germany (☎ 422-4713) 708-1809 Barrington St
Italy (☎ 422-0066) 7-1574 Argyle St
Japan (☎ 429-6530) PO Box 2066
Netherlands (☎ 422-1485) 1306-1959 Upper Water St
Norway (☎ 468-1330) 206-11 Morris Dr
Spain (☎ 429-5680) 1525 Birmingham St
Sweden (☎ 450-5252) PO Box 2027
USA (☎ 429-2480) 910 Cogswell Tower, Scotia Sq

WHERE TO STAY

Budget accommodation

Part of the Hostelling International network, the **Halifax Heritage House Hostel** (☎ 422-3863) is an absolute dream hostel. It's in the middle of town (1253 Barrington St) in a beautiful Georgian building, has a well equipped kitchen, a big common room, a TV, library and shop and is spotlessly clean throughout. What's more it's very cheap – $12.75 for members, and $15.75 for non-members. There are fifty beds but with standards like this they get snapped up pretty quickly so book in advance.

A few doors down at No 1239 is the **YWCA** (☎ 423-6162), for women only. The rates aren't much cheaper than local B&Bs at $26 a single and $47 a double, and the rooms are rather bleak. Very near the citadel, the **YMCA** (☎ 423-9622) has excellent facilities (café, fitness centre, pool) with rooms (a little on the spartan side) going for $31. It's mixed sex, but it's probably not a good idea to stay here as a woman travelling alone.

Mid-range accommodation

Halifax is well endowed with moderately priced guest houses and B&Bs, most of them about a ten-minute walk from downtown. The most central mid-range hotel, at 1515 South Park St, is the **Lord Nelson** (☎ 423-6331) overlooking Halifax's Public Gardens. Built in 1928 it has a beautiful Edwardian-style entrance lobby: high ceilings, oak panelling, shining brass lifts etc. Unfortunately the charm is left behind when you go up to the rooms (which are modern and nothing special) but they're good value at $60 a double.

Queen Street Inn (☎ 422-9828) has the distinct feel of an English country B&B. This lavishly decorated Georgian house has six rooms (starting at $55), some of them with antique four poster beds. There are a few B&Bs scattered along the busy Robie St (running parallel to Barrington St, a few blocks behind the citadel). At No 1722 there's the cosy **Virginia Kinsfolk** (☎ 423-6687), owned by the welcoming Lucy and Dirk Russel. It's small (only three rooms) so it's advisable to book in advance. Singles are $35 a night, and doubles $45 and the price includes a huge breakfast. You'll get a discount if you're a senior citizen, or if you stay for three or more nights. Further along the road at No 2138 you've got the **Fountain View Guest House** (☎ 422-4169). It's clean, comfortable and excellent value, with singles for $25 and doubles for $30. Down in Halifax's South End and close to the train station there's the **Twin Elms Bed & Breakfast** (☎ 423-8974) at 5492 Inglis St. Singles are $30 and doubles are $44, the price including continental breakfast. It's a lovely Victorian house, in the middle of Halifax's stately residences and near to Point Pleasant Park.

Upmarket hotels

Halifax's top range hotels are quite good value, and prices are usually negotiable outside July and August. Best in town is probably the **Delta Barrington** (☎ 429-7410) on the corner of Duke and Barrington Sts. This is where John Major stayed in the 1995 G7 Summit, with a huge suite being created especially for him and his posse. They give excellent discounts if you book early enough, with rooms going for $89 depending on availability. Just over the road is Canadian Pacific's **Château Halifax** (☎ 425-6700). If you're expecting an old railway hotel you'll be disappointed – this highrise block was built in 1972 and is at the opposite end of town from the train station. It's quite stylish inside, though, and many of the rooms have great views over the harbour. Doubles start at $125. Right down by the waterfront, next to the Historic Properties, is the **Sheraton** (☎ 421-1700). Starting prices are $115, with all the usual frills thrown in.

WHERE TO EAT

Budget food

There's a good supply of pubs selling cheap lunches, usually around the $8 mark. In the middle of town, on the corner of Granville and Duke, is the **Split Crow** which serves snacks and cheap beer. It's heavily patronised by raucous locals who for some reason seem to enjoy the live folk bands and terrible comedians usually performing there. Further south at 1222 Barrington St is the **Granite Brewery** which claims to provide 'the perfect English pub atmosphere', kitting the place out with one-arm bandits and a dart board. The food is okay and the beer is excellent, most of it brewed on the premises.

Not to be missed is the **Hungry Hungarian** at 5215 Blowers St. Don't let the dubious fairy lights around the window put you off; the food here is simple, tasty and cheap. The house speciality is goulash in its many varieties; most dishes are around $6. Finally there's **Bud the Spud**, a burger and hotdog vendor outside the public library on Spring Garden Rd. It's become a bit of local institution and, when I stumbled on Bud by accident, I was amazed at the huge line-ups queuing on the pavement.

Mid-range and upmarket restaurants

Fish lovers will find themselves in culinary nirvana. Unsurprisingly this local staple features heavily on just about every menu; the quality is generally good, and the prices always moderate. Make the most of the ocean's delicacies while you can – you've got over 6000km to go before you see another one.

One of the best fish restaurants in town is **The Five Fishermen** at 1740 Argyle Street. It's housed in an old barn-like building that, in 1819, used to be the Church of England's National School for 'the instruction of the poor.' After that it was the Victoria College of Art for a while, when one of its main patrons was the lady from that true-life story, *The King and I*. Today it's famous for its eat-as-much-as-you-can mussel bar and generally delicious food. Prices are around $12-$15 a head. Another good fish place, though a little more expensive, is the **Sail Loft Bar and Grill**. It's at the end of Cable Wharf and has spectacular views over the harbour, particularly at night with Dartmouth, Halifax's sister town, twinkling on the other side of the water. A favourite with locals is **Salty's**, also on the waterfront, next to the Historic Properties. Neither the menu nor the decor are overly inspired but the food is decent and inexpensive and it's always packed out.

If you're looking for something a bit more imaginative, head for **Sweet Basil Bistro** at 1866 Upper Water St. It's owned by a Frenchman and there's an obvious French feel to the place. The mouthwatering menu features fish, veal and home made pasta dishes, delicious salads and incredible desserts. I'd especially recommend the lobster with lemon, fresh basil and fettucini (followed by the homemade ice cream). Three courses will cost around $25. There isn't a wide selection of vegetarian restaurants in Halifax; the best is **Satisfaction Feast** at 1581 Grafton St.

WHAT TO SEE

Halifax's sights are on a rather modest scale. In fact there isn't really that much to do here except stroll around and admire the colonial architecture, take in a couple of parks and a museum or two. The tourist office gives away maps with a suggested walking tour and descriptions of the points of interest along the way.

The Citadel
The star-shaped fortress at the top of the hill is a good place to start; there's a superb view from here over the harbour and the city, and you'll be able to get your bearings and take in the lie of the land. The citadel (open daily 9am-5pm year-round, with an entrance charge of $2 June-August) is supposed to be Canada's most visited historic site. There have been four forts here since 1749. The current one was completed in 1856. If you visit in summer you'll see students dressed up as members of the 78th Highlanders and the Royal Artillery, and you can visit the barrack rooms, furnished as they were in the 1860s. Beware of the eardrum-splitting gun that's fired at the citadel every day at noon.

Old Town Clock
This rather beautiful clock tower stands just below the citadel. It was presented to Halifax as a gift by Prince Edward in 1803 – a fitting present, given his legendary obsession with punctuality.

St Paul's Church

You'll walk past this pretty, white-timbered church many a time while wandering around Halifax. It's right in the centre of town, at the south end of the Grand Parade. Opened in 1750, it is the oldest building in Halifax and the oldest Anglican church in Canada. Look out for the piece of metal embedded in the north wall above the door; it's a bit of the *Mont Blanc* that exploded in Halifax harbour over $3^{1}/_{2}$ kms away in 1917.

Halifax City Hall

Across from St Paul's Church at the other end of the Grand Parade is Halifax's Victorian City Hall. During July and August you can drop in and take afternoon tea with the mayor, Walter Fitzgerald, from Monday to Thursday 3.30-4.30pm.

Province House

Charles Dickens visited Province House in 1842 and said 'it was like looking at Westminster through the wrong end of the telescope.' Presumably he was referring to the business conducted inside and not the building, which is Georgian, sandstone and delicately understated. Built in 1819, it is Canada's oldest and smallest seat of government. It's a stone's throw from the Grand Parade, down George St, and is open to the public Monday to Friday 9am-6pm and weekends 9am-5pm from mid-June to mid-September; and Monday to Friday only, 8.30am-4.30pm for the rest of the year. Entrance is free.

Historic Properties

Down by the waterfront is a collection of beautifully renovated wharves and warehouses, known as the Historic Properties. The oldest is Privateers' Warehouse, built in local granite and ironstone in 1813 (the Privateers were the British Crown's licensed pirates). The area, which

---

The Halifax Explosion

On the morning of 6 December 1917 two ships collided in Halifax harbour. One of them, the French *Mont Blanc*, was carrying relief supplies for the war: 2300 tonnes of pitric acid, 10 tonnes of gun cotton, 35 tonnes of benzol and 200 tonnes of TNT. The result was the biggest man-made explosion the world had ever seen.

Before she exploded the ship drifted to one of Halifax's piers and burned away for twenty minutes. This left plenty of time for crowds to gather round and watch the spectacle. When the big bang came more than 1900 people were killed instantly. Of the survivors, many were horrifically maimed – 25 limbs were later amputated and more than 250 eyes had to be removed. The force of the blast razed half the city to the ground, leaving thousands of Haligonians homeless. Incredibly, all but one of the men aboard the *Mont Blanc* survived the disaster, having rowed to shore in the right direction.

This tragic accident proved to be a precursor of atomic warfare; Oppenheimer studied the effects of the Halifax Explosion while developing America's bombs for Hiroshima and Nagasaki.

had been falling into a state of dereliction following years of disuse, has been successfully transformed into an attractive collection of shops, pubs, eating places and artists' studios. It's a lively to place to hang around on a sunny day.

The Maritime Museum of the Atlantic

Down by the water's edge at 1675 Lower Water St, this museum has some good displays depicting the maritime history of the region. Particularly fascinating is the section on the *Titanic*. When this unfortunate ship sank on 15 April 1912, a huge rescue operation got underway from Halifax. Two hundred and nine bodies were recovered and brought to the city, and embalmers were brought in from all over the Maritimes to cope with the work. About 55 bodies were claimed; the rest were buried in unnumbered graves. The privileges of First Class travel were upheld even in the face of death: the bodies of ordinary passengers were simply tagged before being brought into Halifax; the bodies of First Class passengers were immediately embalmed and laid in coffins.

Point Pleasant Park

A few miles out of town is the splendid Point Pleasant Park, 186 acres of forestland on the tip of the Halifax peninsula. The interior of the park has a good network of trails and footpaths (much more accessible than on the more famous Stanley Park at the other end of the country) and the shoreline boasts a sandy beach from which you can bathe. Look out for the heather close to the southern shores; it grew from seeds accidentally brought over in the mattresses of the Scottish Highland Regiment and has flourished ever since. Incidentally, Halifax still rents this park from the British Government on a 999 year lease for the bargain rate of one shilling a year.

MOVING ON

By rail

Trains leave Halifax for Montreal daily except Tuesday at 2pm. The journey takes nineteen and a half hours. The VIA information number is ☎ 429-8421 (or ☎ 1-800-561-3952 when calling from outside Halifax). To get to the rail station from downtown, take the No 9 bus running south along Barrington St.

By air

The cheapest way of getting to the airport is on the Airbus (☎ 873-2091). Tickets are $11 and the bus picks passengers up at all the major downtown hotels. The information number for Halifax International Airport is ☎ 873-1223. Useful airline numbers include Air Canada: ☎ 429-7111; Canadian Airlines International: ☎ 427-5500 and KLM Royal Dutch Airlines: ☎ 455-8282.

Quebec City

Nothing struck me as so beautiful and grand as the location of the town of Quebec, which could not be better situated even were it to become, in some future time, the capital of a great Empire. Frontenac, in a letter, 1672.

Quebec City, spilling down Cap Diamant's slopes onto the banks of the St Lawrence, has to be one of the most picturesque cities in North America, and it's certainly the only one to be listed as a UNESCO World Heritage Site. Inside the old quarter, Quebec's much-vaunted European flavour exceeds expectations: its narrow, cobblestoned streets are lined with 17th and 18th century houses; 95% of the population is of French ancestry and many inhabitants speak English with a strong French accent. It's all wonderfully exotic and more than a little disorienting.

It would be shameful in the extreme not to visit Quebec City while in Eastern Canada, but two or three days should be enough to savour its charms before moving on. This is, after all, a city that makes a living out of its history and after a while you can begin to feel that you're trapped in a little time bubble.

HISTORY

Cartier lands at Stadacona

Quebec City is the oldest European settlement in Canada though it was, of course, inhabited long before Jacques Cartier first landed on the site in 1535. It was then the location of an Iroquois village named Stadacona, presided over by Chief Donnacona. After spending the winter there, Cartier and his men abducted Donnacona and some Iroquois, and took them back to France. All of the natives except one girl died within a few years of arriving in Europe.

Permanent French base established

It wasn't until 1608 that a permanent European base was established, not by Cartier but by Samuel de Champlain who founded a fur-trading post at the foot of Cap Diamant and named it Quebec. By this time the settlement at Stadacona had vanished, and there was no trace of the Iroquois. Seven years later the first Récollet missionaries arrived, followed by the Jesuits in 1625. The new colony, however, provoked the jealousy and hostility of the British, who blockaded it until it surrendered in 1629. Britain held on to the settlement for just three years before the territory was returned to France in 1632.

Expansion

Back in the hands of the French, the settlement began to expand rapidly as more settlers came out and a church, a school and a hospital were built. It wasn't long before the economy, which revolved around the fur trade, began to diversify: leather manufacturing, ship building and logging were all initiated in the latter half of the seventeenth century. Foreign aggression continued to disturb the city's peace, however, and in 1690 Quebec was unsuccessfully attacked by troops from New England. It was at this point that the city's fortifications began to be built.

Battle on the Plains of Abraham

In 1759 the British were back to launch a massive assault on the city, with the aid of seventy-six warships, 9000 soldiers, 10,000 fire bombs and 40,000 cannon balls. Quebec, under the command of the Marquis de Montcalm, held out for three months before the British – under General Wolfe – managed to land on the western side of Cap Diamant during the night. The ensuing battle lasted less than half an hour; both Wolfe and Montcalm died and Quebec fell to the British. The battle marked the beginning of the end of New France, which was handed over to Britain in its entirety in 1763.

Quebec under the British

The city's French-speaking community of 8000 people suddenly found itself under the rule of an English governor. Despite fears of enforced anglicisation, the Quebec Act of 1774 guaranteed the protection of the Catholic religion and the French language. Apart from an unsuccessful attempt by the Americans to take the city in 1775, Quebec was allowed to develop undisturbed over the next century. The mainstays of its economy were logging and ship building, and it continued to be an important port right through to the 1950s when the St Lawrence was artificially widened to allow ships to reach Montreal.

Quebec today

Largely ignored in favour of Montreal by the immigrant Irish and Scottish merchants at the turn of the century, Quebec City has remained almost completely Francophone. The city, which is the capital of the Province of Quebec, is an important administrative and educational centre, and has spread out well beyond the confines of the old quarters. For most visitors, however, the most visible face of Quebec is that of its narrow streets and old-world charm that draws thousands of tourists here each year. Nonetheless, Quebec does not pander indiscriminately to tourists and its people often seem refreshingly detached from the predominantly English-speaking, camera-clicking crowds wandering through their streets.

ARRIVING IN QUEBEC CITY

Trains from Halifax arrive not at Quebec City but at Lévis on the opposite bank of the St Lawrence. A ferry service (free for VIA passengers) will take you across to Quebec; the terminal is right by the train station. It's a ten-minute ride and ferries leave every half hour during the day and every hour through the night. Trains from Montreal arrive at the beautiful Gare du Palais in the Basse-Ville. Unless you're prepared to hike up to the Haute-Ville (where you'll probably be sleeping), the only way of getting there is by taxi.

LOCAL TRANSPORT

Vieux-Québec is entirely navigable on foot. The only reason you might want to take a bus anywhere is to avoid the walk to the Musée du Québec, or if you want to get out of town to the Montmorency Falls.

The bus service is run by the Société de Transport de la Communité Urbain de Québec, otherwise known as STCUQ (☎ 627-2511). The main point for catching buses is at the Place d'Youville, near the Porte Saint-Jean.

ORIENTATION AND SERVICES

Quebec City is very small and you'll have no problem finding your way around. Most visitors are here to see Vieux Québec which is divided between the Basse-Ville (or Lower Town) at the foot of Cap Diamant and the Haute-Ville (or Upper Town) perched on the top of Cap Diamant. There are steps leading from Place Royale in the Basse-Ville to the terrace beside the Château Frontenac in the Haute-Ville. There's also a funicular from and to the same places. The Haute-Ville is where you'll probably spend most of your time and it's where almost all of the accommodation is located. Part of the Haute-Ville is surrounded by the old city walls. Quebec is, incidentally, the continent's only walled city north of Mexico.

Tourist information

There are two tourist information centres. One is at 12 rue Sainte-Anne (☎ 873-2015), just across from the Château Frontenac. It's open daily 8.30am-7.30pm between 21 June and 5 September, and 9am-5pm for the rest of the year. The other one is tucked away at 60 rue d'Auteuil (☎ 692-2471). It's open daily 1 June to 5 September 8.30am-8pm; 6 September to 9 October 8.30am-5.30pm; 10 October to the end of May, Monday to Friday 8.30pm-5.30pm. Both give away free maps etc, and will ring around to book accommodation for you.

Money

The Caisse Populaire du Vieux-Québec at 19 rue des Jardins changes travellers' cheques and is open seven days a week 9am-7pm weekdays, and to 5pm at weekends. Other banks include the Royal Bank of Canada at 888 rue St-Jean, the National Bank of Canada at 1199 rue St-Jean and the Banque d'Amérique du Canada at 24 Côte-de-la-Fabrique (no commission on travellers' cheques, open at weekends).

Consulates

Finland (☎ 683-3000) 200-801 ch Saint-Louis
France (☎ 688-3820) 1110 ave des Laurentides
Italy (☎ 529-2996) 355-23e rue
Netherlands (☎ 692-2175) 10 rue Ste-Anne
Norway (☎ 525-8171) 2 Nouvelle France, Wolves Crove, PO Box 40
Switzerland (☎ 623-9864) 3293 1er ave
USA (☎ 692-2095) 2 Place Terrasse Dufferin

WHERE TO STAY

Surprisingly for such a popular tourist destination, accommodation in Quebec City is very reasonably priced, and most of it is located right in the heart of the old town.

Budget accommodation

There isn't a wide choice of really cheap places to stay. Most travellers head for the **HI Centre Internationale de Séjour de Québec** (☎ 694-0735) at 19 rue Sainte-Ursule. The dormitories are packed with beds and the place is usually very crowded. Rates are $18 for non members and $15 for members. Another option is the **Auberge de la Paix** (☎ 694-0735) at 31 rue Couillard, where a night in a dorm will cost $18.

Mid-range accommodation

This is where the real bargains are to be found. Many of the city's old residences have been converted to small inns or guest houses, usually containing about 10 to 15 rooms of varying sizes and prices.

One of the most elegant of these is the **Hôtel au Jardin du Gouverneur** (☎ 692-1704). This immaculately furnished house is just behind the Château Frontenac at 16 rue Mont-Carmel, and faces the beautiful Jardin du Gouverneur, once lined by the houses of the city's richest and most important citizens. There's a small room with a private bathroom for $55; the others are around $70-90. At 39 ave Sainte-Geneviève is the **Hôtel Cap Diamant** (☎ 694-0313). The rooms are intriguingly decorated, and they all come with a private bathroom. There's also a sunny conservatory where you can have your morning coffee. Prices range from $55-95.

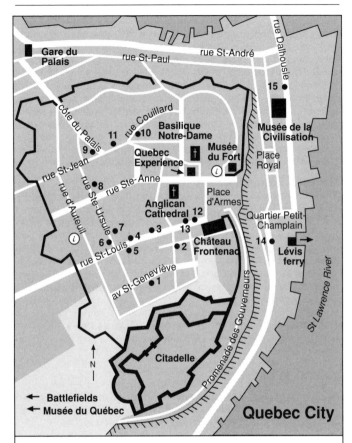

Accommodation

1 Hôtel Cap Diamant
2 Hôtel au Jardin du Gouverneur
3 Auberge Saint-Louis
4 Hôtel La Caravelle
5 Hôtel le Clos Saint-Louis
6 Hôtel l'Hermitage
7 Maison Acadienne
8 HI Auberge de Jeunesse
9 Hôtel Manoir Victoria
10 Auberge de la Paix

Restaurants

11 A la Table de Serge Bruyère
12 Le Continental
13 Aux Anciens Canadiens
14 Le Cochon Dingue
15 Le Café du Monde

0   300m

0   APPROXIMATE SCALE   1/4 mile

Rue Saint-Louis has a good range of accommodation: at No 71 is the **Hôtel le Clos Saint-Louis** (☎ 694-1311) which, although a little on the pink and frilly side, is extremely clean and comfortable. Rooms here range from $55-95, breakfast included. A little further down at No 68 is the **Hôtel La Caravelle** (☎ 694-9022) where the bare stone walls of the bedrooms date back to 1814. Rooms here cost $80-120. The **Auberge Saint-Louis** (☎ 692-2424) at No 48 is considerably more basic and characterless. The rooms are cheap, however, starting at $47, and they all have a private bathroom. Another good street for accommodation is rue Sainte-Ursuline. At No 60 is the **Hôtel l'Ermitage** (☎ 694-0968) which has clean, attractive rooms from $72, and at No 43 is **La Maison Acadienne** (☎ 694-0280) with lovely rooms from $49-94.

Upmarket accommodation

You can't get much more upmarket than the **Château Frontenac** (☎ 692 3861). If you feel like indulging your fantasies of staying in a glamorous hotel, then this is the place to do it. Everything is swimming in luxury, from the vast entrance lobby to the marble bathrooms. The guests, however, look rather out of place in their trainers and jeans: it's the kind of establishment where you'd expect everyone to wear evening dress at the very least. A night at the Château is less prohibitively expensive than you might think: off season 'specials' go for around $99 a double which, divided between two people, is exceptional value. High season prices start at $245. If there's no room at the Château, you could try the elegant **Hôtel Manoir Victoria** (☎ 692-1030) at 44 côte du Palais. This 4-star hotel has recently undergone a $12 million renovation programme; rooms here are from $115.

WHERE TO EAT

Quebec City claims to be the gastronomic capital of Canada and while you can eat very well here, you get the impression that many of the restaurants are in that same little time warp as the rest of the city.

Budget food

My personal lunchtime favourite is the packed-out **Le Casse-Crêpe Breton** at 1136 rue Saint-Jean. After the lengthy process of choosing a crêpe (there's an enormous selection starting at $3) you watch (drooling) as it is cooked in front of you on a big hotplate. There's a lively, intimate atmosphere here and the close proximity of your neighbours ensures that you will make a few friends over lunch. Another cheap and lively place is **Le Petit Coin Latin** at No 8 and a half (!) rue Sainte-Ursule. They do good breakfasts here and there's a pleasant terrace out the back. Finally, if all this French fare is proving a bit too much, you can always grab un macdo at **McDonald's** near the fountain in rue Saint-Jean.

Mid-range and upmarket restaurants

At the upmarket end of the scale, **Le Continental** is one of the best. The same family has been running the restaurant since it opened in 1956, winning numerous culinary awards along the way. It's at 26 rue Saint-Louis – a meal here will cost over $30 a head. In the same price range is **Aux Anciens Canadiens**, a couple of doors down at No 34. The food is very good though the historically themed décor is a bit off-putting. Another venue for a splurge is the very expensive but outstandingly good **A la Table de Serge Bruyère** at 1200 rue Saint-Jean, near McDonald's. Alternatively, if a little more predictably, you might book a table (reservations essential, as are jacket and tie for men) at Le Château Frontenac's **Le Champlain** (☎ 692 3861).

For something more moderately priced, there are plenty of bistros. One of the most stylish is **Le Café du Monde**, down by the port at 57 rue Dalhousie. It's particularly convenient for the Musée de la Civilisation. Another good one, very popular with local people is **Le Cochon Dingue** at 46 boulevard Champlain, just across from the Lévis ferry.

WHAT TO SEE

Haute Ville

• **Château Frontenac** More than a hotel, the towering Château has become the symbol of Quebec and is probably the most photographed building in Canada. It was commissioned for the CPR by Van Horne in 1893, and was designed by an eminent American architect, Bruce Price. There are guided tours ($4.75) around the hotel's magnificent interior leaving on the hour 10am-5pm. If a night at the Château (see p80) doesn't quite fit your budget you should at least treat yourself to the amazing eat-as-much-as-you-like brunch (about $12) served in a beautiful dining room overlooking the St Lawrence River Valley.

• **Terrasse Dufferin** Right next to the Château Frontenac is this long boardwalk skirting the edge of Cap Diamant. The views from here – over the St Lawrence, the Basse-Ville, the Laurentian mountains and even the foothills of the US Appalachians – are absolutely stunning, especially at sunset. The Terrasse extends into the Promenade des Gouverneurs which climbs to the Citadelle and continues to the Plains of Abraham.

• **Citadelle** This massive star-shaped fortress was built over a thirty year period by the British (1820-50). Contained within its wide ditches and thick, squat walls are twenty-five buildings, including the Governor-General's summer residence, the officers' mess and a military museum. Still used as the headquarters of the Royal 22nd Regiment, it is the oldest occupied North American fort. Entrance into the Citadelle costs $4.50; once inside you can take an hour-long guided tour, watch the Changing of the Guard (mid-June to August 10am) or the Beating of the Retreat (July-August, 6pm daily except Monday).

• **Plains of Abraham** It's hard to believe that this undulating parkland was the scene of the violent confrontation between Wolfe and Montcalm in 1759 (see p76), an episode that changed the course of Canadian history. Today it's a favourite area for picnickers and joggers, and only a few monuments, plaques and information boards bear testimony to the famous battle played out on these fields.

• **Musée du Québec** Situated at the far end of the Plains of Abraham, this museum contains the biggest and best collection of Quebec art, covering a period of about three hundred years. Works range from 17th century religious painting through to the latest movements in contemporary art, and the collection also includes sculpture, photography and decorative art. It's open daily 10am-5.45pm late May to 4 September, or Tuesday to Sunday, noon-5.45pm for the rest of the year. The entrance price is $4.75.

• **Musée du Fort** This tiny museum (which hasn't changed much since it opened in 1965) is loads of fun. Visitors are sat down in front of a huge plastic model of 18th century Quebec City; the lights are dimmed and a rippling voice, accompanied by atmospheric music and flashing lights, relates the story of the six sieges of the city, including the famous battle in 1759. The show lasts about half an hour and costs $5.50; it's worth it just for retro value. The museum is at 10 rue Sainte-Anne and is open daily 10am-6pm late June to August; 10am-5pm April, May, September and October, and 11am-3pm for the rest of the year.

• **The Quebec Experience** At the other end of the technical spectrum is this slick 3-D hologram show depicting Quebec's history from the first explorers through to the last few decades. You don your 3-D specs and sit back in a comfy cinema armchair to watch the show, with commentary provided by a hologram of Cartier, who looks so real it's scary. The audio-visual effects are stunning (and occasionally terrifying, the rifle-shot episode for example). Not to be missed on any account. It's at 8 rue du Trésor; admission is $6.50 and it's open daily 10am-10pm 15 May-15 October; otherwise 10am-5pm Sunday to Thursday and 10am-10pm Saturday and Sunday.

• **Basilique Notre-Dame** Notre-Dame is the continent's oldest parish north of Mexico. Work began on the building in 1647 and the cathedral was finally completed in 1844. Sadly, it burnt to the ground in 1922 but has since been rebuilt on the original 17th century plans. The interior is wonderfully light in tone, with its pale walls, shining gold-leaf altar and sky-blue ceiling.

• **Anglican Cathedral of the Holy Trinity** This church is supposed to be modelled on London's St Martin's in the Fields (though unfortunately they forgot to build a café in the crypt). There are some interesting features inside such as the benches made of oak imported from the royal forest in Windsor and the rather underused Royal Seat, reserved exclusively for the use of the British monarch.

Basse-Ville

To get to the lower town you can walk down the steps starting at the Terrasse Dufferin, or you can take the funicular running next to them.

• **Quartier Petit Champlain** This little warren of winding streets full of craft shops and the like is wholly given over to tourism. It's Quebec at its cutest and quaintest. At the centre of the quartier is the **rue du Petit-Champlain**, the city's oldest street (dating from 1685).

• **Place Royal** This is where Quebec City was originally founded back in 1608. The square has been extensively restored over the past few decades and is another example of Quebec's carefully groomed prettiness. Take a look inside the **Eglise Notre-Dame-des-Victoires** on the southern side of the square; note the curious high altar sculpted to look like a castle. At 1 Place Royale is the **Maison des Vins** which was built in 1689. It is still operated by a vintage wine specialist, and there's free wine tasting for the tourists.

• **Musée de la Civilisation** If you have time for just one museum in Quebec, make it this one. The building alone won awards for its architectural excellence and the museum's exhibits are very innovative, particularly in this town that seems so firmly rooted in the past. The exhibitions are mostly temporary and cover a diverse range of historical, sociological and scientific themes. The clever use of space, light and technology makes the museum a pleasure to walk around. It's near to Place Royale at 85 rue Dalhousie and is open daily 24 June to early September 10am-7pm; otherwise Tuesday to Sunday 10am-5pm. Entrance is $6, or free on Tuesdays (5 September-23 June).

Montmorency Falls

A few kms east of the city are the spectacular Montmorency Falls. At 83m high, they are one and a half times the height of Niagara Falls. You can take a cable car from the foot of the cliffs up to the beginning of the waterfall which you can cross on a rather wobbly bridge. This is the third bridge to be built here; the second one collapsed five days after it was completed in 1855, causing three people to plunge down the falls to their deaths. Nearby is the Manoir Montmorency, a former residence of William, Duke of Kent, who was Queen Victoria's father. You can get the No 50 or 53 buses to the falls from the Haute-Ville.

FESTIVALS

• **Carnival de Québec**, early February. Eleven days of freezing madness featuring a mass roll in the snow wearing bathing suits, a canoe race across the frozen St Lawrence and the world's largest ice sculpture competition.

• **Festival d'Eté**, early July. A ten-day whirl of street parties, concerts, singing, dancing and drinking. Excellent fun.

• **International Jazz and Blues Festival**, last week in June. Concerts all around the city in bars, restaurants, outdoor stages, halls etc.

• **Saint-Jean-Baptiste Day**, 24 June. Provincial holiday – parades and celebrations.

• **Les Médiévales de Québec**, mid-August. A five-day celebration of the Renaissance and Middle Ages. Lots of dressing-up in silly clothes.

MOVING ON

There's a frequent daily train service from Quebec's Gare du Palais to Montreal, just under three hours away. There's also a daily service to Montreal (except Wednesday) and to Halifax (except Tuesday) from Lévis on the opposite bank of the St Lawrence River. For information on trains from either Quebec or Lévis call ☎ 692-3940 (or ☎ 1-800-361-5390 when calling from outside Quebec City).

Montreal

This is the first time I was ever in a city where you couldn't throw a brick without breaking a church window. Mark Twain, Speech in Montreal, 1881

Montreal is a delicious, feel-good city. Famous throughout Canada for its party atmosphere, it is positively spilling over with buskers, jazz cellars, wine bars, night-clubs and throngs of beautiful people. It's not an entirely frivolous place, however, and even casual visitors are aware of the complex balance of relationships contained within the city: between the English and French speaking inhabitants, for example; between the North American and European influences, and between the claims of Canada and Quebec.

You can see or feel Montreal's contrasts all around: in the architecture, the food, the newspapers, the snatches of conversation you hear on the streets. But far from producing a feeling of tension, it all adds up to a very rich and full-flavoured city that is one of the most appealing and intriguing in North America.

HISTORY

Early settlement

The site of present-day Montreal was first occupied by the Iroquois Indians who called their settlement Hochelaga (meaning 'place of the beaver'). The first European to arrive was Jacques Cartier who stopped off at the island in 1535 on his way to seek the North-West Passage. He climbed the mountain that rose out of the island's centre, named it Mont Réal and then promptly left. About seventy years passed before the French returned, only to discover that Hochelaga had mysteriously vanished. The site was subsequently chosen as a fur-trading base, erected by Samuel de Champlain in 1611.

French colonists arrive

It wasn't until 1642 that a permanent settlement was established outside the confines of the fur trade. This was created by Paul de Chomedey, the Sieur de Maisonneuve, who brought fifty-three French colonists out with the intention of converting the natives to Christianity. They built houses, a church and a hospital, and named the new community Ville-Marie. By 1672 the population had reached 1200, a figure that began to multiply rapidly during the first half of the eighteenth century when land grants enticed French settlers out in their droves.

The British take over

In 1756 Europe became engulfed in the Seven Years' War. The fighting spread to the North American colonies, and in 1760 the British took control of Montreal. When the war ended three years later, all of New France was ceded to Britain under the Treaty of Paris. Scottish and Irish immigrants flocked to Montreal to make their fortunes, and it wasn't long before the Brits started nudging the French out of their position in Montreal's business life. All this was briefly interrupted in 1755 when American troops marched in and occupied the city for several months. When they retreated, life in Montreal carried on in much the same way as before.

The French were feeling increasingly frustrated at the disappearance of their power and political representation and in 1837 Louis-Joseph Papineau led an uprising against the British. The rebellion was brutally crushed but resentment, of course, remained strong.

The economic hub of Canada

Following Confederation in 1867, Montreal emerged as the economic, financial and transportation centre of the new dominion. Expansion and rapid industrialisation followed, and as the city entered the 20th century it was firmly established as Canada's most important metropolis. Prosperity and success endured, culminating in a massive spate of architectural development in the 1960s in preparation for Expo '67 – a colossal affair that brought a staggering fifty million visitors into Montreal.

Unrest breaks out

Meanwhile, resentment within the Francophone community continued to bubble away. Despite being in the majority, they had been manoeuvred into a subordinate, disadvantaged position in most levels of society, and the Anglophones appeared to remain indifferent to this injustice. While movements such as René Lévesque's Parti Québecois began to gather momentum, it was the dramatic action of the extremist FLQ that brought the crisis to a violent head in October 1970. Following a wave of terrorism, they kidnapped and murdered a Quebec cabinet minister, Pierre Laporte. The assassins were captured and arrested but the shocked government realised that drastic measures would have to be taken to avoid similar explosions of violence. Laws were introduced to protect the French language, and the general 'Frenchification' of Montreal got underway. Many Anglophones felt threatened by what was going on, and over 100,000 left the city over the next few years.

Montreal today

The commercial and financial damage brought about by the Anglophone exodus was quickly repaired by a new wave of French-speaking entrepreneurs. Today they control about 60% of Montreal's economy, a balance more acceptable to most Francophones. Montreal is no longer Canada's biggest city – having been overtaken by Toronto in the late 1960s. Nevertheless it continues to be a thriving and affluent metropolis, despite being hit by the recession in the early 1990s. In 1995 a US research team found it to be 'the world's most liveable city' (an honour it shares with Melbourne, Australia). Secession continues to be the focal issue in Quebec's politics, but after the defeat of the 1995 sovereignty referendum it remains to be seen which direction the independence movement will now take.

ARRIVING IN MONTREAL

By air
Most international flights arrive at **Mirabel Airport**, about 50km north of Montreal. From here the Autocar Connaisseur bus will take you to the city centre for $14.50. It leaves every twenty or thirty minutes, Monday to Friday, 7am-1am. A more costly option is to come in by taxi, for around $50.

Flights from Canada and the US arrive at **Dorval Airport**, which is 22km southwest of the city. Again, the Autocar Connaisseur bus company runs a shuttle service from the airport to downtown – it's a twenty-minute ride and costs $9. Buses run daily, 7am-1.30am, every twenty or thirty minutes. A taxi from the airport to downtown will cost around $25.

By train
The VIA Rail station is bang in the centre of town, in the large underground complex beneath the Queen Elizabeth Hotel.

LOCAL TRANSPORT

Montreal has a good public transport system, although I'd recommend wandering around on foot as the most pleasurable way of getting about the city. Its métro was designed by engineers from the Paris métro; stations are signalled by a white arrow on a big blue sign but they're so carefully hidden you may get half way to your destination before you find one. Once underground, it's all very clean, efficient and safe.

There's also an extensive bus network, which uses the same fare system as the métro: a single ticket costs $1.75, or you can buy six tickets at métro stations for $7.50, valid on both buses and the métro. Public transport starts to wind down at 12.30am, though some buses operate all through the night. The public transport information number is ☎ 288-6287.

Alternatively you can hire bikes at Vélo Aventure (☎ 847-0666) down at the port, next door to the IMAX cinema. Rates are $6 an hour or $20 a day.

ORIENTATION AND SERVICES

It comes as a surprise to many visitors when they discover that Montreal sits on an island. The Isle de Montréal is 32km long and 16km wide and is the largest of 234 islands that make up the Hochelaga archipelago in the St Lawrence River.

To orientate yourself in the city forget about conventional directions and pay no attention to the sun's position in the sky: Montreal has its own definitions of north, south, east and west and they make navigation a lot easier. The old port is down in the south. Mont Royal, the extinct volcano known by everyone as 'the mountain', is a few kms north. So, the streets between the mountain and the quays are deemed to run from north to south, and the streets crossing them at right angles east to west.

The city is divided into two main areas: downtown Montreal and Vieux Montréal. **Downtown** begins a few blocks south of the mountain and is basically everything within the square formed by rue Sherbrooke in the north, rue St Antoine in the south, blvd St Laurent in the east and ave Atwater in the west. This is the modern, high rise, high tech heart of the city. **Vieux Montréal**, down by the port, is where the city's oldest streets were first laid out in 1672. Today it's Montreal's most picturesque, photogenic and tourist-packed quarter.

Finally, a word on street numbers. For east-west streets, 0 is at blvd St Laurent, with numbers increasing as they move east or west from this point. Addresses are suffixed with *est* (east) or *ouest* (west) to designate which side of the boulevard they're on. North-south street numbers start down by the St Lawrence and increase as the streets move north.

Tourist Information

There's a large and very efficient Infotouriste Centre (☎ 873-2015) at 1001 rue du Square Dorchester (about a ten-minute walk from the train station). It's open daily, 8.30am-7.30pm June-August, and 9am-5pm for the rest of the year. It's stocked with masses of brochures and leaflets, and there's also an accommodation desk where the staff will ring around to find vacancies for you.

A second, much smaller tourist office is located on the corner of the Place Jacques Cartier in Vieux Montréal, open daily 9am-7pm June-August, and 9am-1pm then 2-5pm for the rest of the year.

Money

There are numerous banks downtown, including several next to the train station. The following charge no commission for exchanging foreign currency: Banque Nationale du Canada at 1001 rue Sainte-Catherine Ouest; Banque Nationale du Canada at 600 rue de la Gauchèterie Ouest; Thomas Cook at 625 blvd René Lévesque Ouest.

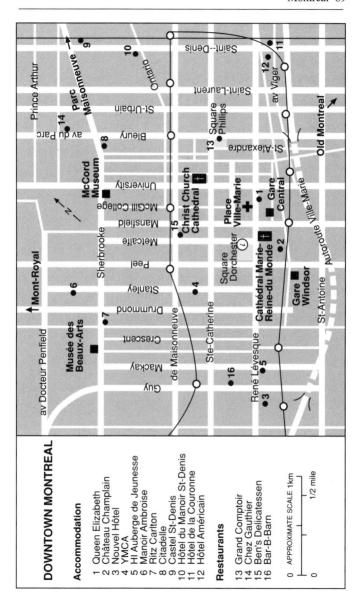

Consulates
Austria (☎ 845-8661) 1030-1350 rue Sherbrooke Ouest
Belgium (☎ 849-7394) 850-999 blvd de Maisonneuve Ouest
Britain (☎ 866-5863) 901-1155 rue University
Denmark (☎ 877-3060) 1 Place-Ville-Marie, 35th floor
Finland (☎ 397-7600) 3400-800 carré Victoria
France (☎ 878-4381) 2601-1 Place-Ville-Marie
Germany (☎ 286-1820) 3455 rue de la Montagne
Italy (☎ 849-8351) 3489 ave Drummond
Japan (☎ 866-3429) 2120-600 rue de la Gauchèterie Ouest
Netherlands (☎ 849-4247) 1500-1245 rue Sherbrooke Ouest
Norway (☎ 874-9087) 1155 blvd René Lévesque Ouest
South Africa (☎ 878-9217) 2615-1 Place-Ville-Marie
Spain (☎ 935-5235) 1456-1 Westmount Sq
Sweden (☎ 866-4019) 800 carré Victoria
Switzerland (☎ 932-7181) 1572 ave Dr Penfield
USA (☎ 398-9695) 455 blvd René Lévesque

WHERE TO STAY

There are plenty of places to stay in Montreal and you can generally get some good deals, particularly in the mid-priced range. Be warned, though, that the best places get snapped up very quickly in July and August, and if you're planning on coming during the Jazz Festival (beginning of July) you should book well ahead.

Budget accommodation
The Hostelling International **Auberge de Jeunesse** (☎ 843-3317) has recently moved to a beautifully renovated old house on the southern corner of rues Mackay and René Lévesque (1030 rue Mackay). Rooms contain three to ten beds, and each one has its own private bathroom. Rates are $16 a night for members, and $20.56 for non-members. The mixed sex **YMCA** (☎ 849-8393) is considerably pricier, with singles at $35 and doubles at $54. It's in a superb location, though, at 1450 rue Stanley and has excellent facilities including a cafeteria and a 22-metre swimming pool. Also very central is the **McGill University Residence** (☎ 398-6367) at 3935 University. Rooms are available only during the summer months, and cost $36.50 a single ($26.50 for students). Another student residence is the **Auberge Quartier Latin** (☎ 982-9016) at 3475 rue Saint-Urbain. Studios, with private bathrooms and kitchenettes, cost $35 – excellent value.

Mid-range hotels
Le Nouvel Hôtel (☎ 931-8841) is a slightly scaled down version of a smart hotel with suitably scaled down prices: doubles cost $79. The

rooms are spacious and smart and come with phone/TV/room service etc. It's central, too, at 1740 blvd René Lévesque. For something with a bit more character, try **Le Manoir Ambroise** (☎ 288-6922). It's a lovely Victorian house converted into a small hotel. The rooms are big and attractively decorated, and the guest book is full of enthusiastic comments such as 'C'est fantastique!' It's situated at the quiet end of rue Stanley (No 3422, at the foot of Mt Royal) and is just a stone's throw from the centre of town. Doubles with a private bathroom cost $65-70, including continental breakfast.

Over in the Francophone enclave to the east of town, rue St-Denis is a mecca of little hotels and guest houses dotted between the bars and restaurants that make this area so trendy. You can get some good bargains along here: at No 2006, the **Hôtel du Manoir St Denis** (☎ 843-3670) has small but comfortable double rooms (with fridges) for $54 (singles $42). The same rates apply in the **Hôtel Américain** (☎ 849-0616), a tastefully restored old house at No 1042 (at the southern end of the street, very close to Vieux Montréal).

Just across the road at No 1029 is the **Hôtel de la Couronne** (☎ 845-0901) in a similar building, with rooms at similar prices (doubles start at $54). For unbeatable value, try the **Castel St Denis** (842-9719) at No 2099, run by the delightful Mr Imam. The rooms are simple, clean and excellently priced, starting at $45 a double.

Upmarket hotels

The classiest joint in town is the **Ritz Carlton** (☎ 842-4212) at 1228 rue Sherbrooke Ouest. It opened in 1912 and its fantastically opulent interior seems to have changed little since then. An added touch of glamour: it was here that Elizabeth Taylor married Richard Burton in 1964. Doubles start at a prohibitive $190 but it's worth going in for a drink at the piano bar (or even just a trip to the loos).

If you like the idea of stepping off the train right into your hotel you can do just that at the **Queen Elizabeth** (☎ 861-3511) which is literally right on top of the station. It's a large, stylish hotel and is always busy with a high-powered international crowd. It's cheapest to stay at the weekend when you can get a room from $130.

Just round the corner at 1 Place du Canada is the Queen Elizabeth's sister hotel, **Le Château Champlain** (☎ 878-9000) which looks exactly like a giant cheese grater and is referred to as such by all Montrealers. Rooms here start at $120.

La Citadelle (☎ 844-8851) has all the amenities of a top hotel but, with only nine rooms on each floor, has a much more intimate feel to it than most establishments. Its top-floor pool has excellent views over the city. The hotel is just on the edge of downtown at 410 rue Sherbrooke Ouest. Rooms start at $95.

WHERE TO EAT

Montreal is blessed with a wealth of eating places ranging from gourmet establishments to dirt-cheap delis. While it shares the North American obsession with bagels, and although European immigrants have imported interesting specialities (notably smoked meat), the majority of Montreal's restaurants are firmly rooted in the city's French heritage. Many restaurants have a fixed-price table d'hôte which is considerably cheaper than ordering à la carte.

Budget food

Cheap restaurants are few and far between in **Old Montreal** (where there aren't even any fast food joints). You can try **Chez Better** at 160 Notre-Dame Est which serves German sausages and fries for about $10 a head, or the very popular **Steak Frites** at 12 Saint-Paul Est.

   Downtown, the choice of cheap options is enormous. You can find all the usual fast food outlets lined along Ste Catherine St, among many other places. Over in the **Grand Comptoir** at 1225 Square Phillips you can eat a splendid bistro lunch for around $7. Enormously popular with Montrealers is the **Bar-B-Barn** (1201 Guy) which serves delicious pork ribs. (Be warned that the lunchtime queues are out of the door at weekends). **Ben's Delicatessen**, the most famous of the city's innumerable smoked-meat sandwich restaurants, is enshrined as a local institution. It's at 900 Maisonneuve and is open 7am-4am. Finally a word must be said about rue Prince-Arthur which, between Laval and Saint-Laurent, is packed with super-cheap restaurants (mainly Greek, Vietnamese or Italian). Many of them are BYOBs (bring-your-own-booze) which makes a night out there even cheaper.

Mid-range and upmarket restaurants

Enjoying a prime location on the Place Jacques Cartier in Old Montreal, **La Marée** (☎ 861-9794) serves excellent but expensive fish dishes. Despite being in the heart of touristville it is heavily patronised by locals. The table d'hôte starts at $29; reservations are essential. Round the corner at 443 Saint-Vincent (and located in a former morgue) is **Claude Postel**, a favourite haunt of Montreal's bourgeoisie. The gourmet French restaurant is a little stingy with its portions but the food is superb. The three-course table d'hôte is very reasonable at $24. Along the same lines but not quite as upmarket is **Bonaparte**, also in Old Montreal at 443 Saint-François-Xavier (from $22 a head). Downtown there's the long-established **Beaver Club** at the Queen Elizabeth Hotel and the outrageously posh restaurant at **The Ritz** where you can count on spending about $50 per person. A little more affordable is **Chez Gauthier** (3487 ave du Parc) where you can feast on good bistro food in a pretty, wood-panelled room from about $18.

NIGHTLIFE

Montreal's dazzling nightlife scene is concentrated in several different areas, each with its own character and crowd.

Rue Crescent (between Sainte Catherine and Maisonneuve) is an out and out cruising street. Traditionally regarded as the preserve of the Anglos, it's packed with pubs, nightclubs and a dolled-up crowd whose main pursuits seem to be drinking, dancing and attempting to pull. Favourite spots include the **Sir Winston Churchill** at No 1459 and **Thursday's** at No 1449.

The **blvd Saint-Laurent** is considerably more sophisticated (and Francophone) and has some of the most interesting nightspots in town. **Le Balattou** (No 4372) is a hot, smoky and immensely popular African nightclub, while further down at No 3556 is **Le Zoo** where a self-conscious clientele come to dance within a self-conscious interior (check out the leopardskin-clad mannequins hanging from the ceiling).

Rue Saint-Denis has a more studenty, bohemian feel to it. There are some excellent jazz bars here, including **Le Central** at No 4479 and **Les Beaux Esprits** at No 2073.

There's also a thriving gay scene in Montreal, most of it centred in what's known as the '**Gay Village**'. The core of the village runs along Sainte-Catherine between Saint-Denis and Papineau. One of its most famous clubs is **KOX** at No 1450, which attracts a good number of straights as well as gays.

WHAT TO SEE

Vieux Montréal

Old Montreal (see map p94) is a magnet for tourists with its cobblestoned streets, immaculately restored buildings, churches, boutiques, cafés and restaurants. It contains some of the best examples of 18th century architecture in North America and, despite the crowds, is completely irresistible. The Infotouriste Centre at the corner of Place Jacques Cartier hands out free walking tour booklets which give a detailed account of the district's main historic and architectural features. The highlights are as follows.

• **Notre-Dame Basilica** This Gothic Revival extravaganza at 116 Notre-Dame Ouest was the biggest religious building in North America when it was completed in 1829. It was designed by James O'Donnell, a New York-Irish architect who was so proud of his work he converted to Catholicism so he could be buried in it. The interior is a dazzling spectacle of gold leaf and stained glass, and the main altar is breathtaking. Note also the beautiful vaulted ceiling, and the huge 5772-pipe Casavant organ (remember St-Hyacinthe? See p145).

• **Château Ramezay** More a big house than a château, this is nonetheless a fine old residence. It was built in 1705 for the Governor of Montreal, and has since been used as a furs and spices store for the French West India Company and a base for American revolutionaries trying to get Montreal to join forces with the US. It's now a museum featuring mainly 18th and 19th century furniture and costumes. It's located at 280 Notre Dame Est, and is open daily 10am-8pm June to September (and Tuesday to Sunday 10am-4.30pm for the rest of the year). Entrance is $5.

• **Bank of Montreal** At 119 rue Saint-Jacques stands Canada's oldest banking institution. This is where George Stephen and Donald Smith were directors before leaving to form the CPR Syndicate; the bank continued to be an important source of funds throughout the railway's construction. This domed, neo-classical building, modelled on the Pantheon in Rome, is particularly grand inside with its marble counters, massive columns and bronze trimmings everywhere.

• **Marché Bonsecours** Montrealers clearly delighted in these neo-classical, temple-style buildings. The old market hall at 350 rue Saint-Paul Est is a very striking example, with its doric columns and silver dome. The line of Georgian sash windows is a bit of a leap in period, but the overall effect is lovely.

• **Notre-Dame-de-Bonsecours Chapel** There's none of the grandeur here of the Notre-Dame Basilica, but this pretty little church at 400 Saint-Paul Est is well worth a visit. It was a favourite of Montreal's

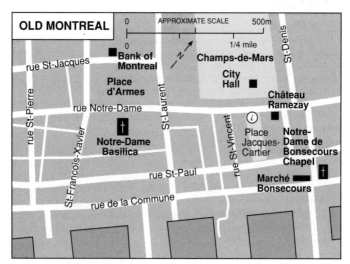

sailors who would pray here for a safe voyage, and then bring votive offerings on their return. Many of these are still there, such as the carved model ships hanging from the roof of the nave.

• **Old Port** No longer used commercially, the old port has recently been landscaped and redeveloped with gardens, cycling paths, exhibition salles and an IMAX cinema. The views along the river are splendid and a look-out tower gives excellent views over the city. You can also see one of the old grain silos – a huge, grey block that apparently sent the visiting Le Corbusier into raptures.

Downtown

The pace of life shifts up a few gears as you move into the hustle and bus-tle of downtown Montreal. While many streets are dominated by sky-scrapers, there are more than enough department stores, bars, museums, restaurants and even churches to give Montreal a softer edge. The prolif-eration of young people here makes it as lively by night as it is by day.

• **Le Musée des Beaux Arts** Many of the paintings in this wonderful museum were acquired from the private collections of Montreal's turn-of-the-century business magnates. The European collection, in particular, is excellent and includes works by El Greco, Canaletto, Renoir, Sizley, Monet, Giacometti, Dali and Picasso.

   The museum is at 1380 rue Sherbrooke Ouest, and is open Tuesday to Sunday 11am-6pm, Wednesday and Saturday evenings until 9pm. Entrance is a steep $12.

• **McCord Museum of Canadian History** Founded in 1919 when David Ross McCord donated his collection of Canadiana to McGill University so that it might form the basis of a history museum. The exhibits, ranging from china and jewellery to native costumes, are inter-esting and very well displayed, but you can't help wishing there was more of it. The museum is at 690 rue Sherbrooke Ouest and is open Tuesday to Sunday, 10am-5pm. Entrance is $5.

• **McGill University** Just over the road from the McCord museum, this is one of Canada's most prestigious universities. The campus with its limestone buildings and well-tended gardens extends to the foot of the mountain and is a very pleasant place to stroll around.

• **Christ Church Cathedral** This Anglican cathedral, on the corner of Sainte-Catherine and University, quietly sums up some of the remarkable contrasts of Montreal: the graceful old building, containing some beauti-ful stained glass William Morris windows, is set on top of a shopping mall. This connects it to a towering glass sky scraper next door, which is where the church's offices are located!

• **Rue Ste-Catherine** This is the main shopping street in Montreal. It's always incredibly busy but has a vibrant rather than stressed atmosphere to it. Don't miss the Eaton department store at No 677, whose wonderful art deco dining room (9th floor) has remained unchanged since it opened in 1931.

• **Place-Ville-Marie** Designed by the man who created the pyramid in the Louvre, Place-Ville-Marie is a complex of towers built over the railway tracks. The most arresting one is the famous crucifix-shaped skyscraper, supposedly a symbol of the city's roots in Catholicism. (It also provides a handy landmark.) The tower houses hundreds of offices, including the headquarters of VIA Rail.

Underground City
Each year more than 40 million tonnes of snow are ploughed up from Montreal's streets. Hardly surprising, then, that most Montrealers take to their incredible Underground City during these winter months. This eighteen-mile system of shops, cinemas, restaurants, hotels and banks has even become something of a tourist attraction but be warned: it's notoriously difficult to find your way around, so be sure to equip yourself with a map (available at the tourist office) before venturing down.

• **Sun Life Building** Right next door to Place-Ville-Marie is the former headquarters of the massive Sun Life Insurance company, who objected so strongly to Montreal's new language laws that they moved their head offices to Toronto in the 1970s. This was the biggest building in the British Empire when it was erected in 1917, and despite being dwarfed by surrounding skyscrapers today, it remains an impressive sight. It is also where the crown jewels were hidden during World War II.

• **Cathédrale Marie-Reine-du-Monde** Opposite the Sun Life Building is the green-roofed scale model of St Peter's in Rome; it's exactly one third of the original's size. It was built in the late 19th century in a flagrant attempt to overshadow the Notre-Dame Basilica in Old Montreal. Note the thirteen copper statues above the entrance: these are of the patron saints of Montreal's parishes.

• **Windsor Station** When Van Horne decided that Montreal needed a new railway station to house the terminus of the transcontinental line, he got Bruce Price to draw up the plans. (Price was a leading American architect who went on to design the Château Frontenac and other CPR hotels.) The result was Windsor Station, a huge Romanesque building whose grandness reflected Montreal's importance as the railway centre of

(**Opposite**): Street performer in Quebec City (see p75). Despite losing the referendum in 1995, many Québecois still find plenty to smile about.

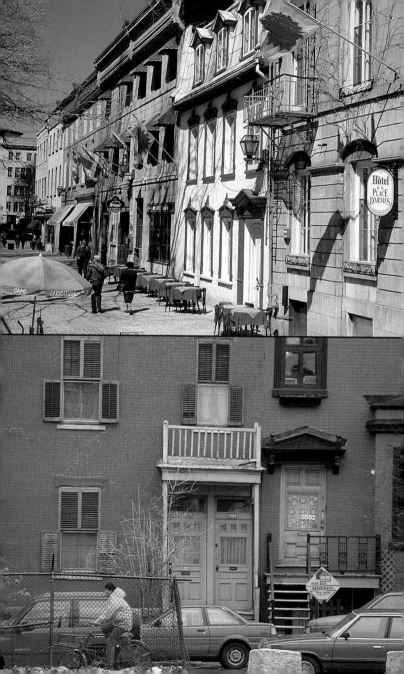

Canada. Although inter-city trains moved over to Central Station after World War II, it continued to be used by commuter trains until 1993 when the construction of the new Forum put a stop to its activities. A new purpose for the building is currently being sought; in the meantime it stands sad and empty.

A downstairs office at the station (Room G-1) houses the Canadian Pacific Archives, a massive collection of photographs and documents pertaining to CPR history. Members of the public aren't encouraged to come wandering in off the street, but if you're interested you can phone them (☎ 395-5135) and arrange a visit.

Mont Royal

You can't come to Montreal without going up its little mountain which at just 232m is not a taxing climb. You will be rewarded with superb views over the city, a little like those over Paris from the Sacré Coeur. Besides the views, the expanse of parkland at the top of the hill is a fine place to wander about. You can also take in **St Joseph's Oratory**. This magnificent basilica was built at the request of Brother André, who is reputed to have performed miraculous healings. He was beatified by Pope John Paul II in 1982, and the site has since become an important pilgrimage destination for North Americans.

Maisonneuve

A few kms east of downtown is the Maisonneuve area, the site of three major attractions: the Olympic Stadium, the Biodôme and the Botanical Gardens. The best way to get out there is by taking the métro to Pie IX; everything is well signed from the métro exit.

● **Olympic Stadium** Mention the stadium to most Montrealers and you'll get a raising of the eyebrows and shrug of exasperation. The giant complex, with its 175-metre inclined tower supporting the supposedly retractable roof was built at colossal expense for the 1976 Olympic Games. Not only did it leave the city with an enormous debt but it didn't even work very well and the controversial roof is scheduled to be replaced by a permanent structure. Still, the tower is an impressive construction and the shuttle ride up to the observation desk at the top is good fun. Open daily 10am-6pm, (and until 9pm mid-June to 4 September). For more information, phone ☎ 252-8687.

● **Botanical Gardens** Among the largest in the world, the thirty outdoor gardens include the beautiful replica of the old Ming Gardens of Shanghai, Montreal's twin city, designed by experts brought over from

---

(**Opposite**): It's not just Quebec's language, food, and culture but even the architecture is different, like these Gallic-looking houses in Quebec City (**top**) and Montreal (**bottom**).

China. The gardens also house an **Insectarium**. The botanical gardens are open daily year-round, 9am-6pm (and until 8pm 24 June-4 September). It costs $7 to get in.

• **Biodôme** This amazing environment museum contains four different North American ecosystems under one roof: Tropical Rainforest; Laurentian Forest, St Laurent Marine Ecosystem and (most interesting) Polar World. The habitats are home to thousands of plants and animals, living as though in their natural environment. Opening times are 9am-6pm daily, year-round (and until 8pm in summer); entrance price is $9.50.

FESTIVALS

• **International Fireworks Competition**, late May to early June. Spectacular displays in the beautiful setting of the Parc des Iles.
• **Montreal International Jazz Festival**, late June-early July (11 days). Outstanding, world-class cultural event attracting well over a million tourists annually. Two thousand international musicians (including lots of big names) and over three hundred shows, many of them free.
• **Just for Laughs Festival**, mid-July. The world's largest comedy festival, a fascinating insight into the contrasts of Anglo and Franco humour.
• **Montreal World Film Festival**, late August to early September. New films screened practically around the clock. At the end of the festival prizes are awarded, the top one being the Grand Prix des Amériques.

MOVING ON

By rail
The service between Montreal and Toronto is the busiest in Canada . A good number of trains run daily between the two cities. Several trains a day also leave Montreal for Ottawa and for Quebec City, and there's a daily (except Tuesday) service to Halifax via Lévis (opposite Quebec City). For more information call VIA on ☎ 871-1331 (or ☎ 1-800-361-5390 when calling from outside Montreal). Note that there is also an Amtrak rail service from Montreal to New York and Washington – the Amtrak toll-free information number is ☎ 1-800-872-7245.

By air
Montreal's two international airports serve hundreds of internal and world-wide destinations. Autocar Connaisseur (☎ 934-1222) run a shuttle bus to both airports – they pick up passengers at all the major hotels. Other useful telephone numbers include Dorval Airport: ☎ 633-3105; Mirabel Airport: ☎ 476-3031; Air Canada: ☎ 393-3333; Canadian Airlines International: ☎ 636-3890; American Airlines: ☎ 397-9635 and British Airways: ☎ 287-9133.

Toronto

The country round this town, being very flat, is bare of scenic interest; but the town itself is full of life and motion, bustle, business and improvement. Charles Dickens, *American Notes*

Toronto's had a considerable amount of bad press over the years and many people have agreed with Peter Ustinov's unflattering conclusion that it is 'a kind of New York run by the Swiss'. Yet the city is nowhere near as boring or sanitised as this stereotype makes it out to be. On the contrary you'll see beggars on the street and crazies on the underground, you'll hear lots of loud music pumping out of ghetto blasters, and you'll see the funkiest people this side of Camden Town. Toronto, you'll quickly realise, is a crowded, noisy and very exciting place to be and fulfils European expectations of a big North American metropolis more than any other city in Canada.

One of the best things about Toronto is that it doesn't keep going on about its history – possibly because it has very little to go on about, but the welcome result is a moving, dynamic and forward-looking environment where new theatre, art and music flourish. It also boasts some outstanding museums, architecture and other attractions (notably the CN tower). There really is plenty to do and see here, the only drawback being the vast amounts of money required to do it and see it.

HISTORY

Early settlement
The site was first occupied by the Huron Indians who named it Toronto, meaning 'meeting place'. Lying on a sheltered harbour on the north shore of Lake Ontario, it was part of the connecting land route to Lake Huron. In 1750 the French set up a fur-trading post here and built a stockade to protect their trading operations but the British ejected them in 1759 and destroyed the fort. They proceeded to ignore the place for several decades. However, when Loyalists to the British Crown started fleeing America after the War of Independence, many came and settled in the area.

Bought from the natives
In 1788 the Governor-in-Chief of Canada officially bought the site of Toronto from the Mississauga Indians. What was to become the nation's biggest city was a bargain at £1700, a few bales of cloth and some axes.

The new purchase was renamed York and a few years later became the capital of Upper Canada. The first of the city's grid-patterned streets were laid out and the community slowly began to take shape.

America invades

When war broke out between England and America in 1812, York was invaded by 1700 US troops who pillaged the town and burnt down the Parliament Building. In revenge, British troops tried to burn down the building occupied by the US President in Washington. They didn't succeed, but the damaged walls had to be white-washed which is how it came to be known as the White House. After the war ended in 1814, colonists began to come over in greater numbers: the city's population grew from 700 in 1816 to over 9000 in 1834. In this year the city was incorporated and given back its old name of Toronto.

Industrial and economic boom

With the arrival of the Grand Trunk and Great Western railways in the 1850s, Toronto entered a period of rapid economic expansion. It quickly emerged as an important agricultural, manufacturing and distribution centre and as its population and industrial clout boomed, expensive new buildings were erected at a similar pace. Following the difficult years of the 1930s' Depression, Toronto's economic strength was reaffirmed when the St Lawrence Seaway was opened in 1959, bringing with it a mass of trade and investment. The next few decades saw the construction of a multitude of gleaming skyscrapers and Toronto's business world was further enlarged by the arrival of many firms from Montreal, in flight from Quebec's language laws.

Toronto today

Toronto is Canada's biggest city with over 750,000 people living in the city proper, and 3.4 million in Greater Toronto. Its population is astoundingly multicultural as a result of Toronto's policy of welcoming immigrants from around the globe, and in 1989 the United Nations identified it as the most ethnically diverse city in the world. Racial relations are exemplary, giving weight to Toronto's claim that it is 'a city that works'. It is the financial, industrial and commercial capital of Canada and is also the most expensive city in the country to live in.

ARRIVING IN TORONTO

By air

Most flights to Toronto arrive at the massive Pearson International Airport, 25km northwest of the city centre. Airport Express buses will bring you into town for $14, stopping at all the major hotels. Buses leave every 20 minutes from 6am to 1am, and every hour in between these times. You can, of course, do the forty-minute ride in a taxi but this will set you back around $45. Commuter flights from Ontario and Quebec arrive at the Toronto Island Airport from which a ferry and shuttle bus take travellers to the railway station.

By rail

Trains arrive at Union Station on Front Street, near the CN tower. It's right at the southern end of town but if you need to go north, you can catch the subway here. This huge, imposing building was opened by the Prince of Wales (the future King Edward VIII) in 1927 and is still the grandest railway station in Canada.

LOCAL TRANSPORT

Toronto's public transport system – a network of buses, streetcars and the subway – is probably the best in Canada. It's operated by the Toronto Transit Commission (TTC) – their telephone information line is ☎ 393-4636. Single tickets cost $2, a book of five costs $6-50 or you can get a day pass for $5. Note that you need the exact fare, or a ticket or token (available at subway stations).

The subway is open 6am-1.30am, and there are regular Blue Night Network buses running along Bloor-Danforth and Yonge when the subway is closed.

ORIENTATION AND SERVICES

Toronto's downtown layout is very uncomplicated: it's contained within a rectangle formed by Front St in the south, Bloor St in the north, Jarvis St in the east and Spadina Ave in the west. A couple of blocks south of Front St is the harbour front. The biggest and busiest north-south street is Yonge St; the streets running across it at right angles are divided into East and West at this point. The distance between Bloor and Front is about $2^1/_2$ km, while Jarvis to Spadina is just under 2km.

Asking directions
When you ask for directions you'll notice that most Canadians refer to a street or avenue just by its name, so Yonge St is simply 'Yonge' and University Ave is just 'University.' This is especially true in Toronto, where it's even written like this on tourist maps.

Tourist Information

The main tourist office (run by the MTCVA – Metropolitan Toronto Convention and Visitors' Association) is down by the harbour at 207 Queen's Quay West, Suite 590. There are also several tourist kiosks around the city, eg outside the Eaton shopping mall (Yonge at Dundas) or at the City Hall. You can make enquiries by phone on ☎ 203-2500, or toll-free from anywhere in North America on ☎ 1-800-363-1990. As well as the usual tourist information, they have some surprisingly enlightened publications such as a guide for gay and lesbian travellers and a list of free activities in Toronto.

Money

There is no shortage of banks in Toronto; whichever part of town you're in you'll find one nearby. In addition, Thomas Cook has numerous foreign exchange branches in the city including 100 Yonge St (15th Floor), Sheraton Centre Hotel Lobby, 123 Queen St West and 9 Bloor St West.

Consulates

Australia (☎ 323-1155) 314-175 Bloor St East
Austria (☎ 863-0649) 1010-360 Bay St
Belgium (☎ 944-1422) 2006-2 Bloor St West
Britain (☎ 593-1290) 1910-777 Bay St
Denmark (☎ 962-5661) 310-151 Bloor St West
Finland (☎ 964-0066) 604-1200 Bay St
France (☎ 925-8041) 400-130 Bloor St West
Germany (☎ 925-2813) 77 Admiral Rd
Italy (☎ 977-1566) 136 Beverley St
Japan (☎ 363-7038) Suite 2702, Toronto Dominion Bank Tower
Netherlands (☎ 598-2520) 2106-1 Dundas St West
South Africa (☎ 364-0314) 2515-2 First Canadian Place
Spain (☎ 967-4949) 400-12 Bay St West
Sweden (☎ 963-8768) 1504-2 Bloor St West
Switzerland (☎ 593-5371) 601-154 University Ave
USA (☎ 595-1700) 360 University Ave

WHERE TO STAY

Budget accommodation

Options for cheap accommodation are somewhat limited. **Hostelling International Toronto** (☎ 971-4440) has recently moved from Church St to 90 Gerrard West (near the corner of Bay) and now occupies several floors of a nurses' residence. The resulting ambience is rather strange and travellers seem a bit unsure about the place. The check-in queues are probably the longest in Canada but, no doubt, these little teething problems will disappear with time. Rates are $20.95 for members, and $25.23 for non-members.

At 96 Gerrard East the **Neil Wycik College Hostel** (☎ 977-2320) rents private rooms to travellers from May to August at $31.50 for a single or $38 for a double. It's very clean, and the facilities are excellent (roof-top sun deck, sauna, breakfast café, laundry, kitchens). Another summertime possibility is the **University of Toronto Residence Service** (☎ 978-8735), based at Rm 240, Simcoe Hall, 27 Kings College Circle. They have over 800 rooms located in various parts of the city, most of them around the $40 mark.

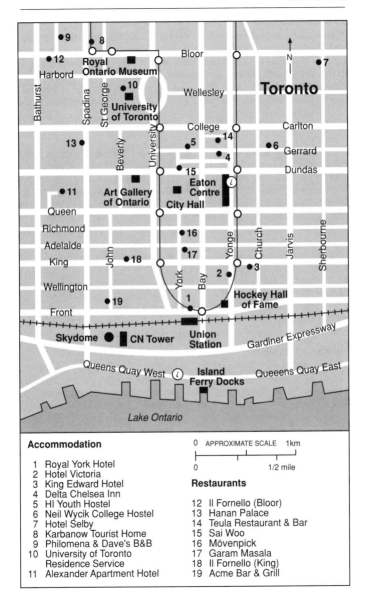

Accommodation

1 Royal York Hotel
2 Hotel Victoria
3 King Edward Hotel
4 Delta Chelsea Inn
5 HI Youth Hostel
6 Neil Wycik College Hostel
7 Hotel Selby
8 Karbanow Tourist Home
9 Philomena & Dave's B&B
10 University of Toronto
   Residence Service
11 Alexander Apartment Hotel

0   APPROXIMATE SCALE   1km

0   1/2 mile

Restaurants

12 Il Fornello (Bloor)
13 Hanan Palace
14 Teula Restaurant & Bar
15 Sai Woo
16 Mövenpick
17 Garam Masala
18 Il Fornello (King)
19 Acme Bar & Grill

Mid-range hotels

Toronto has a very diverse range of good value, mid-priced accommodation. At the southern end of Yonge St (No 56) the modern **Hotel Victoria** (☎ 363-1666) has 48 nicely furnished, comfortable rooms starting at $69 at the weekend ($75 weekdays). Going for more of a period look is the **Hotel Selby** (☎ 921-3142) whose building dates from 1882. It has 67 rooms, many with open fireplaces, and most of the bathrooms have beautiful, free standing baths. Guests also have the use of kitchen and laundry facilities. Singles here start at $49, doubles at $59, and it's at 592 Sherbourne (at Bloor).

At the other end of town near the corner of Queen and Bathurst is the **Alexander Apartment Hotel** (☎ 504-2121) at 77 Ryerson Ave. It's a block of 60 self-contained studios, quite small but spotlessly clean and well-equipped (they all have a TV, phone, private bathroom and kitchenette). Doubles start at $55. Excellently located (not far from the Royal Ontario Museum) is the 20-room **Karabanow Tourist Home** (☎ 923-4004) at 9 Spadina Rd. It's a lovely old house (though the garish, 1970s decor does clash a bit with the Victorian fireplaces) and its very convenient for public transport, being literally right next door to Spadina subway. Singles are $49 and doubles $56.

If you'd prefer to be removed from the hustle and bustle, **Philomena & Dave's B&B** (☎ 962-2786) is on a quiet, leafy street just a few minutes' walk from Spadina subway at 31 Dalton Rd. The rooms are beautiful but there are only five of them, and the owners stress that telephone reservations are essential before turning up. Singles are $40, doubles $55.

Upmarket hotels

If you want to do things in true style there's only one place to stay: the **Royal York Hotel** (☎ 368-2511) opposite the railway station. Built by Canadian Pacific Railways in 1929, the one-time tallest building in the British Empire is splendidly luxurious inside. This is where the rich and famous stay when they're in town. Guests have included the Queen, Bob Hope, Ronald Reagan, Dolly Parton and His Holiness the Dalai Lama of Tibet. A night at the hotel is surprisingly affordable, with weekend rates from $139 a double.

Other upmarket hotels include the massive **Delta Chelsea** (☎ 243-5732) at 33 Gerrard West, which has lots of special facilities for children and doubles from $130, and the very elegant **King Edward Hotel** (☎ 863-9700) at 37 King East, where doubles start at $235.

WHERE TO EAT

Toronto has some fine restaurants but many of these are far from the centre, out in the neighbourhoods. Downtown seems to be dominated by chain restaurants serving predictable but adequate food.

Budget food

As you may well imagine, Chinese restaurants are superabundant in Toronto. A walk down Spadina will leave you dazed and confused, unable to choose from the dazzling cornucopia of eateries. **Hanan Palace** at No 412 is exceedingly good and exceedingly cheap, with lunch time specials at $4.99. One of the oldest and best known restaurants in the area is **Sai Woo** (130 Dundas West).

Garam Masala at 100 Adelaide is a very decent Indian restaurant. Its eat-as-much-as-you-want lunch buffet ($6.95) makes it a big hit with local Torontonians. If your palate can't handle all this ethnic diversity there's always the burgers and Coke option at the **Acme Bar & Grill** (86 John St).

Finally, **Yonge St** is lined with hundreds of cheap bagel, submarine, burger and numerous other fast-food joints.

Mid-range and upmarket restaurants

If you fancy a splurge you might as well go right to the top and visit the world's highest revolving restaurant, in the CN Tower. Prices at **360 Revolving Restaurant** are suitably steep (around $35 a head) and reservations are essential (☎ 868-1977).

For around $20 a head you can dine among the tropical plants and Swiss art of **Mövenpick** (165 York St, south of Richmond). This immensely popular restaurant serves seasonal Swiss delicacies as well as tamer fare, like pork chops and mashed potatoes, and it has a near-legendary dessert buffet. At around the same price, **Teula Restaurant and Bar** (opposite the Delta Chelsea) serves lots of fresh market cuisine, with some excellent lamb and beef dishes. A very successful Italian chain is **Il Fornello** where you can indulge in delicious clay oven pizzas in a stylish decor. There are several branches around town, eg 486 Bloor West and 155 King East.

NIGHTLIFE

One of the liveliest stretches of town after dark is Queen West, between University and Spadina (see p107). Places to look out for are the **Black Bull** at No 298 (live bands); the **Horseshoe Tavern** at No 370 (more live bands); **Rivoli** at No 332 (lounge bar); the **Bamboo** at No 312 (African music) and the **Big Bop** at No 651 (nightclub). The city's trendy gay village runs down Church St.

Toronto claims to be 'the third largest **theatre** centre in the English-speaking world' after London and New York. There's certainly an enormous variety of shows being put on, from glitzy musicals *(Phantom* et al) to the best of contemporary theatre (particularly from the Canadian Stage Co). Check the local papers for listings.

WHAT TO SEE

CN Tower

Never mind the five-mile queues, never mind the exorbitant entrance fee, the CN Tower is something that has to be done while in Toronto. This long, spindly telecommunications tower that looks as if it might snap in two in a high wind is the tallest free-standing structure in the world at 553m high. When your turn finally comes you ascend the first 442m to the Observation level in a glass elevator on the outside of the tower. Once you're up you can enjoy the staggering views over the toy-town city from either an indoor or outdoor viewing deck. The particularly brave can also take a stroll across the gut-churning glass floor. Not being particularly brave myself, it took me half an hour to edge my way to the centre, at which point I nearly fainted when a 22-stone adolescent suddenly attempted a somersault, apparently to test the strength of the glass).

Serious height enthusiasts can go up an extra 100m to the Space Deck. I am told that on a clear day you can see as far as Niagara Falls, 137kms away. The entrance to the CN Tower is on Front St, about five minutes' walk west of the railway station. It costs $12 to get to the Observation level, and a further $3 to get to the Space Deck. The tower is open daily 10am-midnight in summer, and 10am-10pm for the rest of the year.

Skydome

Right next door to the CN Tower is Toronto's answer to Montreal's Olympic Stadium: the Skydome also with a fully retractable roof. The huge arena is home territory for the Toronto Blue Jays (baseball) and the Toronto Argonauts (football) and is the venue for numerous concerts and shows. It's certainly an impressive building but it's debatable whether it's worth parting with $9 for the behind the scenes 'Tour Experience' in the arena (daily, on the hour, 10am-6pm in the summer).

Hockey Hall of Fame

Continuing the sporting theme is this shrine to ice hockey on the corner of Front and Yonge. It's filled with a dazzling display of memorabilia (trophies, photos, movies etc) which seems to send the Canadians and Americans wild. Opening hours are Monday-Wednesday and Saturday 9am-6pm; Thursday and Friday 9am-9.30pm (or 6pm in winter); Sunday 10am-6pm. Entrance costs $8.50.

City Hall

Unlike many daring new edifices erected in the 1960s, this one continues to be raved about today. It's comprised of two tall, thin buildings curving towards each other with a short, dome-covered building in between them. City Hall is at Nathan Phillips Square (on Queen St West), which turns into a skating rink in winter. The old city hall still stands at the east side of the square (on the corner of Bay and Queen), its Romanesque grandeur somewhat diminished by its towering neighbours.

Queen West

Starting a few blocks west of the City Hall, Queen St West suddenly goes all young and trendy – a change in tone due mainly to the close proximity of Canada's biggest art school, the Ontario College of Art. Cafés, nightclubs, bookshops and restaurants are interspersed with art studios and fashion design workshops. This very lively and slightly downbeat area stretches between University and Spadina and is known simply as 'Queen West'.

Longest street in the world

The biggest and brashest thoroughfare in Toronto, **Yonge St** is packed with skyscrapers, hotels, theatres, upmarket boutiques, scruffy discount stores, exclusive restaurants, greasy diners, thousands of people and much much more. It's also the location (at Dundas) of the main entrance to the Eaton Centre, a veritable mega-mall that swallows up a million shoppers each week.

Not only is Yonge St one of the oldest streets in Toronto; it is also the longest street in the world. Starting near Toronto's harbour front you could drive north along Yonge (petrol supplies permitting) all the way to Rainy River, Ontario – a distance of 1900km. If you were to drive that distance from London you'd end up in Morocco!

Royal Ontario Museum

A few blocks north of Chinatown is the Royal Ontario Museum (ROM). The easiest way to get there is to take the subway and get off at Museum, then follow the signs to the entrance (Bloor at University). The enormous museum contains both arts and science based collections, including dinosaur skeletons (most of them from the Alberta Badlands), a display of precious gems and exhibitions on the ancient civilisations of Egypt, Greece and Rome. Best of all is the internationally famous Far Eastern art collection, which includes works dating from 150 BC (the Shang Dynasty) through to the early 20th century (the era of the Manchu Emperors). At the time of writing, a large part of this collection, including the magnificent Ming Tomb, has been out of bounds for almost a year but will be back on view in a brand new gallery from March 1996. Don't miss the stunning display of Chinese Temple Art, a group of tall, carved figures imaginatively presented in a darkened room. The painted carvings date from the 12th century, and the biggest is an imposing 3m tall.

Entrance into the museum costs $7 and opening hours are: 10am-6pm, Monday to Saturday ; 11am-6pm on Tuesday and 10am-8pm on Sunday; (closed Mondays in the winter).

Art Gallery of Toronto

This wonderful museum is a pleasure to visit. Good use of space and light makes it an airy and stress-free environment. The first rooms you come to house the nineteenth and early twentieth century collection, including works by Renoir, Degas, Sisley, Matisse, Monet and Picasso. Monet's gorgeous *Vétheuil in Summer* seems to light up in increasingly golden hues the further you stand back from it. Note also his *Charing Cross Bridge: Fog* which depicts a London fog the like of which I've never seen before – all pinks, greens and blues. In the same gallery look out for Otto Dix's startling *Portrait of Dr Heinrich Stadlemann*.

Up on Level 2 there's a very good collection of paintings by the Group of Seven (see below). Their work powerfully evokes the vast wilderness of northern Ontario, which you pass through on the train journey between Toronto and Winnipeg. On the same level, a little further along from Andy Warhol's gun-slinging *Elvis*, is the Henry Moore Sculpture Centre which houses the world's largest public collection of Moore's work. The sculptor insisted on natural, overhead lighting and the effect is beautiful; his mammoth bronze women bathed in sunlight make an arresting sight.

The museum is at 317 Dundas St (on the edge of Chinatown) and is open as follows: Wednesdays and Fridays 10am-10pm; Thursdays, Saturdays and Sundays 10am-5pm; closed Mondays and Tuesdays. Entry is $7.50; Wednesdays free 5-10pm.

The Group of Seven

If you plan to spend any length of time in Canadian art galleries you had better get to grips with the Group of Seven, still Canada's artistic pride and joy. The movement championed by the Group was initiated by the commercial artist, Tom Thomson, in 1912, following a trip to the Mississagi Forest Reserve in Northern Ontario. Thomson developed a bold new approach to painting Canada's wilderness, characterised by heavy colours, expressive patterns and a move away from similitude. His style was embraced by several of his friends who shared his frustration with the conservative nature of Canadian art, which had barely moved on from the nineteenth century. Together the artists began painting the wild and rugged terrain of Ontario's northern interior, where they honed their hallmark style of vibrant colours and stark, swirling landscapes.

In 1920, three years after Thomson's tragic death in a boating accident, his fellow artists – Frank Carmichael, Lawren Harris, AY Jackson, Franz Johnston, Arthur Lismer, JEH Macdonald and FH Varley – formed the Group of Seven and staged their first exhibition. They were wildly successful and their influence grew rapidly over the following years. Talent and innovation were helped by clever self-promotion and influential friends, which provoked resentment among Canada's established artists. The public, on the other hand, adored them, perhaps responding to their romantic evocation of the lonely, wild frontier.

The Group's work was to dominate Canadian art for the next thirty years. The irony of their success is that whilst they had set out to liberate Canadian art from the constraints of naturalism, their influence was so great that it stifled the development of alternative styles, and became as restrictive as the artistic establishment they had replaced. Nonetheless, they engendered an important sense of national pride and showed that Canadian painters did not always have to look to Europe for the way forward.

Casa Loma

One of Toronto's quirkiest and most fascinating attractions is this grandiose mansion standing on a hillside. It was built in 1911 for Sir Henry Pellat, a self-made multi millionaire who embarked on a four-year orgy of spending to make his 98-room castle as ornate and opulent as it could possibly be. The palatial interior is fabulously over the top with a mixture of mediaeval-style banquet halls, secret passageways, marble bathrooms and fluffy boudoirs. Sir Henry, alas, had enjoyed the comforts of his castle for just ten years when bankruptcy forced him and his wife to move out and sell up. Casa Loma is a short uphill walk from Dupont subway. It's open daily 10am-4pm, and entrance is $8.

Toronto's ethnic neighbourhoods

Officially deemed by the UN to be the most ethnically diverse city in the world, Toronto is made up of an exotic patchwork of cultural neighbourhoods. The largest ones are as follows:

• **Corso Italia**: Torontonians of Italian origin are outnumbered only by those of British extract. The Latin culture has been kept very much alive in 'Little Italy', centred along St Clair between Bathurst and Bloom.

• **Chinatown**: Toronto's Chinese population is the second biggest in the world outside Asia, the biggest being in San Francisco. Starting with Sam Ching, a laundry shop owner who was Toronto's first Chinese immigrant at the turn of the century, the community has grown to 350,000 people – more than twice the population of Halifax. It's an exhilarating place to wander around, especially at the weekend when the street markets are in full swing and the shoppers are out in their thousands. All signs and prices are in Chinese and there's barely a Westerner in sight.

• **The Danforth**: East along Danforth Ave (between Pape and Woodbine) is the heart of 'Little Athens', where you'll find white-walled restaurants, little Greek bars and the National Bank of Greece.

• **The Jewish Community**: Centred mainly in the suburb of North York, Toronto's thriving Jewish community has no fewer than 60 synagogues and a fabulous supply of kosher delis.

• **Little Poland**: West of downtown, along Roncesvalles Ave the shops are stocked with Polish pastries and other delicacies. There is also a statue of the first Polish pope and a monument in honour of the 20,000 Poles who died in World War II.

• **West Indies in Toronto**: Spreading around the suburbs north of Highway 401 is the 300,000 strong Caribbean community. Over a million visitors a year come to see the community's Caribana carnival in July.

The Islands

Having expended vast amounts of energy and money cramming in Toronto's many attractions, most visitors find a trip to the islands a well deserved break. For just $3 for a return ticket, you can take a 15-minute ferry ride to one of three interconnecting islands – Ward's Island, Centre Island, or Hanlan's Point – where you can wander around the parkland, take a picnic, stroll along the beach and generally unwind. It's worth it for the view alone: Toronto's downtown skyline is breathtaking from the ferry. The Island Ferry Docks are right at the bottom of Bay St on the lakeshore; you can walk from Union subway or go one stop from there on the connecting Harbourfront LRT line.

FESTIVALS

• **du Maurier Ltd Downtown Jazz Festival**, late June to early July. Canadian and international jazz musicians.
• **International Dragon Boat Race Festival**, late June. Boat races and lots of hoopla on Centre Island.
• **Caribana**, late July to early August. Massive Caribbean festival of music and dance, with a fabulous parade.
• **Toronto International Film Festival**, mid-September. Highly regarded festival showing new films from around the world.

MOVING ON

By rail

The Canadian leaves Toronto for Vancouver on Tuesdays, Thursdays and Saturdays. The journey takes three days and three nights. There are frequent daily services to Montreal (4 hours), Ottawa (just over 4 hours) and Niagara Falls (2 hours). In addition, Amtrak connections provide a service to New York and Chicago. The VIA information number is ☎ 366-8411 (or ☎ 1-800-361-1235 when calling from outside Toronto). The Amtrak number is ☎ 1-800-872-7245.

By air

To get to Pearson International Airport take the Airport Express bus (☎ 905-564-6333). It picks up passengers from 14 downtown locations, including most of the major hotels. Useful airline numbers include Air Canada: ☎ 925-2311; Canadian Airlines International: ☎ 798-2211 and American Airlines: ☎ 283-2243.

Winnipeg

The manners of Winnipeg, of the West, impress the stranger as better than those of the East, more friendly, more hearty, more certain to achieve graciousness, if not grace.
Rupert Brooke, *Letters from America*, 1916.

Winnipeg is a convenient place to take a break, being right in the middle of the country; it lies midway between the Atlantic and the Pacific, just 20km from the longitudinal centre of Canada. Its short but hot summers coax the crowds out of the malls and onto the streets and Winnipeg in July is a lively and vibrant city. Out of season, however, it's a drab and chilly place. Winters are long and bitterly cold, and the intersection of Winnipeg's two main streets has the unenviable reputation of being the windiest spot in the world.

The city is described in Carol Shields' *The Republic of Love* as 'a place with a short tough history and a pug-faced name' and receives less than flattering treatment at the hands of the English writer, Mark Lawson, in *The Battle for Room Service*: 'it was somehow just one of those places that sounded as if it might be Indian for shit-hole.' The people of Winnipeg, however, are known for their warmth and friendliness. Perhaps this is the result of a conscious effort on the part of the locals to live up to the provincial slogan, 'Friendly Manitoba', but each time I've visited Winnipeg I've had some wonderful strangers take me under their wing. I'm inclined, in the end, to agree with one of Shields' characters who declares: 'I love Winnipeg because the people here are the salt of the earth. You walk down Portage and you get smiles from everyone, even the cops.'

HISTORY

The fur trade

Winnipeg is situated where the Red and Assiniboine Rivers meet. This junction, known as The Forks, was an important centre of the fur trade: in 1738 Sieur de la Vérendrye erected a post here, which was later taken over by the French-owned North West Company. It soon became a playing field for the bitter antagonism between the Nor'westers and their rivals, the Hudson's Bay Company.

The Red River Colony

In 1812 the Earl of Selkirk of the HBC set about creating a settlement near The Forks, which he named the Red River Colony. The life of the new settlers, most of whom had come from Scotland, was not an easy one. The Nor'Westers felt threatened by their presence and systematically attempted to destroy the colony. The aggression reached a head in 1816 when the Seven Oaks Massacre left 21 of the settlers dead. The problems were in a large part resolved when the North West Company and the Hudson's Bay Company amalgamated in 1821 (keeping the HBC name). The Red River Colony began to grow in size, this time populated mainly by local Métis (of French and Indian extract).

The Riel Rebellions

After Canada became a dominion in 1867, the new government purchased the land occupied by the Red River Colony from the Hudson's Bay Company. They somewhat insensitively began to reorganise the settlement without consulting its inhabitants. The Métis staged a rebellion (see p32) organised by Louis Riel which resulted in the creation of the province of Manitoba but also in the exile of Riel. When a second Métis rebellion broke out fifteen years later, Riel was summoned back to lead his people once more. This time the results were less successful and Riel was hanged for high treason.

The boom years

When it became clear that Winnipeg was going to be an important stop on the new transcontinental railway, it became in 1881 the site of a feverish and undisciplined land boom. Thousands of speculators rushed in to buy and sell lots and as the value of land rocketed, vast fortunes were made overnight.

Over the following years a steady flow of immigrants arrived to settle and farm the land, the influx reaching an all-time high between 1901 and 1914. In just a few decades it had grown from a small settlement of 241 people in 1871 to Canada's third largest city in 1911, with a population of 136,000. The Winnipeg Grain Exchange was exporting grain all around the world, and the city was the transportation, distribution and financial centre of western Canada.

Winnipeg today

By 1915 the boom was over and Winnipeg entered a period of recession. Poor working conditions and a burgeoning trade union movement resulted in the abortive Winnipeg General Strike in 1919, Canada's most famous strike to date. The situation didn't improve as Canada entered the 1920s in the grip of the world-wide Great Depression.

The economy picked up after the Second World War and Winnipeg once more established itself as the transportation hub of the west. Its prosperity has been undermined, however, by the westward shift of economic development into cities like Saskatoon and Regina. Today Winnipeg has a population of 600,000 and is the seventh biggest city in Canada.

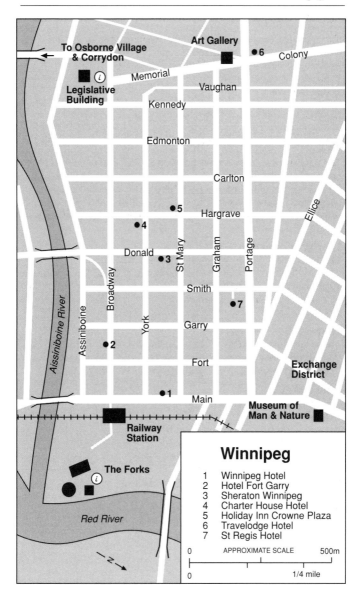

To Osborne Village & Corrydon

Art Gallery

● 6 Colony

Legislative Building (i)

Memorial

Vaughan

Kennedy

Edmonton

Carlton

● 5 Hargrave

● 4

Donald ● 3 St Mary

Graham

Portage

Ellice

Smith ● 7

York

Garry

Assiniboine

Broadway

● 2

Fort

● 1 Main

Exchange District

Aissiniboine River

Museum of Man & Nature

Railway Station

The Forks (i)

Red River

→ z

Winnipeg

1 Winnipeg Hotel
2 Hotel Fort Garry
3 Sheraton Winnipeg
4 Charter House Hotel
5 Holiday Inn Crowne Plaza
6 Travelodge Hotel
7 St Regis Hotel

0 APPROXIMATE SCALE 500m

0 1/4 mile

LOCAL TRANSPORT

The local bus service is operated by Winnipeg Transit (☎ 986-5700). Tickets are $1.35 and the exact fare must be given. There are two free shuttle services to and from The Forks, one (No 96) running up and down Portage, and the other (No 99) looping around Broadway, Memorial, Portage and Main.

If you'd rather get around by bike, River City Cycle (☎ 227-2453) rents bikes for $5 an hour or $18 for 12 hours.

ORIENTATION AND SERVICES

The train station is very central, on Main St, and is no more than 10 minutes' walk from most hotels. The lay-out of the city has developed around the Red and Assiniboine Rivers – the downtown area slots into the corner where the two rivers meet. The two busiest thoroughfares are Main St (north-south, parallel to the Red River) and Portage Ave (east-west, parallel to the Assiniboine).

Tourist information
There's a large Tourism Winnipeg office (☎ 943-1970, or ☎ 1-800-665-0204 toll-free from anywhere in North America) at The Forks, open 10am-6pm daily. Inside the Legislative Building there's a Travel Manitoba information desk (open 8am-9pm daily from May to August, and 8.30am-4.30pm Monday to Friday in September and October).

Money
There are plenty of banks about, including the Bank of Montreal inside Portage Place Mall and the Royal Bank of Canada at Portage and Garry. The Custom House Currency Exchange is at 231 Portage Ave.

Consulates
Austria (☎ 489-3850) 889 Erin St
Belgium (☎ 261-1415) 15 Acadia Bay
Britain (☎ 896-1380) 111 Aldershot Blvd
Denmark (☎ 837-1099) 111 Mountbatten Ave
Finland (☎ 942-7457) 127-167 Lombard Ave
France (☎ 837-9583) 64 Athlone Dr
Germany (☎ 947-0958) 208-310 Donald St
Italy (☎ 943-7637) 309-283 Portage Ave
Japan (☎ 284-0478) 680 Wellington Cres
Netherlands (☎ 489-0467) 69 Shorecrest Dr
Norway (☎ 489-0456) 336 Lindenwood Dr E
Spain (☎ 831-6033) 1025 Buchanan Blvd
Sweden (☎ 233-3373) 1035 Mission St

WHERE TO STAY

Budget accommodation

The **HI Ivey House International Hostel** (☎ 772-3022) is at 210 Maryland, about a 15-minute walk west of downtown. It's a small but clean and friendly hostel in an old house with big sunny rooms. Rates are $12 for members and $16 for non-members. A few doors down at No 168 is the **Backpackers' Guest House International** (☎ 772-1272) – it has 35 beds, a games room in the basement, laundry facilities and bike rental. Rates are $11.77 (but it may be closed from November to March – phone in advance). It's about a 25-minute walk from the train station to the hostels, or you can take the No 29 bus to Broadway and Sherbrook (Maryland St is one block west of here).

If the hostels are full up or you're feeling brave, the **Winnipeg Hotel** (☎ 942-7762) is virtually opposite the train station at 214 Main. Doubles are $17 without a shower, and $21 with a private shower; but be warned that the rooms are a little insalubrious and the bar downstairs can get rowdy at night.

Mid-range accommodation

The **Charter House Hotel** (☎ 942-0101) at 330 York Ave is excellent value. It's quite large with spacious, clean rooms from $54. Its restaurant, the Rib Room, gets crowded with locals as well as guests.

The **St Regis Hotel** (☎ 942-0171) at 285 Smith was built in 1911 at the height of the immigration boom. The rooms aren't exactly flash but they're clean, come with a TV and private bathroom and are very cheap for what you get – rates start at $49. The **Travelodge Hotel** (☎ 786-7011) at 360 Colony St has spacious, well-equipped rooms from $64.

Upmarket hotels

The **Sheraton Winnipeg** (☎ 942-5300) is at 161 Donald St. It's the only hotel I've been to where it's actually cheaper to stay in high season: rates are $79 in July and August and go up to $110 the rest of the year. The atmosphere is very relaxed and informal for a big international hotel.

Close to the railway station at 222 Broadway, the **Hotel Fort Garry** (☎ 942-8251) is quite possibly the best value hotel in Canada. It was built in 1913 by the Grand Trunk Pacific as their answer to the CPR's château hotels. It's wonderfully grand inside and, following a recent takeover, its prices have been slashed in an attempt to win customers: just $59 a double at weekends or $69 during the week, the price of an ordinary B&B in the UK. The **Holiday Inn Crowne Plaza** (☎ 942-0551) is big, smart and modern and comes with all the usual comforts of an upmarket hotel. It's noted for its excellent restaurant, Between Friends, and is at 350 St Mary Ave. Weekend rates start at $79 and weekday rates are from $128.

WHERE TO EAT

Budget food
Over in the Exchange District there's the **Old Spaghetti Factory** – excellent value and conveniently located. There are also plenty of cheap food stalls at **The Forks** market. For a really cheap eat you could do worse than try **VJ's Drive In**, a shack opposite the railway station serving home made burgers, hot dogs and fries, and apparently famous throughout the prairies.

Mid-range and upmarket restaurants
Some of the best places to eat are out of downtown in the surrounding neighbourhoods, where Winnipeg's ethnic communities are concentrated. One of these is **Corrydon Ave** which is lined with Italian cafés and restaurants (to get there take the No 18 from Main St). **Civita**, at No 691, has an Italian-meets-Californian feel to it – the food is superb and moderately priced and the atmosphere and service very friendly. Another highly recommended restaurant is **Sette Bello** at No 788, whose chef used to work at Civita. It serves traditional Italian food and does a roaring trade – booking is advised on a Saturday night (☎ 477 9105).

Closer to the city centre, on the south side of the Assiniboine River, is **Osborne Village** which has a number of good value, interesting eating places. One of the best is the **Tap & Grill** (137 Osborne St) whose unpromising name and exterior conceal a beautiful tropical plant-filled room where delicious Mediterranean grills are served. The Village is about a 10-minute walk from the Legislative Building; alternatively take the No 16 bus from Graham at Vaughan.

If you'd rather stay downtown you could try the food courts or restaurant-bars at **The Forks**. The **Mondetta World Café** serves an astonishingly wide range of food (from East African eggplant with garam masala to 'Japanese pork dumplings') in a super-stylish interior that becomes a nightclub late at night. Also at The Forks is the **Prairie Oyster**, a better than average Canadian grill which claims to use 'only the freshest of ingredients.'

WHAT TO SEE

The Forks
Right behind Union Station is The Forks, where the Red and Assiniboine Rivers meet. It used to be a railway service and repair site but has recently been converted to a market. The buildings are full of food, crafts, jewellery, clothes, restaurants, cafés and the like, bearing more than a passing resemblance to London's Covent Garden, and there are plenty of street entertainers outside. It's very lively and has a great atmosphere, especially in the summer.

Manitoba Museum of Man and Nature

This is Winnipeg's best museum by a long shot. It concentrates on the province's natural and human history, and highlights include a re-creation of the Arctic Tundra with an impressive polar bear display, a Grasslands gallery with a big tepee and other items typical of life on the plains and, best of all, a full-size replica of the ketch that brought the founders of the Hudson's Bay Company to Canada (you can climb on board and wander around).

The museum is at the Centennial Centre on Main St, opposite the City Hall. It's open daily 10am-6pm June and July, and Tuesday to Friday 10am-4pm, weekends 10am-5pm for the rest of the year. Admission is $4, or $9 for an Omni Pass which also gets you into the attached **Planetarium** (excellent shows for all ages) and **Touch the Universe** (a hands-on science gallery).

Winnipeg Art Gallery

The gallery houses mainly temporary exhibitions of modern Canadian art which change every six to eight weeks. One of the rooms is used exclusively for Inuit collections, and the museum has a reputation for showing the most comprehensive range of Inuit art in the country. It's located at 300 Memorial Blvd, and is open daily 11am-5pm, and until 9pm on Wednesdays. From 19 June to 4 September it opens at 10 am. Entrance is free on Wednesdays, otherwise it's $3.

Legislative Building

Dating from 1919, Manitoba's seat of government is an imposing building. Its large dome is topped by Winnipeg's most famous symbol: the Golden Boy, a four-metre gilded statue of a messenger carrying a sheaf of grain in one arm and a torch in the other (and supposedly embodying the spirit of youth and enterprise). There are free guided tours around the building, which stands close to the Art Gallery at 450 Broadway.

Exchange District

In the boom years of 1880-1915 large numbers of banks, warehouses and other commercial buildings sprang up in Winnipeg. The centre of this expansion was the Exchange District, where the old buildings, with their elaborate advertisements painted on the walls, have recently been renovated and gentrified. They now house offices, shops, restaurants and pubs. It's an interesting place to wander around and certainly contains the best examples of Winnipeg's otherwise uninspiring architecture.

Assiniboine Park

About 8km west of downtown is this 376-acre park, containing a zoo (admission $3 or free on Tue; over 1000 animals), a conservatory (excellent tropical plants) and the Leo Mol Sculpture Garden (religious and wildlife sculptures by this 'internationally renowned' sculptor). To get to the park take the No 66 bus from Broadway at Smith.

Prairie Dog Central Steam Train

This beautiful turn-of-the-century train makes two 36-mile round trips every Sunday between June and September. The Prairie Central's steam engine was built in Scotland in 1882, and for 36 years pulled CPR passenger trains between Fort William and Kenora. These days it runs north from the CNR station at St James, a Winnipeg suburb, to Grosse Isle, and while it can hardly claim to be the most scenic rail ride in the country it's certainly one of the most stylish; the polished oak and mahogany inside the old coaches are magnificent.

Trains depart at 11am and 3pm and the fare is $13. It's not possible to make advance reservations so be there as early as possible. To get to the station, take the No 21 Express bus from the north side of Portage. For more information on the Prairie Dog, phone ☎ 832-5259.

Union Station

Winnipeg's railway station (which was, incidentally, designed by the same architects as New York's Grand Central Station) keeps one of its gems hidden away upstairs: the old Countess of Dufferin built in 1872, the first locomotive in the Canadian West. The gallery where she's kept is open to the public and also has a display on the story of the transcontinental railway though rather irritatingly the narrative ends half way through, as it had to make room for something else.

FESTIVALS

• **Winnipeg Jazz Festival**, end of June. Week-long programme of indoor and outdoor jazz concerts.
• **Red River Exhibition**, last week in June. Manitoba's largest fair: music, parades, shows and games.
• **Folk Festival**, mid-July. Huge gathering of Canadian and international folk musicians.
• **Folklorama**, middle two weeks in August. A multicultural celebration of the peoples of the world – over 40 pavilions throughout the city, with singing, dancing, arts and crafts, ethnic foods and more.

MOVING ON

The **Canadian** leaves for Vancouver (about 40 hours from Winnipeg) on Wednesdays, Fridays and Sundays, and for Toronto (about 30 hours) on Wednesdays, Saturdays and Mondays. The **Hudson Bay** leaves Winnipeg for Churchill on Sundays, Tuesdays and Thursdays – the journey takes $34^1/_2$ hours. The VIA information line is ☎ 1-800-561-8630.

Edmonton

Edmonton, the headquarters of the Hudson Bay Company's Saskatchewan trade...is a large, five-sided fort with the usual flanking bastions and high stockades. It has within these stockades many commodious and well-built wooden houses, and differs in the cleanliness and order of its arrangements from the general run of trading forts in the Indian country. Butler, *The Great Lone Land,* 1872

Situated on the northern edge of the prairies, Alberta's provincial capital is a city grown rich from wheat and oil. Despite its affluence, however, of all the cities along the line it has the least to recommend itself to the rail traveller. It's not that there's nothing to do or see here; on the contrary there are some great attractions but, unfortunately, most of them are far from the city centre, and reaching them by public transport can be tedious. The downtown area is a little lifeless owing to the collapse of a large number of shopping outlets since the opening of the giant West Edmonton Mall. This shopping complex, the largest in the world, ranks as Edmonton's number one tourist attraction – a fact that may well start the warning bells ringing... Finally, Edmonton is so close to Jasper that there seems little point, for west-bound travellers anyway, in delaying the spectacular ride through the Rockies.

HISTORY

Fur-trading outpost
Edmonton began life in 1795 when the Hudson's Bay Company erected Edmonton House as a fur-trading base. This was established to compete with the nearby Fort Augustus, founded a few months earlier by the HBC's great rival, the North West Company. The two companies traded with the local Cree and Blackfoot Indians for beaver pelts, otter and muskrat furs and Edmonton quickly became the headquarters of the fur trade in the western prairies. It was also a major stopping-off point for travellers to the North or to the Pacific.

Sold to the Dominion
It wasn't until the Hudson's Bay Company sold the best part of its land to the Dominion of Canada in 1870 that settlers began to set up home outside the HBC stockade. Businesses sprang up and by the 1890s the new town was operating coal mines, saw mills and a boat-building factory. In 1897 the Yukon gold rush brought thousands of fortune-seekers to Edmonton en route to the gold fields. Many stayed and by the turn of the century Edmonton's population had grown to 4000.

Booming provincial capital

Following its incorporation as a city in 1904, Edmonton became Alberta's capital when the province was created in 1905. By now it was home to 9000 people, a number that grew rapidly in the next few decades. Although it had been ignored in favour of Calgary by the Canadian Pacific Railway, it was a major stop on two new lines by 1915. It also became an important transportation and supply centre with the construction of the Alaska Highway in 1942. Shortly after this, Edmonton's success was assured when oil was discovered at Leduc Number One Well in 1947. Over the following years, oil was struck in thousands of wells within a 160-km radius of the city and Edmonton became known as 'Oil Capital of Canada'.

Today almost 800,000 people live in Greater Edmonton making it Canada's fifth largest city. The wealth bestowed on it by the oil industry has transformed the downtown district into a jumble of glass-plated skyscrapers. As the impact of oil on Edmonton's economy begins to scale down, businesses such as forestry, pharmaceuticals and electronics are starting to play a more important role.

LOCAL TRANSPORT

Everything in downtown Edmonton is within walking distance but for visits to out-of-town attractions such as the famous Mall you'll need to use Edmonton Transit (☎ 496-1611) – a mixture of bus and light-rail networks. Fares are $1.35.

ORIENTATION AND SERVICES

Downtown Edmonton, which is surprisingly small, sits on the northern bank of the North Saskatchewan River. The railway station is in the north-west corner of the city centre; most of the centrally located hotels are within ten to twenty minutes' walk from here.

The city's biggest and busiest thoroughfare is Jasper Ave. The other avenues and streets are numbered, not named: avenues run from east to west, their numbers increasing as you go north; streets run from north to south with their numbers increasing as you move east.

Tourist information

The main office is in the Edmonton Convention Centre (☎ 496-8400) at 9797 Jasper Ave. It's open daily 8.30am-4.30pm. Alberta Tourism (☎ 427 4321) has an office at the City Centre Building at 10015-102nd St.

Money

All the major banks can be found along Jasper Ave. There's an American Express office there too, at No 10305, and a Thomas Cook Foreign Exchange on the main floor of ManuLife Place, 10165-102 St.

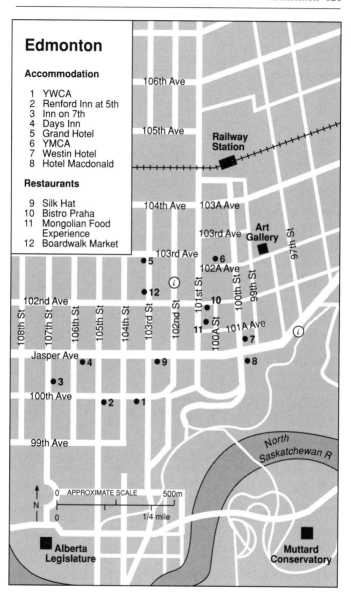

Edmonton

Accommodation

1 YWCA
2 Renford Inn at 5th
3 Inn on 7th
4 Days Inn
5 Grand Hotel
6 YMCA
7 Westin Hotel
8 Hotel Macdonald

Restaurants

9 Silk Hat
10 Bistro Praha
11 Mongolian Food
   Experience
12 Boardwalk Market

Consulates

Belgium (☎ 425-0184) Suite 1500, 10250-101 St
Denmark (☎ 426-1457) Suite 1112, 10235-101 St
Finland (☎ 426-7865) Westin Hotel, Lower Level, 10135-100 St
France (☎ 428-0232) Suite 300, 10010-106 St
Germany (☎ 422-6175) ManuLife Place, Suite 1220, 10180-101 St
Italy (☎ 423-5153) Suite 1900, Royal Trust Tower, Edmonton Centre
Japan (☎ 422-3752) Suite 2480, ManuLife Place, 10180-101 St
Netherlands (☎ 428-7513) 10214-112 St
Norway (☎ 440-2292) 2310-80 Ave
Sweden (☎ 482-2561) Suite 305, 11523-100 Ave
Switzerland (☎ 426-2292) 11207-103 Ave

WHERE TO STAY

Budget accommodation

The very central **Grand Hotel** (☎ 422-6365) at 10266-103 St has 76 basic but clean rooms starting at $23 for a room with a sink, going up to $38 for a room with a private bath. The mixed sex **YMCA** (☎ 421-9622) at 10030-102A Ave has dorm beds for $15 and singles for $30. Facilities there include a cafeteria and a fitness centre. The women-only **YWCA** (☎ 429-8707) at 10305-100 Ave has dorm beds for $13.38 and singles for $29.43.

Mid-range hotels

The **Renford Inn at Fifth** (☎ 423-5611) has 106 clean spacious rooms and an indoor pool. It's situated on a quiet street at 10425-100 Ave. Regular rates start at $69 but when business is at a low ebb rooms often go at the discount price of $45. **Days Inn** (☎ 423-1925) at 10041-106 St has been recently refurbished throughout – the rooms are immaculate, big and light. Rack rates start at $71-95 but 'specials' (around $55) are often available during quiet periods. The **Inn on 7th** (☎ 429-2861) at 10001-107 St has well-equipped if rather pink rooms from $69.

Upmarket hotels

Hotel Macdonald (☎ 424-5181) at 10065-100th St was built in 1915 by the Grand Trunk Railway but by 1983 it had fallen into a state of chronic disrepair and had to close down. CPR Hotels came to the rescue with a $20 million renovation package and the hotel was reopened a few years ago – exquisitely refurbished, all ivories, whites, Edwardian understatement and stunning views over the river valley. Rates start at $129.

Over the road is Edmonton's other top hotel, the **Westin** (☎ 424-5181) at 10135 100th St. It's a lot more modern and ritzy than the Macdonald and the lobby sports a photo of a cuddling Charles and Di who stayed there in 1983. Rooms start at $95.

WHERE TO EAT

Budget food

Downtown, a good place to head for is the small pedestrianised section of 100A St (where it meets 101A Ave) where you'll find lots of little bistros and restaurants, many with outside terraces. Among them are the intimate **Bistro Praha** (main dishes around $6) and the **Mongolian Food Experience** where you watch your choice of meat (from $1.80 per 100gms) cooked in front of you on a big hot plate.

Not far from here is the Boardwalk Market on 103rd St at 102nd Ave where you'll find another collection of reasonably-priced restaurants including the **Old Spaghetti Factory**, **Bones** (good for ribs) and **La Crêperie**, as well as some fast food outlets.

Over at 10251 Jasper Ave is the **Silk Hat** – this is one of the oldest restaurants in Edmonton and each table still has its own little jukebox dating from the 1950s. A meal of burgers and fries or pancakes is about $6.

Mid-range and upmarket restaurants

One of the nicest places to eat in is the Hotel Macdonald's **Harvest Room**, which has beautiful views over the river. A meal here will set you back around $25, but the food is excellent. Another good place for a splurge is **La Ronde**, Edmonton's revolving restaurant on top of the Holiday Inn Crowne Plaza, where you can eat from around $30.

WHAT TO SEE

Downtown

• **Edmonton Art Gallery** Centrally located at 2 Sir Winston Churchill Square, the gallery houses mainly temporary exhibitions focusing on contemporary Canadian painting. The permanent collection ('From Sea to Sea') features examples of Canadian painting from the late 19th century to today, including works by the Group of Seven and Emily Carr. Admission is $3 (free Thursday evenings) and it's open 10.30am-5pm Monday to Wednesday; 10.30am-8pm Thursday and Friday, and 11am-5pm at the weekend.

• **Alberta Legislature** This beautiful neo-classical building is worth a visit, if only for the tranquillity of its gardens and fountains. It was built in 1912 on the site of Fort Edmonton (the stockade belonging to the Hudson's Bay Company) at 97th Ave and 107 St. There are free guided tours inside – for details call ☎ 427-7362.

Out of town

• **Provincial Museum of Alberta** While not exactly world-class, this museum has some interesting displays falling into three broad categories: natural history, habitat groups and human history. Highlights include some life-size dinosaur models and hundreds of examples of Canadian taxidermy at its best. 'Human history' is rather weak consisting mainly of a collection of Victorian furniture, though the fine Indian beaded clothing in this gallery livens things up a bit. The museum is open daily 9am-8pm; entrance is $5.50. It's at 12845-102nd Ave: to get there take the No 1 or 2 bus west along Jasper Ave.

● **West Edmonton Mall** This mother of all malls is listed in the *Guinness Book of Records* as being the 'largest shopping mall in the world' and having the 'world's largest car park.' It's certainly big, covering an area of forty-eight city blocks. Inside, not only can you shop 'til you drop: you can also do a spot of bungy-jumping, take a submarine ride, watch some performing dolphins, take a whirl on the ice rink, lose your money at the casino and wrap it all up with a penitential visit to the chapel. It's quite a fun place to visit and is very well designed with lots of natural lighting to stop you from feeling claustrophobic.

A shopping mall's really just a shopping mall no matter how much you jazz it up but that doesn't stop 37,000 tourists a day from visiting this one. To join the crowds take bus No 10 west along Jasper Ave.

● **Muttard Conservatory** Highly recommended as a post-mall relaxation exercise. The conservatory, which consists of four pyramid-shaped greenhouses, is on the southern bank of the river, not too far from downtown. The plants inside represent three climatic zones: arid, temperate and tropical (the fourth one houses a changing display). It's a lovely, peaceful place to stroll around and the plants are glorious, especially in the tropical pyramid; one local told me she goes there to cheer herself up in the middle of Edmonton's bitterly cold winters.

Admission to the conservatory costs $4.25. It's at 9626-96 A St and is open year round: daily 11am-9pm June-August; for the rest of the year 11am-9pm Sunday to Wednesday and 11am-6pm Thursday to Saturday. To get there take the No 51 bus on 100 St opposite the Hotel Macdonald.

● **Fort Edmonton Park** This 'living museum' represents four periods of Edmonton's past with reconstructions of the old Hudson's Bay Company fur-trading fort and three streets (1985 Street, 1905 Street and 1920 Street). The fort is excellent and gives a very clear picture of how life and trade were organised in these early outposts. The park covers a large site and transport is provided by way of an old steam locomotive and a tram.

It's quite a distance from downtown. To get there take the LRT southbound to University then the No 39 or 32 bus to the park. It's open daily from late May to early September, 9.30am-4.30pm Monday to Friday and 10am-6pm at weekends. Entrance is $6.50.

• **Edmonton Space & Science Centre** This excellent complex includes Canada's biggest planetarium and a huge IMAX theatre. Shows are screened on various scientific topics with the help of fabulous state-of-the-art audio visual effects. There's also an observatory, a centre for live demonstrations and facilities for going on simulated trips in space. Brilliant stuff. For information on schedules call ☎ 451-7722. The centre is open year round 10am-10pm, daily June to September and closed Monday for the rest of the year. To get there take the No 5 bus west along Jasper Ave.

FESTIVALS

• **Jazz City International**, late June to early July. Good selection of jazz artists, Canadian and international.
• **Klondike Days**, last week in July. Big and brash celebration of the good old gold rush days.
• **Folk Music Festival**, early August. Internationally renowned event attracting huge crowds. A wide range of styles represented.
• **Fringe Theatre Event**, mid-August. More than 800 performances are spread over nine days. The quality is highly variable, as with any fringe festival, but on the whole it's worth visiting.

MOVING ON

The Canadian leaves for Vancouver on Thursdays, Saturdays and Mondays, and for Toronto on Tuesdays, Fridays and Sundays. For more details call VIA on ☎ 1-800-561-8630.

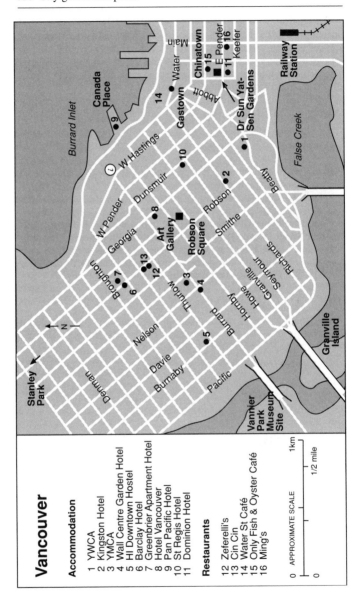

Vancouver

Accommodation

1 YWCA
2 Kingston Hotel
3 YMCA
4 Wall Centre Garden Hotel
5 HI Downtown Hostel
6 Barclay Hotel
7 Greenbrier Apartment Hotel
8 Hotel Vancouver
9 Pan Pacific Hotel
10 St Regis Hotel
11 Dominion Hotel

Restaurants

12 Zeferelli's
13 Cin Cin
14 Water St Café
15 Only Fish & Oyster Café
16 Ming's

APPROXIMATE SCALE

0   1/2 mile   1km

Burrard Inlet

Canada Place

Stanley Park

False Creek

Granville Island

Vannier Park Museum Site

Chinatown

Railway Station

Dr Sun Yat-Sen Gardens

Robson Square

Art Gallery

Gastown

Vancouver

A great sleepiness lies on Vancouver as compared with an American town; men don't fly up and down the streets telling lies, and the spittoons in the delightfully comfortable hotels are unused; the baths are free and their rooms are unlocked. Rudyard Kipling, *From Sea to Sea*, 1900

Vancouver just doesn't have to try. In front is the ocean, behind are the snow-capped mountains and in between is this bustling city full of cafés, restaurants, boutiques and healthy, long-limbed people. It is utterly seductive.

The city is situated on a peninsula in the south-west corner of British Columbia. It has a mild, temperate climate and its inhabitants have a reputation for taking a laid-back attitude to life (it is said that Vancouver is more Californian than Canadian). Its easy-going ambience, however, conceals a vigorous commercial, financial and industrial sector that has made it the economic hub of western Canada. Its port handles 65 million tonnes a year, real estate in the city is undergoing a massive boom and its population is the fastest-growing in North America. Still, to most visitors Vancouver is primarily a place of parks, beaches, relaxation and outstanding natural beauty.

HISTORY

Early visitors
It is thought that Coast Indian tribes inhabited the area as early as 5000 BC and developed a number of fishing communities. The first European to visit the site where Vancouver now stands was the Spanish sailor, José Navéz, in 1791. The following year the English explorer, Captain George Vancouver, made a fleeting one-day visit on his way to search for the Northwest Passage. The site was then largely ignored by Europeans until the 1858 Fraser River gold rush brought fortune-seekers to the area.

Gastown
Of these, three intrepid Englishmen decided to stay and set up (rather curiously) a brickyard on the shore of the Burrard Inlet. The venture failed, but a more astute entrepreneur moved in to establish the highly successful Hastings Saw Mill. A small settlement soon sprang up and became known as Gastown after a garrulous local bar-owner named 'Gassy' Jack Deighton. In 1869 it was incorporated as a town under its official name of Granville, only to go up in flames later that year.

CPR terminus

The rapidly rebuilt Granville would probably have remained a small coastal town if it hadn't been for Van Horne's decision, on a visit to the area in 1884, to make it the terminus of the new transcontinental railway instead of Port Moody (about 20kms away). He also decided that Vancouver would be a more fitting name than Granville. Thus, Vancouver officially came into existence on 16 April 1886 and the first through train from Montreal arrived on 23 May the following year. The railway brought a massive boom to the town which by the end of the century out-stripped Victoria in size and commercial importance. Before long it had also replaced Winnipeg as the most important city in western Canada.

Vancouver today

Vancouver's commercial success has been built on its fishing, lumber and minerals industries and on its huge port which is today the largest on the west coast of North America. Most exports are bound for Asia and include wheat, timber, ore and cellulose. In just over a hundred years Vancouver has grown from a tiny outpost to Canada's third largest and fastest growing city. Almost 500,000 people live in the city proper, and around 1.7 million live in Greater Vancouver.

ARRIVING IN VANCOUVER

By air

Vancouver International Airport is 12km south of the city centre – about a 20-minute drive. An Airport Express bus runs daily between the airport and downtown, from 6am until midnight. It departs from Level 2 and tickets cost $8.25. The same ride by taxi will cost around $23.

By rail

Trains arrive at the stately Pacific Central Station. It's a bit of a walk from downtown but directly linked to the centre by the Sky Train (Vancouver's fully automated light rail transit – fares are $1.50). Otherwise there are plenty of taxis at the station (about $7 to downtown).

LOCAL TRANSPORT

Local transport is operated by BC Transit (☎ 521-0400). In addition to their vast network of buses they run a ferry service (known as the SeaBus) across the Burrard Inlet between downtown and North

---

(**Opposite**) **Top**: The CN Tower (see p106), the tallest building in the world, dominates Toronto's skyline and gives a toy-town view of the rest of the city (**bottom right**). Christ Church Cathedral (**bottom left**) in Montreal (see p95) is reflected in the glass plate of its towering neighbour. (**Overleaf**): These brightly-coloured clapboard houses in Halifax (see p73) are typical of the Maritime Provinces.

ROSS ST
羅士街
41

COLLEGE ST.
書院街
219

Vancouver, and the state-of-the-art driverless Sky Train between Vancouver and the suburb of Surrey. Single zone fares are $1.50 for all three modes of transport.

ORIENTATION AND SERVICES

Downtown Vancouver is located on a small peninsula framed by Burrard Inlet to the north and False Creek to the south. Stanley Park covers the western tip and the city centre pretty much fills the rest of the peninsula, spilling south onto the other side of False Creek. The main downtown artery is Robson St; the focal point of the waterfront is Canada Place.

Tourist information
The excellent Vancouver TouristInfo Centre (☎ 683-2000) is at 200 Burrard St, close to the waterfront. As well as providing the usual information the office has a foreign exchange and accommodation booking service. It's open daily 8am-6pm from June to August, and Monday to Friday 8.30am-5pm for the rest of the year.

Money
There's no shortage of downtown banks, with a cluster around Georgia at Burrard and Howe. Foreign exchange offices include American Express at 1040 W Georgia St, International Foreign Exchange at 1169 Robson St and Custom House Currency Exchange at 375 Water St.

Consulates
Australia (☎ 684-1177) 602-999 Canada Place
Austria (☎ 687-3338) 202-1810 Alberni St
Belgium (☎ 684-6838) 570-688 W Hastings
Britain (☎ 683-4421) 800-1111 Melville St
Denmark (☎ 684-5171) 755-777 Hornby St
Finland (☎ 688-4483) 1100-1188 W Georgia St
France (☎ 681-4345) 1201-736 Granville St
Germany (☎ 684-8377) 704-999 Canada Place
Italy (☎ 684-7288) 705-1200 Burrard St
Japan (☎ 684-5868) 900-1177 W Hastings St
Netherlands (☎ 684-3549) 821-475 Howe St
New Zealand (☎ 684-7388) 1200-888 Dunsmuir St
Norway (☎ 682-7977) 1200-200 Burrard St
Sweden (☎ 683-5838) 1100-1188 W Georgia St
Switzerland (☎ 684-2231) 790-999 Canada Place
USA (☎ 685-4311) 1095 Pender St W

(Opposite): In Toronto (see p109) the 350,000-strong Chinese community is twice the size of Halifax and forms the second largest Chinatown in the world.

WHERE TO STAY

Budget accommodation

Due to open in the summer of 1996 is the brand new **HI Vancouver Downtown Hostel** (☎ 684-7101) at 1114 Burnaby St, at Thurlow. The hostel has 220 beds in small shared rooms for up to four people. The rates are very reasonable: $15 for members and $19 for non-members. The original **HI hostel**, out by Jericho Beach (☎ 224-3208; 1515 Discovery St) will continue to operate – it has 350 dorm beds, rates are the same. To get there take the No 4 bus from Granville St.

Another brand-new establishment is the **YWCA** (☎ 662-8188) at 733 Beatty St in the trendy Yaletown area. It's more like a hotel than a hostel: the rooms, all private, have phones and mini fridges and cost from $40 for singles and $44 for doubles. The **YMCA** (☎ 681-0221) has singles from $32 and is centrally located at 955 Burrard St.

Mid-range hotels

Excellently located at 1348 Robson St, seconds from the shops and cafés and a short walk to Stanley Park, is the **Barclay Hotel** (☎ 688-8850). It has pleasant rooms at fair rates, starting at $69. Across the road at No 1393 is the **Greenbrier Apartment Motor Hotel** (☎ 683-4558) with spacious self-catering apartments from $108. Another choice location is offered by the **Dominion Hotel** (☎ 681-6666) in Gastown, at 210 Abbot St. It's a charming old building that has seen better days, with rooms starting at $58.

Probably the best-value place in Vancouver is the **Kingston Hotel** (☎ 684-9024) at 757 Richards St. The rooms are immaculate throughout, and there's a laundry room for guests' use. Rates start at $45 including continental breakfast. The **St Regis Hotel** (☎ 681-6341) is beginning to show its age but it's basically clean, serviceable and very central at 602 Dunsmuir St. Rooms start at $75.

Upmarket hotels

Vancouver's most flamboyant place to stay has to be the new five diamond **Wall Centre Garden Hotel** (☎ 331-1000). This 35-storey building is sheathed in glass from top to bottom; each room has floor to ceiling windows that can be opened and $300,000 worth of BC art is scattered around the building. It's at 1088 Burrard St and standard rates start at a cool $350, though 'Super Saver' rates of over half this price are sometimes available, even in summer. Another glitzy five diamond job is the **Pan Pacific** (☎ 662-8111) down in Canada Place. Rooms start at $345 for a city view and $375 for a harbour view. On a more measured note is the beautifully refined **Hotel Vancouver** (☎ 684-3131) at 900 Georgia St. This old CPR railway hotel is now a heritage building, and is one of the most elegant establishments in the city. There are rooms from $215.

WHERE TO EAT

Budget food

There's a branch of the good old low-price pasta chain, **The Old Spaghetti Factory** at 53 Water St in Gastown which is worth visiting just for the bizarre decor. For a really cheap meal you could try **The Only Fish & Oyster Café**, located on the somewhat run down fringes of Gastown at 20 East Hastings St. The fish is really fresh and very cheap.

Chinatown is highly recommended with thousands of places to choose from, most of them very cheap: your best bet is simply to wander down E Pender St at lunchtime and pick a crowded restaurant. One of the most popular dim sum joints is **Ming's**, at 147 E Pender St (at Main).

There are numerous food courts in all the city's malls (eg the Royal Centre Mall on Burrard at Dunsmuir or the Harbour Centre on W Hastings St) plus no fewer than five branches of **McDonald's** around town (including W Georgia at Burrard and Dunsmuir at Granville).

Mid-range and upmarket restaurants

Vancouver has a superabundance of eating places and the food's usually good. One of the most stylish restaurants in town is the excellent **Azure** at the Wall Centre Garden Hotel, specialising in Mediterranean seafood. The menu is mouth-watering if a little on the pricey side (around $30 per person); adjoining it is **Indigo,** a slightly cheaper continental-style bistro.

There's a proliferation of restaurants along Robson St, one of the best being **Cin Cin** at No 1154, serving the type of food the locals like to call 'West Coast' (fish, grills, pasta). Again, prices are high here as in the trendy **Zeferelli's** nearby at No 1136 which is also 'West Coast' and very good. A cheaper option (around $15) is the **Cactus Club Café** below Zeferelli's. It's very lively and the Tex/Mex menu isn't bad at all.

Gastown's another place with plenty of eating spots, including the **Water Street Café** with its very pleasant outdoor terrace which looks onto the steam clock. If you want to eat in Stanley Park be prepared for high prices; **The Tea House** at Furguson Point serves wonderful seafood and has stunning views over English Bay, but it's expensive.

WHAT TO SEE

Vancouver is a relaxing place to spend time in. It's not packed full of museums and obligatory sights. The best thing to do here is just wander round and soak up the atmosphere in the city's many 'people's places' (to use Vancouver-speak).

Robson St to English Bay

A good way to get a feel for the city is to take a walk down Robson, starting at Robson Square. This is Vancouver's liveliest street: it's lined with clothes boutiques, bookstores, record shops, cafés and restaurants, and by night it's packed with young people out on the town. If you turn left off Robson down Denman (more cafés, restaurants etc) you'll end up at English Bay Beach. The views from here are lovely and it's a very relaxing place to go and lie with a book in summer.

The walk to English Bay from Robson Square takes about half an hour; alternatively the No 1 bus takes the same route.

Canada Place and Harbour Centre

Canada Place, down by the waterfront, was built as the pavilion for Expo '86. The complex, with its roof of billowing sails, was designed to resemble a large ship and is worth visiting if just for its excellent vantage point over the harbour. You can get an even better view, though you have to pay $7 for it, from the 500 ft-high observation platform at the nearby Harbour Centre at 555 W Hastings St. It's open daily 8.30am-10.30pm (and until 11.30pm at weekends).

Vancouver Art Gallery

The highlight of the gallery is the excellent collection of works by Emily Carr whose swirling greens and blues depict the landscape and Indian communities of the West Coast. Also to look out for are the 80 prints of Goya's 'Disasters of the War' series in which he documents the brutal occupation of Spain by Napoleon's forces (1810-14).

The gallery is on the corner of Hornby and Robson and is open 10am-6pm Monday to Friday; until 9pm on Thursday, until 5pm on Saturday and 12-5pm on Sunday. Entrance is $6 (or 'pay as you wish' Thursday evening).

Gastown

Vancouver's oldest quarter was given a huge facelift in the 1970s in a generous move to give the tourists somewhere else to spend their cash. The result is decidedly twee (dubious looking gas lamps, brand new cobble stones etc) but it's still a lively, fun place to take a stroll, especially Water St, the core of the area. Not to be missed is the hilarious spectacle of crowds of tourists silently waiting – breath held, cameras poised – for the **steam powered clock** on Water St to start chiming and hissing vapour, which it obligingly does every 15 minutes (see p161).

Chinatown

Chinatown is a vibrant and frenetic tangle of streets packed with restaurants, markets, bakeries, herb shops and thousands of Chinese people. The main thoroughfares are Pender and Keefer Sts (a 20-minute walk from Robson Sq, or a short bus ride on the No 22 from Burrard). If the relentless bustle gets too much for you the **Dr. Sun Yat-Sen Classical Chinese Garden** will sort you out. Modelled on the Ming Dynasty gardens in the City of Suzhou, and incorporating the Taoist philosophy of yin and yang, the garden is an oasis of harmony and tranquillity. It's located at 578 Carrall St, next to the Chinese Cultural Centre. Entrance is $4.50 and opening hours are 10am-3pm daily.

Vancouver's Chinese immigrants

When Andrew Onderdonk began work on his section of the transcontinental rail line through the Fraser Valley, he knew he had a serious labour shortage on his hands. British Columbia's population was very small and Onderdonk needed at least 10,000 men. The solution was found in the large numbers of Chinese labourers in California who had worked on the Union Pacific Railway and were more than willing to come and work for Onderdonk at a cheaper rate than the locals. When still more workers were needed they were shipped over from Canton – between 1881 and 1885 more than 15,000 Chinese came to work on the railway.

Once the line was completed many of these stayed on to the disgust of British Columbians, who regarded the Chinese with contempt. In an attempt to curb immigration the Chinese 'head tax' imposed on new arrivals was increased to a drastic $100 in 1900. Two years later, as anti-Chinese feelings reached hysterical proportions, a Royal Commission on Chinese and Japanese Immigration produced a report which concluded that Asians were 'obnoxious to a free community and dangerous to the state' and, accordingly, 'unfit for full citizenship.' In 1903 the head tax was raised to $500 and the Immigration Act of 1923 effectively banned Chinese immigration (the day the act was passed is known as 'Humiliation Day' by Canadian Chinese). Amazingly, it was not until 1947 that this appalling legislation was repealed, and not until 1967 that the final restrictions on Chinese immigration were removed.

Granville Island

The island was developed as an industrial site in 1915, largely to provide space for the railway yards of the Canadian Northern Railway and the Great Northern Railway. After years of disuse it received a handsome redevelopment package from the federal government in 1972 and was soon transformed into a colourful and lively centre of markets, cafés, artists' workshops and boatyards. The area works much better than Gastown, partly due to the fact that it is as popular with locals as with tourists. To get there take the No 50 bus along Granville St.

Vannier Park museum site

Near Granville Island to the south of False Creek is a park containing three of the city's main museums: the Vancouver Museum, the Macmillan Planetarium and the Maritime Museum. The grounds are very pretty and there's an attractive coast path leading from the park to Kitsilano Beach. To get there take the No 22 bus from Burrard St and get off at the first stop after the bridge.

• **The Vancouver Museum** Concentrating on local history, the museum takes you through the city's settlement and development with exhibits ranging from clothes and canoes to photographs and replicas of turn of the century shops. The displays are quite well presented and the accompanying text is thoughtfully written but the museum has a very parochial air to it and is, on the whole, a bit disappointing. It's open daily 10am-7pm May to September, and Tuesday to Sunday 10am-5pm for the rest of the year. Entrance is $5.

● **Macmillan Planetarium** The planetarium shares the same building as the Vancouver Museum and specialises in astronomy and rock laser shows (tickets cost $6). It also has an observatory next door where you can look at the stars under the guidance of astronomers for free. For schedules, call ☎ 738-STAR.

● **Maritime Museum** In addition to the usual wooden models and old photos is the *St Roch* – a gem of an exhibit. This two-masted arctic patrol ship, built in 1928, was only the second vessel to navigate the treacherous North West Passage (and the first to do it in both directions). There are guided tours around the ship every half hour. The museum is open daily 10am-5pm; entrance is $5.

Stanley Park

Visit Stanley Park and you begin to see why Vancouverites look so happy: they have 1000 acres of green space on their doorstep to unwind in. Situated on the tip of a peninsula, most of the park is surrounded by ocean. You can walk all the way round its edge on the 10km seawall promenade, or take a bus on the road running parallel. From the eastern side are excellent views over Vancouver's downtown skyline, and from the west are equally fine views of the mountains looming over West

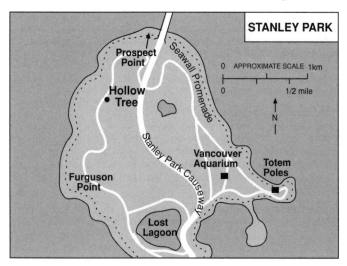

Vancouver across the Burrard Inlet. Points of interest to look out for include the Lost Lagoon which is home to numerous Canada geese, ducks and swans, a collection of magnificent totem poles, Prospect Point (excellent views) and the Hollow Tree (a huge red cedar thought to be up to 1000 years old). Also inside the park is the amazing **Vancouver Aquarium**. Entrance is a steep $9.50 but with 6000 marine species represented (including sea otters, beluga whales, sea lions and sharks) it's an absolutely fascinating place. The aquarium is open daily 9am-8pm late June to early September and 10am-5.30pm for the rest of the year.

UBC Museum of Anthropology

Located way out of town on the university campus, this outstanding museum is well worth the trip. Its modern, award-winning buildings house a vast collection of artifacts with an emphasis on the cultures of BC's Pacific Coast Natives. Exhibits include masks, jewellery, textiles, ivory carvings and an amazing collection of totem poles. Particularly arresting is 'The Raven and the Beast', an enormous sculpture designed by the contemporary Haida artist, Bill Reid. The museum is open Wednesday to Sunday 11am-5pm and until 9pm on Tuesday. Entrance is $5 (free on Tuesday evenings). To get there take the No 10 bus from Granville to its final stop, near to the campus.

Royal Hudson Steam Train

Between June and September the old Royal Hudson steam train runs from North Vancouver to Squamish, a distance of 40 miles. The railway follows the edge of Howe Sound, a stunning fjord dotted with little islands, framed by a backdrop of mountains. You can go both ways by train, or incorporate a cruise, either going or returning aboard the *MV Britannia*. Trains leave the BC railway station on the North Shore at 10am daily, and boats depart at 9.30am from the North Foot of Denman St. Advance reservations are essential. The round trip by rail costs $36, and the cruise and rail trip costs $62. For more information call BC Rail (☎ 984-5246).

The Royal Hudson was a class of CPR locomotive that pulled passenger trains between Revelstoke and Vancouver. Originally known simply as Hudsons, they got their 'Royal' after the visiting King George VI and Queen Elizabeth were transported around Canada on a train hauled by a Hudson locomotive. Following the tour, the CPR requested and were granted royal permission to put the image of a crown on the front of the running board and to rename the engines 'Royal Hudson.' The Royal Hudson running today between Vancouver and Squamish is Locomotive 2860.

The route it takes follows the first leg of the Vancouver – Prince George line operated year-round by British Columbia Railway. This was originally run by the Pacific Great Eastern, or PGE, a company that was notorious throughout the province for inefficiency and incompetence. Things got off to a bad start when, only half completed, construction of the line was 'temporarily' put on hold for 28 years, from 1928 to 1956! When it was finally up and running, passengers discovered that trains were prone to letting in rain, taking unscheduled stops in the middle of nowhere, showing a spectacular disregard for timetables or simply not turning up at all. Hardly surprising, then, that the PGE soon became known as the 'Prince George Eventually.'

FESTIVALS

• **International Dragon Boat Festival**, late June. Lively three-day event featuring boat races, music and theatre shows.
• **International Jazz Festival**, late June to early July. Balmy summer evenings of jazz and blues – a highly pleasurable festival.
• **Firework competition**, early August. Another Benson & Hedges-sponsored music and firework extravaganza.
• **International Comedy Festival**, early August. Usually has an excellent line-up; great location, too, on Granville Island.
• **Vancouver Fringe Festival**, usually first two weeks in September. Excellent range of material encompassing drama, comedy, dance and musicals. Very popular.

MOVING ON

By rail
The Canadian leaves Vancouver for Toronto on Mondays, Thursdays and Saturdays; the journey takes three days and three nights. There's also a service between North Vancouver and Prince George, operated by British Columbia Railway (☎ 984-5246) and an Amtrak connection from Vancouver to Seattle (☎ 1-800-872-7245).

By ferry
BC Ferries (☎ 669-1211) run frequent services from Vancouver to Victoria and Nanaimo on Vancouver Island, and to the southern gulf islands. They also operate the famous Inside Passage service between Port Hardy, on Vancouver Island, and Prince Rupert.

By air
The Vancouver Airporter bus (☎ 244-9888) runs between major downtown hotels and Vancouver International Airport. Note that you will be stung for an airport improvement fee when flying out of Vancouver: this is $5 for destinations within BC, $10 within North America and $15 if you're travelling outside North America. Useful numbers include Airport Customer Service Information: ☎ 278-7788; Air Canada: ☎ 643-5600; Canadian Airlines International: ☎ 665-4400 and American Airlines: ☎ 685-5722.

PART 5: ROUTE GUIDE AND MAPS

Using this guide

You can follow your route on the strip maps in this guide and read about the points of interest along the way in the accompanying text. Where something of interest is on only one side of the track, it is identified by the letters N (north), S (south), W (west) and E (east). Note that in some cases these compass directions are only approximate. Since the direction of travel from Toronto to Vancouver is due west, when you're on this journey north is on the right-hand side of the train.

Railway subdivisions
Each line is divided into subdivisions. These are usually about 125 miles long which was the average distance a steam train could travel in twelve hours when the railways were built. If you take the train all the way from Halifax to Vancouver, you'll pass through twenty subdivisions. These are shown as —— **RAILWAY SUBDIVISION** —— in the text.

Mile markers
The mileage within each subdivision is indicated by mile markers at the side of the track. Subdivisions run from east to west or south to north, so Mile 0 will always be at the eastern or southern terminal of a subdivision. When you reach the end of a subdivision the next one begins. This is known as a railway divisional point and the miles go back to 0. The mile markers are usually white rectangular boards on metal posts or telegraph poles. They can be on either side of the track.

Signal masts
You'll also notice numbers marked on signal masts along the way. You can work out which mile you're at by inserting a decimal point before the

---

Miles or kilometres?
While travelling through Canada you may well be struck by the odd mixture of kilometres and miles, feet and metres in use throughout the country. Conversion to the metric system from the British Imperial system began here in 1971 and while the process is more or less complete, many traces of the old method of measurement remain. The result can be a little confusing; for instance, VIA's timetables give all distances in kilometres, but the CN subdivisions are still broken down by miles and marked by mile posts at the side of the track.

last digit. For instance, if the number on the signal mast is 562 that means you're at Mile 56.2.

Station names

Of course the fool proof way to find out where you are is to look out for the names of the stations you're passing. These are conveniently announced on signposts a mile before each station. The names of sidings or junctions are often displayed by the track as well.

Stops

Most of the stops are for only a few minutes, giving the crew just enough time to whisk the passengers on and off. Longer stops are always indicated in the timetable and are shown in this guide in brackets after the station name. You'll notice that some of the stops in the timetable have asterisks after them; these are 'flag stops' which means the train will stop here only when someone wants to get on or off. Flag stops are also marked by an asterisk in this guide, eg **Clearwater***.

Time zones

Most of the routes described take you through at least two time zones; the Canadian takes you through four. When you enter a new time zone this will be indicated in the text using the following abbreviations: AT (Atlantic Time); ET (Eastern Time); CT (Central Time); MT (Mountain Time); PT (Pacific Time). See page 40 for more on time zones.

Speed calculations

You can work out how fast you're travelling by measuring the time it takes the train to get from one mile marker to the next one, then consulting this table.

Seconds	kph	mph	Seconds	kph	mph
36	170	100	80	72	45
38	153	95	85	68	42
40	145	90	90	64	40
42	138	86	95	61	38
44	138	86	100	58	36
46	126	78	105	55	34
48	121	75	110	53	33
50	116	72	115	50	31
52	111	69	120	48	30
54	108	67	130	45	28
56	103	64	150	39	24
58	100	62	160	37	23
60	96	60	170	34	21
65	88	55	210	27	17
70	82	51	240	24	15

The Ocean:
Halifax to Montreal

The Ocean follows the meandering lines of the old Intercolonial Railway, indeed the line loops around so much, swinging off to tiny villages, that it was said the contractors were paid by the mile. It's a line with a history – the first passenger train ran from Halifax to Lévis, opposite Quebec City, back in 1876. The train following this route has been known as the Ocean since 1904 making it the longest running train in Canada. It takes you through three provinces and two time zones and, as you might expect, past a good deal of water: you'll see plenty of lakes, harbours, bays and rivers, including the great St Lawrence, which the train follows for a large portion of the journey. The trip from Halifax to Montreal takes nineteen and a half hours.

Mile 0: Halifax [AT] For a detailed guide to Halifax, see p67.

Mile 4 (S): The train passes **Fairview Cemetery** where 125 victims of the *Titanic* tragedy are buried. There's also a large common grave here for the unidentified men and women who died in the Halifax Explosion (see page 73).

Mile 18-27: As you leave the city you move into a landscape of spruce forest and lakes. Look east at Mile 18 for a view of Kinsac Lake, and west between Mile 24 and 27 for lovely views over Shubenacadie Lake.

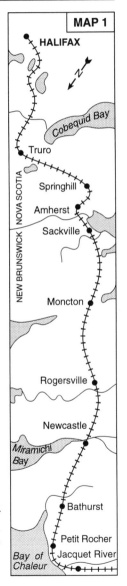

Mile 63: Truro There was an Acadian settlement here as early as 1701 but these unfortunate people were forced to make way for New England settlers in 1755. S i n c e then it's become a major railway centre, and a thriving farming, lumbering and dairy area. It's a pretty town though the train station situated in the middle of an ugly shopping mall would suggest otherwise.

——— RAILWAY SUBDIVISION ———

Mile 11: Just after crossing the Debert River the train swings around a great, sweeping curve of track known as the **Grecian Bend**, apparently laid at the behest of an influential local ironworks owner.

Mile 23 (N): Folly Lake Formed by a melting glacier 10,000 years ago, it's supposed to be a watering spot for moose and bear.

The expulsion of the Acadians
Acadia (or Acadie) was the name given to the original French settlements on the Atlantic Coast, dating from around 1610. This land was also claimed by the British who renamed it Nova Scotia. They finally acquired Acadia in the Treaty of Utrecht in 1713, though they more or less left it alone until 1750-60, when thousands of New England settlers were moved in to colonise the area.

Britain demanded of the Acadians an oath of unconditional allegiance to the British Crown but the French refused vowing neutrality instead. In response, the Acadian population was rounded up, herded onto ships and forcibly deported. Up to 10,000 of these people were expelled between 1755 and 1762, and the event has gone down as one of the greatest tragedies of the French-speaking people of Canada.

Mile 25: For the next five miles the train rides high above the Wallace River, along the Wentworth Valley. As you leave the valley behind, look south for a view of Sugarloaf Mountain in the distance.

Nova Scotia
Nova Scotia is Canada's second smallest province, covering just over 55,000 square miles. It sits in the North Atlantic Ocean on a lobster-shaped peninsula, surrounded by 7579km of coastline. One of the three Maritime Provinces, practically everything about Nova Scotia – its history, its climate, its industries, its people – is intricately bound up with the sea. The first Europeans in the area were fishermen, lured over by the legendary supplies of cod here and the first towns were set up as ports, first by the French and then by the British. The biggest, Halifax, was and remains an important naval base, as well as being the province's capital.

It's an area of great natural beauty, particularly around the coast with its incredible variety of fjords, bays, coves, inlets, mud flats, sand dunes, beaches, lagoons and salt marshes. This rugged terrain, added to the province's isolation from central Canada, lends a remote and slightly sleepy feel to the place – qualities that draw significant numbers of tourists here each year. Nova Scotia's population is 873,00; about 75% of these are of British extract, and 11% of French descent (with German and Dutch origin making up the rest). The average income per capita is less than 80% of the national average, but Nova Scotians generally claim to enjoy a good quality of life in an unspoilt environment.

Mile 59: Springhill Jct* Springhill used to be an important coal mining centre but its pits were dogged by tragedy: in 1891 125 miners were killed in an explosion; in 1956 39 died in an accident; just two years later a tunnel collapsed killing a further 74 men. Today the pits are all shut down, but the bravery of the men who once worked there is still honoured in the Springhill Miners' Museum.

Mile 76: Amherst The town was once a booming industrial centre of Nova Scotia, but large numbers of the population left for New England after World War I, and the local economy has never recovered its former success.

Mile 80: Here you cross the Missaquash River which separates Nova Scotia from New Brunswick.

Mile 81(N): On top of the hill you can see **Fort Beauséjour**, built by the French between 1750 and 1755, then promptly captured by the British the year it was completed. This low-lying building doesn't exactly dominate the skyline, so keep your eyes peeled if you want a glimpse of it.

Mile 86: Sackville This is a small, pretty town with old timbered houses and (surprisingly, for its size) a university, Mount Allison, founded over 150 years ago. What's more, this university was the first in Canada to grant degrees to women, when Grace Anne Lockhart was made a Bachelor of Science here in 1875. Sackville is surrounded by the saltwater **Tantramar Marshes**. Keep a look out for Canada geese, marsh hawks, blue-winged teal, black ducks and numerous other waterfowl; the area is a national wildlife reserve and is one of the densest breeding grounds in the world for many species.

Mile 125: Moncton (20-minute stop) The original name of this town was The Bend; sadly it was renamed Moncton (losing a 'k' along the way) in 1855, in honour of General Robert Monckton, a British commander who became lieutenant-governor of Nova Scotia. Efforts to officially respell the town's name in the 1920s were vigorously opposed by the locals, and Moncton it remained. Today about a third of the population is French-speaking. The twenty-minute stop provides a good opportunity to stretch your legs.

'From Moncton, westward, there is much along the line worthy of description, but thousands of Railway tourists will see it all with their own eyes in a year or two – the deep forests of New Brunswick, the noble Miramichi River with its Railway bridging on a somewhat gigantic scale, the magnificent highway scenery of the Baie des Chaleurs, the Restigouche and the wild mountain gorges of the Matapédia'.
Rev Grant, *Ocean to Ocean* (1873)

———— **RAILWAY SUBDIVISION** ————

Mile 62: Here you cross the **Miramichi River** and then, immediately after, the Little Miramichi. Anglers reportedly flock to these waters from all over the world, lured by their silver Atlantic salmon.

Mile 66: Newcastle The local economy revolves around the town's thriving salmon fisheries. It also boasts a large radio station which met its moment of glory during World War II when it was selected as the British government's receiving station.

New Brunswick

The official name of this province is New/Nouveau Brunswick. Over a third of its population of 715,000 is French-speaking, and New Brunswick is Canada's only officially bilingual province. It was originally administered as part of Nova Scotia, but when its population expanded with the arrival of about 14,000 English Loyalists after the American War of Independence, it was made a separate province in 1784. It's bordered by Quebec to the north and Maine (USA) to the west, and is connected to Nova Scotia by the Chignecto Isthmus.

In the early decades of Confederation, New Brunswick was the most prosperous region of Canada. Its economy was based on the massive boat-building industry centred in Saint John, which exploited the enormous quantity of timber available from the province's interior forest land. However, when ships started to be built with steel its fortunes declined rapidly, and have never properly recovered, due in some part to Canada's national policies which restrict individual provinces from setting their own competitive tariffs. New Brunswick is one of the Maritime Provinces, along with Nova Scotia and Prince Edward Island. Its capital is Fredericton.

Mile 110: Bathurst This small copper-mining and fishing town marks the beginning of the Caraquet coast. The sandy beaches and old Acadian fishing villages along this coast have made the area a popular tourist resort.

Mile 138: Jacquet River* This town was founded by a Mr J Doyle in 1790 who, according to local legend, was its only inhabitant for many years. To the north is the Bay of Chaleur; the train will hug its shores for the next 35 miles. The views over the bay are particularly pretty between miles 165-170.

Mile 154: Charlo* This little fishing and forestry town has its own local airport with regularly scheduled flights to Montreal.

Mile 173: Campbellton The town was originally settled by the dispossessed Acadians back in 1757, but they were once more forced out of their homes by the English a few years later.

The skyline at Campbellton is dominated by the 300-metre high Sugarloaf Mountain – a huge lump of volcanic rock – but it may be too dark to get a good look by the time you arrive.

Mile 12: Matapédia (ET) Matapédia gets its name from a Micmac word which means 'the river that breaks into branches'. You are now in Quebec Province.

The **Micmac** (sometimes spelt mi'kmaq) people occupy the coastal regions of the Gaspé and Maritime Provinces. It is not certain how long they have been there, though it could be anything up to 10,000 years. Their settlements were traditionally located around bays or rivers, and their community and economy revolved around fishing and hunting. As with most native tribes, however, their society was virtually dismantled with the arrival of the Europeans. Attempts by the government to integrate Micmacs with white Canadians resulted in few advantages for the natives and the loss of most of their land, villages and customs. Today there are about 20,000 people of Micmac origin living in this part of Canada.

Mile 47: Causapscal A lumbering and farming village touched by romance. It was here that Donald A Smith of the CPR (see p56) fell in love with and married his beautiful Indian bride.

Mile 60: Amqui Again, this place-name is derived from a Micmac word, this time meaning (intriguingly) 'place of amusement'.

Mile 76: Sayabec* The train passes through this town late at night but, if you haven't gone to bed yet, you may be able make out the striking silhouette of Sayabec's church (E), standing on a hillside.

Mile 105: Mont-Joli The moose and deer hunting capital of Quebec, this little town is also known as 'Gateway to the Gaspé'.

Mile 123: Rimouski With a population of around 30,000, this is the first sizeable town since Moncton. The Roman Catholic cathedral is the

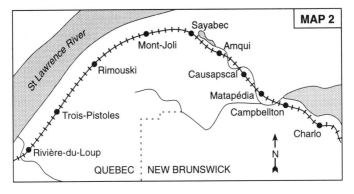

centre of the diocese. Much of the town was destroyed by a fire in 1950 but there are few signs of this left today.

Mile 161: Trois-Pistoles No one knows for sure how this village got its name, but legend has it that a sailor sent to fetch water from a stranded ship lost the silver goblet he was carrying, which was worth three gold *pistoles* (a French coin). These days Trois-Pistoles is a popular whale-watching spot: beluga, blue and finback whales are all common in this part of the St Lawrence.

Mile 188: Rivière-du-Loup This town used to be called Fraserville but the large packs of wolves that once gathered around the river gave the place its more poetic name.

———————————— RAILWAY SUBDIVISION ————————————

Mile 41: La Pocatière This small town of about 5000 people is home to a modern, avant-guarde cathedral containing works by an eminent Quebec sculptor.

Mile 78: Montmagny Probably the most noteworthy feature of this biscuit-manufacturing town is its curious ten-sided church.

Mile 114: Lévis (for Quebec City)   [10-minute stop]
If you're not getting off here be sure to wake yourself up for one of the most striking views of the whole trans-Canada trip. The train pulls into Lévis just as dawn is breaking. Pull up the blinds and look across the river: you'll see a beautiful walled city, a fairy tale castle and church spires dotted all around; Quebec City of course, with its towering Château Frontenac and the rooftops of its cathedrals and churches – a

---

Quebec

Quebec is Canada's largest province, covering 1.65 million square km. The UK would fit into this vast area seven times over, but Quebec's population is a fraction of the UK's at 6.5 million. The province stretches right up to the Hudson Strait, not far from the Arctic Circle, but most of the land is covered by the Canadian Shield (see p27) and is virtually uninhabitable. Subsequently, almost all Quebeckers live in the fertile valley of the St Lawrence River, with over a third in Montreal alone.

Quebec is unique in North America in being an almost wholly French-speaking region: over 90% of its people have French as their mother tongue. Its distinctness from the rest of Canada has given rise to a vigorous separatist movement over the last few decades, and Quebec has been teetering on the brink of independence in recent years (see p33). In the 1995 referendum Quebeckers voted to stay with Canada by just 1%, a figure that proves that the uncertainty of Quebec's future is far from over. If Quebec becomes a separate nation it will break up the rest of Canada into two blocks, as the province separates Ontario from New Brunswick, Nova Scotia, Newfoundland and Prince Edward Island. Quebec also borders four American states: Maine, New Hampshire, Vermont and New York.

breath taking panorama. If you *are* getting off here you can take the ferry from Lévis to Quebec City; the ferry terminal is right next to the train station. For more details on Quebec City see page 75.

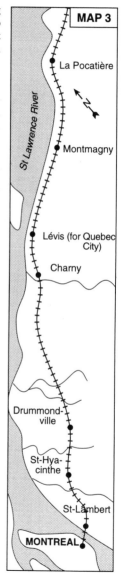

──────── **RAILWAY SUBDIVISION** ────────

Mile 8: Charny As you pull out of Charny the train crosses a wide bridge over the Chaudière River. The river takes its name from the 'boiling waters' of its falls, the tallest being forty metres high.

Once out of Charny you move into a rural landscape of forests or pastures dotted with tiny villages, pretty church spires or farms. This fertile land stretches most of the way from here to Montreal.

Most of the trees that you pass along this stretch are maple trees, used to produce that great Canadian staple, maple syrup. A hole is bored in each tree so that the sap can be removed, drop by drop; this is then heated under controlled temperatures and the sap turns into syrup. It's then transferred to a cute glass bottle that ends up on your break-fast table next to your pancakes.

Mile 98: Drummondville Note the huge hydroelectric station the train passes just before you get to this busy industrial town.

Mile 40: St-Hyacinthe The mileage suddenly goes down to Mile 40 following a railway junction just before the town. The great gothic building to the south is the St-Hyacinthe Seminary, supposedly modelled on Amiens Cathedral. It is said of St-Hyacinthe that until very recently it had a higher concentration of religious institutions than any other town in the world. It's also the birthplace of Canada's greatest organ builder, Joseph Casavant.

Mile 50: There's a dramatic change of scenery as two of the **Monteregian Hills**

suddenly loom up out of nowhere. These huge volcanic mounds were formed 120 million years ago when the area was covered by sea. Particularly impressive is the dark and somewhat menacing Mont Rouge, towering over the track at **Boloeil** (Mile 56). Altogether there are seven of these hills, the western-most being Mont Royal in Montreal.

Mile 55: As you cross the Richelieu River spare a thought for the victims of the terrible rail accident at this spot in 1864. A Grand Trunk train carrying mainly German and Polish immigrants was unable to stop for the rising drawbridge and went plunging between the gap into the river. About a hundred passengers died.

Mile 70: The Ocean crosses the St Lawrence Seaway into greater Montreal, stopping briefly at the suburb St-Lambert. Look north as you cross the bridge for excellent views of Montreal's skyline. A few miles on from St-Lambert you're in Montreal's Central Station. For more information about **Montreal**, see page 85.

The Corridor route:
Montreal to Toronto

VIA's modern LRC (Light, Rapid & Comfortable) trains travel along the old Grand Trunk inter-city route, following first the St Lawrence River (which drifts in and out of sight) to its source at Lake Ontario, and then the shores of the lake as far as Toronto. The journey takes four hours.

Mile 0: Montreal [ET] See p85.

Mile 11: Dorval The train makes a brief stop just outside Montreal, near the southern international airport. Moving out of Dorval the tracks run parallel to the highway (Route 20) which will remain in view for the next hour or so.

Mile 21 & 23: Here you cross the Ottawa River. Look north for fine views down the river to the Lake of Two Mountains studded with little islands. In the distance you can see the Laurentian Highlands.

Mile 25: Around here the urban landscape peters out and the train moves into a rural setting. The land is as flat as a pancake, and the only things to look at are trees and farms.

Mile 37: Coteau This small agricultural village is also the south-west terminus of the Soulanges Canal, part of the St Lawrence Seaway system.

Mile 41: The train crosses the boundary between Quebec and Ontario.

Mile 58: The peculiar igloo-shaped buildings you can see standing by the track are used by the government to store sand to sprinkle on the roads in the winter.

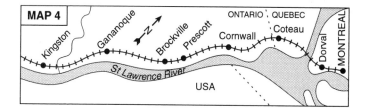

Mile 65-105: The track running along this stretch was re-laid in the late 1950s when the original track was submerged by the artificial widening of the St Lawrence River. This was part of the construction of the huge **St Lawrence Seaway**, a system of canals and locks connecting the Atlantic Ocean to the St Lawrence River and the Great Lakes. The biggest section is the one you're now running alongside (though it's just out of sight), linking Montreal with Lake Ontario; it can take vessels of up to 222.5m long and 23.2m wide. The railways weren't the only thing submerged by the Seaway – over 500 homes and 6500 people had to be relocated to two newly built towns (you'll pass one of them, Ingleside, at Mile 80).

Mile 68: Cornwall　Site of one of the province's oldest courthouses (1833) and a restored 'Regency Cottage' museum.

If you look south here you can make out the original route of the track before it was re-laid.

Mile 109 (S):　Over the trees you can see a huge bridge – this is the International Bridge linking Canada with the US. Right by the bridge are several enormous grain elevators.

Mile 112:　A large water storage tower announces your arrival at **Prescott**. In stark contrast to this modern edifice is Prescott's beautiful stone station, about a hundred and fifty years old.

Mile 125: Brockville　(Or 'Gateway to the Thousand Islands') Between here and Kingston the St Lawrence River is dotted with hundreds of little islands, covered with rock and trees. The area – an exten-

---

Ontario
Sandwiched between Quebec and Manitoba, Ontario sprawls over a million square km, from the Great Lakes in the south up to Hudson Bay in the north. A large part of this area is Shield country, with its boreal forest, granite outcrops and countless lakes. Ontario is an Iroquoian word meaning 'shining waters', a most appropriate name since the province contains a full quarter of the world's fresh water.

It is the most populated province in Canada (with nine million people), and has been so since the first census was taken in 1871. It is also the wealthiest, with the highest degree of urbanisation and industrialisation, and the most diversified economy. Its manufacturing sector is particularly important, with about half of all goods produced in Canada coming from Ontario. Another major source of revenue is the rich mineral deposits discovered with the construction of the railroad across the Canadian Shield.

Ontario attracts many tourists each year, being home to the nation's capital (Ottawa), its largest city (Toronto) and the Niagara Falls. Its charms are not exclusively urban, however, and popular wilderness retreats include Georgian Bay, the Thousand Islands and Algonquin Park (a mecca for canoeists, with its 1600km of water trails).

sion of the Canadian Shield – is very beautiful and has attracted tourists since the early 1800s, but unfortunately not much of it can be seen from the train.

Mile 135-145: The rolling pastures suddenly give way to ten miles of beautiful limestone rock and wild-looking trees – a brief glimpse of the scenery covering the Thousand Islands just to the south.

Mile 155: Gananoque The other 'Gateway to the Thousand Islands.' It also has a bridge across the St Lawrence to the US.

Mile 169: The train crosses the **Rideau Canal** which links Kingston with Ottawa. The canal was completed in 1832, and was originally designed (following the War of 1812) to guarantee a supply route north of the US border in the event of another war. In winter this canal turns into a busy skating rink and is used by many locals to skate to work.

Mile 176: Kingston This town's claims to fame include being the former capital of the Province of Canada (1841-67) and the birthplace of Sir John A Macdonald, Canada's first Prime Minister.

Mile 180: As the train passes pretty Collins Bay with all its pleasure yachts bobbing in the water, you get your first glimpse of Lake Ontario.

Mile 182: A big water tower stands by the track (N) with 'Amherst View' written on it. About a mile further on you can snatch a bit of this view for yourself – the beautiful Amherst Island on Lake Ontario (S).

Mile 199: Nepanee Just before you get here look south as you cross the river and you'll see a series of pretty waterfalls. The picturesque view continues with Nepanee's beautiful town hall (S) and then its charming old railway station.

Mile 220: Belleville This town has been, in its time, an important fur-trading, saw-milling and cheese-making centre. Like Nepanee it boasts an attractive, well-preserved station dating from the 1850s.

Mile 233: Trenton Jct This little town was chosen as the base for the Royal Canadian Air Force during World War II and was the train-

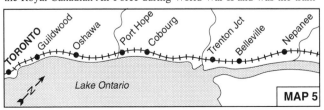

ing centre for Commonwealth pilots. Back in the 1920s, however, not content with the usual saw-milling and lumbering industries, Trenton tried to establish itself as a film production centre. Unfortunately the glamorous plan didn't really take off and only a handful of films were produced here.

Mile 260 (S): Over the next few miles you can catch some lovely views of Lake Ontario.

Mile 265: Cobourg Among this small town's architectural high-lights is a court which is a replica of London's Old Bailey. You may also be interested to know that Cobourg was the site of one of Canada's oldest railways – a 48km track to Peterborough across Rice Lake. The line was not a success; right at the beginning most of the construction team was wiped out by cholera, and then when the track was finally laid in the mid 1850s the 5km Rice Lake Bridge proved rather unstable. When the Prince of Wales visited the area in 1860 it was considered best that he shouldn't cross the bridge in case it collapsed – and collapse it did less than one year later, leaving Cobourg with an inoperable and bankrupt railway.

Mile 268: By now the train is running right alongside the lakeshore: the views are stunning so keep your cameras at the ready.

Mile 270: Port Hope This town has one of the best preserved turn-of-the-century main streets in Canada. You won't see much of it from the train but its beautiful little railway station is equally well-kept.

Mile 271: More stunning views of Lake Ontario – sandy beaches, clay bluffs and holiday homes dotted along the shore.

Mile 300: Oshawa This manufacturing city (predominantly of motor cars) was the birthplace of industrial unions in Canada, following a 4000-men strike at General Motors in 1937. The controversy sur-rounding the company's and the government's response to the strike resulted in two cabinet ministers resigning. Eventually the company gave in to the strikers' demands – this was the first union victory in the country. You can see the GM site on the other side of the rail tracks from the station.

Mile 315: Once more the tracks sweep right by the edge of the lake. Take your fill of the beautiful views before the train heads off into Toronto's suburbs where a stop is made at **Guildwood** at **Mile 321**.

Mile 333: Toronto Your journey ends at Union Station. For more about Toronto, see page 99.

The Canadian: Toronto to Vancouver

This epic journey of 4467 km takes three days and three nights. You'll travel through some of the most diverse landscape contained within a single country. The highlight of the journey is without question the ride through the Rocky Mountains; the stretch between Jasper and Kamloops takes you through some of the most spectacular scenery in the world.

TORONTO TO WINNIPEG

Mile 1-50 [ET]: For the first half hour or so the train chugs through the dismal Toronto suburbs before the landscape gives way to the fertile pastures and picturesque farms that characterise southern Ontario.

Travelling this way in 1872, Rev Grant noted: 'The first half of the journey, or as far as Lake Simcoe, is through a fair and fertile land; too flat to be picturesque, but sufficiently rolling for farming purposes. Clumps of stately elms, with noble stems, shooting high before their fan-shape commences, relieve the monotony of the scene. *(Ocean to Ocean).*

Mile 63: Barrie This not especially attractive city lies on the shores of Kempenfelt Bay which is part of Lake Simcoe. The views over the lake are pleasant, though, and if you happen to be making this journey on a fine winter's day you're likely to see hundreds of people fishing through holes in the ice.

Mile 86: Orilla Squeezed on the narrows between Lake Simcoe and Lake Couchich-

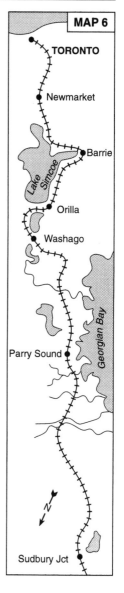

MAP 6

TORONTO

Newmarket

Barrie

Lake Simcoe

Orilla

Washago

Georgian Bay

Parry Sound

N

Sudbury Jct

ing, Orilla is best known in Canada as the subject of Stephen Leacock's *Sunshine Sketches of a Little Town*, which satirises small-town life in Ontario. The book has been a Canadian favourite since its publication in 1912. As you leave Orilla look west for a glimpse of a grand white house standing by the bay; this was Leacock's summer residence and is now a museum containing the manuscript of *Sunshine Sketches*.

Mile 99: Washago Sounding alarmingly like a Vidal Sassoon shampoo, this tiny village is situated on the northern shores of Lake Couchiching. The name is actually taken from the native 'wash-a-go-min' which means 'sparkling waters.' To the west you can see the beautiful **Georgian Bay**, an arm of Lake Huron, one of the Great Lakes. The waters are studded with little islands, and holiday cottages are dotted around the shore.

Mile 100: The Canadian now crosses the Severn River which flows up to Hudson Bay. The river was used by fur traders in the 17th and 18th centuries as a route between the bay and Lake Winnipeg. Beyond the river the landscape alters dramatically as you move into the wild and rugged terrain of the **Canadian Shield** (see page 27). For the next few hours the train winds its way between great outcrops of pink and grey granite, surrounded by a dazzling array of lakes, waterfalls and streams. The scenery is utterly beautiful.

> 'For a distance of 600 miles there stretched away to the north-west a vast tract of rock-fringed lake, swamp and forest; lying spread in primeval savagery, an untravelled wilderness'. Butler, *The Great Lone Land* (1872)

Mile 150: Parry Sound This town has a peculiar history. The land was bought in the mid-nineteenth century by a Mr W H Beatty who laid out a settlement and encouraged families to move there. As it grew into a successful logging centre, Mr Beatty's son became a sort of self-appointed squire. He was known by everyone as 'The Governor,' enforced prohibition on the villagers and even began to circulate his own money!

These days Parry Sound is a bustling tourist resort in the summer. It's known as 'Gateway to the Thirty Thousand Islands' on Lake Huron – the world's largest concentration of islands. You can see some of these (S) over the next few miles.

Mile 215: After crossing the Pickerel River, the train crosses the **French River**, part of a historic fur-trading route. It's still popular with canoeists who share its shallow waters with large numbers of bass, pike and muskellunge.

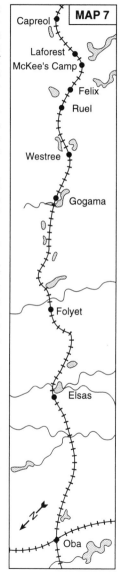

Mile 260: Sudbury Jct As you approach Sudbury look south for a view of the towering 381-metre INCO smokestack. The region's rich nickel and copper deposits were discovered during the construction of the trans-Canada railway and since then Sudbury has become the largest nickel-mining centre in the world.

The mining and smelting were responsible for ravaging the surrounding landscape but extensive reforestation and redevelopment projects have recently improved the environment.

Mile 276: Capreol   **[15-minute stop]**
Besides being a railway divisional point, this small town serves as a distribution centre for Sudbury's mining industry.

———————— **RAILWAY SUBDIVISION** ————————

Mile 5: Moving out of Capreol the train enters the increasingly remote interior of northern Ontario. It's mind-boggling to think that the exposed bedrock you can see is 500 million years old. You can begin to understand why it took more than 20,000 men to get the track from here to the prairies: the train is forced to weave and loop around numerous lakes, all the while cutting through the rock or bogland of the Shield.

The communities that have sprung up along the track remain isolated and sparsely populated (Farlane, for instance, has fewer than forty inhabitants) and most of the stops between here and Winnipeg are flag stops. Only the occasional trapper, fisherman or lumberjack is likely to get on or off.

Mile 86: Gogama This is a typical logging village. The area between here and Folyet (Mile 150) is renowned for moose and bear but it'll probably be too dark to see anything as you travel through.

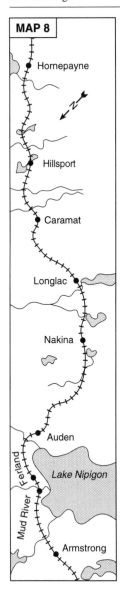

MAP 8

Hornepayne

Hillsport

Caramat

Longlac

Nakina

Auden

Lake Nipigon

Mud River (Ferland)

Armstrong

Mile 258: Oba A railway junction amidst the wilderness! The trans-Canada line crosses the tracks of the Algoma Central Railway (from Sault Ste Marie to Hearst) giving rise to a little railway hotel in this village of a hundred people.

Mile 295: Hornepayne [30-minute stop] Once a gold-mining town, Hornepayne now relies on its pulp mill to keep its workforce employed. It has about 2000 inhabitants.

―――――― RAILWAY SUBDIVISION ――――――

Mile 76: Caramat* Like many sites along the line, Caramat sprang up as a logging town and then almost vanished once the area was logged and the workmen moved on. You can make out an abandoned sawmill (S) across Caramat Lake.

Mile 100: Longlac This former gold-mining settlement sits on the northern banks of Long Lake which drains into Lake Superior. The lake is forty-five miles long and just two miles wide. Almost half the village's population (of over 2000) is French-speaking.

Mile 131: Nakina This little fur-trapping town also boasts an airfield and a radio station.

Mile 210: The Canadian goes over a viaduct high above Jackfish Creek. Look south for fine views over Lake Nipigon, the fourth largest lake in Ontario.

Mile 219: Mud River* Another viaduct takes you across the murky waters that give this little village its name.

Mile 243: Armstrong The landscape by now has become a little monotonous: trees, trees and more trees. This continues for several hours but you'll think fondly of them as you cross the treeless prairies.

Mile 264: Collins* [CT] You've now crossed over into Central Time.

─────────── **RAILWAY SUBDIVISION** ───────────

Mile 67: Flindt Landing* This fishing resort is situated on a little island. Look north to see the cabins and huts.

Mile 78: Savant Lake Another long, narrow lake, 25 miles long and just five miles wide. This settlement is visited mainly by people out fishing.

Mile 139: Sioux Lookout [15-minute stop]. Sioux Lookout sounds as if it's going to be interesting but it's not. There are a few banks and shops across the road from the train station (a once opulent mock-Tudor building which is now falling into disrepair) but nothing much to see around the platform. The place was far more glamorous in days gone by: it was the home of the Ojibway natives who used the nearby hills as a lookout during an attack by Sioux Indians.

─────────── **RAILWAY SUBDIVISION** ───────────

Mile 90: Canyon* The train skirts the shores of Canyon Lake for about ten miles.

Mile 113: Farlane* Look south for a view of Farlane's pretty rail station. This tiny settlement was once a favourite fishing resort of Winnipeg's affluent middle class.

Mile 137: Minaki This used to be a fashionable riverside tourist resort in the 1920s and 30s. The CNR built the elegant Minaki Lodge here which you can see (N) as you cross the Winnipeg River.

Mile 153: Malachi* Look south for a beautiful view over Lake Malachi. The pretty hamlet by the lake is still popular with tourists.

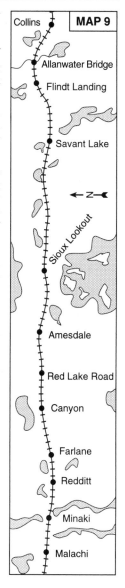

Mile 160: Rice Lake* This is the first settlement after crossing the Ontario/Manitoba border at Mile 159.

You're now in **Whiteshell Provincial Park**, a wilderness area with over 200 lakes. One of these, West Hawk Lake, is 111 metres deep and is supposed to have been created by a giant meteorite. Keep your eyes open for the black bear, deer, moose, coyotes and beavers that live in the park.

Manitoba

Manitoba is in the very centre of Canada, and borders Ontario to the east and Saskatchewan to the west. It covers 650,000 square km, but is sparsely populated with about one million inhabitants – over half of them in its capital city, Winnipeg. Its northern regions are covered by the frozen tundra of the Hudson lowlands, but the province's dominant geographic feature is the Canadian Shield, spreading over half the land. To the south is the flat, fertile wheat belt that provides Manitoba with most of its wealth.

This vast territory was originally part of Rupert's Land, owned by the Hudson's Bay Company who used the intricate system of lakes and rivers for their fur-trading activities. After this land was purchased by the first Canadian government, Manitoba became a separate province largely due to the efforts of the rebellious Louis Riel (see p32). When it was incorporated in 1870 it was known as the 'postage stamp province' because its area was so tiny, covering little more than a small rectangle around Winnipeg. It quickly grew, especially following the completion of the transcontinental railroad which allowed wheat to be exported, and brought in thousands of settlers from eastern Canada and eastern Europe. Today it's one of the most ethnically diverse provinces of Canada, with thousands of Manitobans of Ukrainian, German, French, Italian, Dutch, Polish, Hungarian and Scandinavian origin.

Mile 180: Brereton Lake* The last of the lakes. The trees begin to thin out here, giving way to fields and farms.

Mile 197: Elma* Look south as you approach this little hamlet for a view of a Ukrainian church with its striking, onion-shaped dome. This is typical of the ethnically diverse settlements dotted across the prairies; immigrants were encouraged to come here from all over the world to populate the region once the railway was built, and a large number came from eastern Europe.

Mile 244: Transcona* Just before arriving in this Winnipeg suburb you cross the Red River Floodway on a viaduct 275 metres long. The canal was built to divert floodwaters around Winnipeg following the massive flood of 1950 which forced 100,000 Winnipegers to evacuate their homes.

Mile 252: Winnipeg   [60-minute stop]

The station is right next door to 'The Forks' (the market/restaurant/people-watching centre of Winnipeg) so if you're only getting off for the hour-long stop this is where to go.

If you're staying over in Winnipeg, see page 111 for a guide to the city.

──────── **RAILWAY SUBDIVISION** ────────

WINNIPEG TO EDMONTON

Mile 15: As you pull out of Winnipeg the train rolls into some of the most fertile land in Canada. Enormous fields stretch all around, the flatness broken only by farms and grain elevators standing by the rail track.

Mile 55: Portage-la-Prairie A portage is the connecting overland stretch of a water route. For the fur traders, this area was a portage between the Assiniboine River and Lake Manitoba. The activities pursued at Portage-la-Prairie today are not quite so exotic: it's a food processing centre specialising in mushrooms and frozen foods.

Passing through in 1872, Rev Grant noted: 'Portage la Prairie is the centre of what will soon be a thriving settlement and, when the railway is built, a large town must spring up. On the way to the little village we passed, in less than ten miles, three camps of Sioux – each of them with about twenty wigwams ranged in a circular form. The three camps probably numbered three hundred souls. The men were handsome fellows, and a few of the women were pretty. We did not see many of the women, however, as they kept to the camps doing all the dirty work, while the men marched along the road, every one of them with a gun on his shoulder'.

MAP 10

MANITOBA ONTARIO

Rice Lake

Ophir

Brereton Lake

Elma

Transcona

WINNIPEG

Portage-la-Prairie

Brandon North

←–N–←

Rivers

Mile 128: Brandon North Brandon is Manitoba's second largest city (about 39,000 people) – you can just about make it out, five miles south of the station.

Mile 143: Rivers You approach this little town on a 27 metre-long bridge high above the Minnedosa River. Look out for the colourful grain elevators alongside the track.

Mile 180: For the next twenty-five miles the train follows the **Qu'Appelle Valley**. Look south for lovely views over the lakes and waterways threading through the emerald green land. The name is derived from the French translation of an Indian legend which told of a young man who, on hearing his name called as he crossed the valley, cried out 'Qui appelle?' ('who calls?') The only reply was the echo of his voice: 'qu'appelle....qu'appelle....' He later discovered that the voice he had heard was his lover crying

'The broad, open valley of the Qu'Appelle stretched out along to the west, making a grand break in what would otherwise have been an unbroken plateau of Prairie. Three miles to the south of this valley, and therefore opposite us but farther down, two or three small white buildings on the edge of the plateau were pointed out as Fort Ellice. To the north of the Qu'Appelle, the sun was dipping behind woods far away on the edge of the horizon, and throwing a mellow light on the vast expanse which spread around in every direction'.
    Rev Grant, *Ocean to Ocean* (1873)

out for him at the moment of her death. A cheery little story to ponder on as the train chugs into the shadows of dusk.

Mile 213: Manitoba/Saskatchewan border As the train moves into the Saskatchewan prairies the land gets flatter and flatter. VIA's

Saskatchewan

Saskatchewan is true prairie country – over two thirds of its land is part of the Great Plains, largely composed of fertile, arable soil. It's known as 'the bread basket of Canada' owing to its prodigious wheat production, which meets 60% of the nation's consumption and 12% of total world demand. Saskatchewan has also carved a niche for itself in the manufacturing and distribution of agricultural implements, which it exports around the world. To add to its economic feathers are a range of abundant mineral deposits including uranium, copper, gold and potash.
    The region belonged to the Hudson's Bay Company for two centuries, and was not settled by Europeans until the 1870s. Up until then it had been largely the preserve of the Plains Indians (whose tribes included Cree, Assiniboine, Chipeweyan and Blackfoot) and vast herds of buffalo. After Confederation, the area was first administered by the government as part of the Northwest Territories (most of western Canada) and it wasn't until 1905 that Saskatchewan became a separate province, along with Alberta. Its name was derived from the Cree word for the Saskatchewan River, meaning swiftly-flowing water. It's capital is Regina, and its population is now just over one million.

scheduling thankfully has you travelling through most of Saskatchewan in the dark (in both directions) – presumably to avoid the risk of 'prairie madness' breaking out on the trains.

Mile 280: Melville This town (it's officially a city but the word seems inappropriate for a prairie community of 5000 people) was established by the Grand Trunk Pacific Railway in 1908. It was named after Charles Melville Hays, the GTP president who died with the sinking of the *Titanic*.

──────── **RAILWAY SUBDIVISION** ────────

Mile 129: Watrous This town sprang up on the banks of Manitou Lake to house the thousands of visitors who came by rail to bathe in the lake's mineral-rich (and supposedly curative) waters. The buoyancy of these waters is greater that of the Dead Sea.

> 'After breakfast we entered on a vast plain that stretched out on every side to the horizon. This had once been the favourite resort of the buffalo, and we passed in the course of the day more than a score of skulls that were bleaching on the prairie. All the other bones had of course been chopped and boiled by the Indian women for the oil in them'.
> Cumberland, *The Queen's Highway* (1887)

Mile 191: Saskatoon [20-minute stop]
Saskatchewan's second city (with a population of 185,000) started out as a Temperance Colony in 1882. The Temperance Movement aimed to curb or eliminate the consumption of alcohol in pursuit of a better society. The growth of Saskatoon was slow until the Grand Trunk Pacific brought its northern transcontinental tracks here in 1906. Today it's a small but very prosperous prairie city, its economy revolving around oil and wheat. For those spending time here, attractions include the Ukrainian Museum

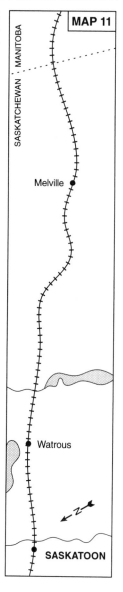

MAP 11

SASKATCHEWAN · MANITOBA

Melville

Watrous

SASKATOON

of Canada, the Western Development Museum and Wanuskewin Heritage Park. However, both eastbound and westbound trains arrive here in the middle of the night, and the station is seven miles out of town – so unless you've got your heart set on visiting Saskatoon, getting off here involves far too much effort and hassle. If you do, however, you ought to book your first night's accommodation in advance. You could try the Patricia Hotel (☎ 306-242) at 345 2nd Ave – the rooms are pleasant and reasonably priced, at around $30-40 a night. A taxi from the station to downtown will cost you around $15.

Mile 247: Biggar   'New York is big, but this is Biggar!' is this little town's slogan. It sprang up when the Grand Trunk Pacific decided to locate a railway divisional point here. As well as being a railway centre Biggar is the tractor manufacturing capital of Saskatchewan.

―――――――――――――― RAILWAY SUBDIVISION ――――――――――――――

Travelling across this area in 1872, Butler was moved to write: 'No solitude can equal the loneliness of a night-shadowed prairie: one feels the stillness, and hears the silence, the wail of the prowling wolf makes the voice of solitude audible, the stars look down through infinite silence upon a silence almost as intense' (*The Great Lone Land*).

Alberta
Alberta is one of Canada's most prosperous and attractive provinces, stretching across the rolling prairies in the east and centre, over to some of the most dramatic Rockies scenery at the province's western border. Jasper National Park, the biggest of the four Rocky Mountain parks, lies entirely within Alberta, and the most heavily visited parts of Banff National Park sit inside the province.
　　Alberta is still less than a hundred years old, created in 1905 along with Saskatchewan. (These provinces are, incidentally, the only two in Canada not to have any salt water coast). It was named after Queen Victoria's fourth daughter, Princess Caroline Alberta, who was married to a former Governor-General of Canada. The two mainstays of Alberta's economy are wheat and oil, the latter bringing a great boom to the two main cities, Calgary and Edmonton, in the 1970s. These cities have been engaged in fierce rivalry for many years, and while Edmonton scored the coup of being made the province's capital, Calgary has managed to win hands down in most other areas. Alberta's population is 2.5 million, and it is the fourth largest province in Canada.

(**Opposite**) **Top**: This elegant, turn-of-the-century steam locomotive shuttles visitors around Fort Edmonton Park (see p124). **Bottom**: West Coast fishing boats moored in the deep sea harbour by Vancouver's Granville Island (see p133). You can sample their catch at the island's excellent fish market. **Overleaf**: The image that has graced a million calendars, chocolate boxes and jigsaw puzzles - Lake Louise, of course, in Banff National Park.

Mile 57: Unity The first attempt to mine potash in Canada took place in Unity. It wasn't an overly successful venture but the subsequent mining of salt was a huge success and continues today. Passing through the area in 1872,

Mile 101: [MT] Saskatchewan/Alberta border As you move into Alberta you also move into the Mountain Time Zone.

Mile 140: Wainwright This town was created by transplanting another settlement, Denwood, 4km from its original location. Everything was moved – houses, stores, the church – to the new site and the settlement was promptly rechristened Wainwright in honour of William Wainwright of the Grand Trunk Pacific.

A huge, brightly coloured grain elevator towers by the railway station; the train always stops here so keep your camera at hand for that classic grain elevator shot. There's a peregrine falcon breeding centre near Wainwright so keep your eyes peeled for a sighting.

Mile 147: Moving out of Wainwright the relentless flatness of the land starts to give way to gently rolling plains. Look north for an impressive view over the mile-wide Battle River Valley. The river looks like a little stream as it snakes along, far below the train. You soon cross it on an 884-metre-long steel trestle, giving you fine views on both sides.

Mile 184: Viking This small town was settled at the beginning of this century by Scandinavians, hence its name. Not far from the town are **The Ribstones**, two massive

---

(**Opposite**): One of Vancouver's oddest attractions is its steam-powered clock (reputed to be the only one in the world) that runs off the city's underground heating system (see p132).

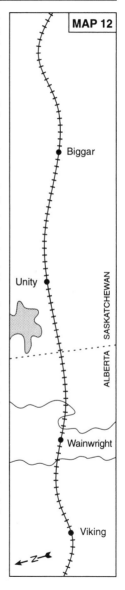

rock carvings created by the Plains Indians about one thousand years ago, depicting a buffalo backbone and ribs.

Mile 205(N)   The train passes Holden. The town's onion-domed Ukrainian Church looms dramatically on the horizon.

Mile 260: Edmonton   [30-minute stop]
The train crosses the North Saskatchewan River on a 500 metre-long bridge, taking you into Edmonton. Your approach to the city is heralded by the enormous oil refineries that have brought Edmonton its wealth. For details on Edmonton, see page 119.

───────────────────── **RAILWAY SUBDIVISION** ─────────────────────

EDMONTON TO JASPER

Mile 32(N):   The train passes another ornate Russian Orthodox church. Strangely, these buildings are almost as much a part of the prairies as the grain elevators.

Mile 44(S):   The train skirts the shores of Wabamun Lake for the next ten miles. Wabamun is the Cree word for 'mirror'.

Mile 45(N):   The tranquillity of the scene is interrupted by the huge power stations on the lakeshore. These are coal-fired power generators; the biggest one is called the Sundance Power Plant.

Mile 67:   The train crosses the Pembina River, once used as a water route to the Cariboo gold fields.

Mile 68: Evansburg   A small coal-mining village named after Harry Evans, a former mayor of Edmonton.

Mile 73-122:   The train crosses five bridges over a series of rivers and creeks. The most impressive crossings are at Mile 121 (over Wolf Creek) and Mile 122 (over the McLeod River); both these bridges are 40 metres high.

Mile 130: Edson   This little lumbering town was established as a railway divisional point in 1910 by the Grand Trunk Pacific. It was named after Edson J Chamberlain, the company's vice-president.

Mile 136(N):   Look down for a view of the pretty Sundance Creek.

Mile 150:   The terrain is becoming increasingly hilly and you can feel the train begin to climb higher. To the south are sweeping views over the McLeod River valley.

Mile 165: At last – the Rocky Mountains! Look towards the front of the train for your first view of the distant snow-capped peaks. The excitement onboard the train is palpable, as all the passengers start 'oohing' and 'ahing' and pressing their faces to the windows.

> 'Looking west, I beheld the great range in unclouded glory...An immense plain stretched from my feet to the mountain – a plain so vast that every object of hill and wooded lake lay dwarfed into one continuous level, and at the back of this level, beyond the pines and the lakes and the river courses, rose the giant, solid, impassable, silent – a mighty barrier rising midst an immense land, standing sentinel over the plains and prairies of America, over the measureless solitudes of this great lone land. Here, at last, lay the Rocky Mountains'.
>
> Butler, *The Great Lone Land* (1872)

Mile 184: Hinton As you pull out of this busy town the views of the mountains suddenly become quite stunning.

Mile 190: The train passes a little village, charmingly named Entrance. It marks, of course, your official entrance into the Rocky Mountains.

Mile 192(N): The **Athabasca River** comes into view. On a sunny day its waters are a beautiful jade-green. The train follows its course from here to Jasper.

Mile 197: For the next eight miles the train skirts **Lac Brulé**, named after Etienne Brulé, the famous 17th century explorer who was the first Frenchman to live among native Canadians.

Mile 200: By now the train is right in the middle of the mountains; they tower above you on both sides of the track. To the north is the Bosche Range and to the south the Miette Range.

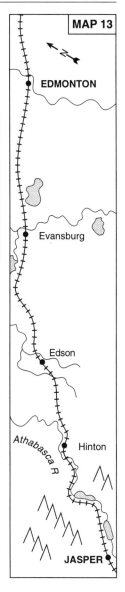

MAP 13

EDMONTON

Evansburg

Edson

Athabasca R   Hinton

JASPER

Mile 206: Here you cross the boundary of **Jasper National Park**. It's staggeringly vast, covering over 10,880 square km, with peaks as high as 3747 metres. It's the biggest of Canada's mountain national parks, and also one of the best for wildlife.

Mile 215: Now known as the **Devona Siding**, this was once the site of Jasper House, a supply post used by travellers crossing the mountains for the fur trade. It was built in 1817 by a merchant called Jasper Hawe whose name has proved a more enduring feature of the region than his store.

'A ride of two miles took us to Jasper's, where we arrived exactly fifteen days after leaving Edmonton... This station is now all but abandoned by the Hudson's Bay Cy. It was formerly of considerable importance, not only from the number of fur-bearing animals around, but because it was the centre of a regular line of communication between Norway House and Edmonton on the one side, and the Columbia District and Fort Vancouver on the other. An agent and three or four men were then stationed at it all the year round...Now, the houses are untenanted, locked and shuttered. Twice a year an agent comes up from Edmonton to trade with the Indians of the surrounding country and carry back the furs'.

Rev Grant, *Ocean to Ocean* (1873)

Mile 216(S): Jasper Lake is less than one mile wide, and is getting narrower and narrower because of the silt deposits carried here from the mountains by the Athabasca River.

Mile 235: Jasper   [70-minute stop]
If you hadn't planned to stop over in Jasper, you might well change your mind during the next seventy minutes. If you've been to Banff, you'll be amazed by the complete absence of taxi drivers, courier guides and general clamour at the train station of this quieter, calmer town. It's a lovely base for some of the best and most beautiful wilderness in Canada.

————————————— **RAILWAY SUBDIVISION** —————————————

JASPER TO KAMLOOPS

Mile 17 [PT]: You're now going through the **Yellowhead Pass** which provides a gap through the **continental divide.** The continental divide is the line following the main ranges of the Rocky Mountains; on one side of the line rivers flow west to the Pacific, on the other side they drain into the Arctic or the Atlantic. It is also the border between Alberta and British Columbia and is the point at which you move from Mountain Time into Pacific Time.

Mile 22(S): The shimmering **Yellowhead Lake** appears, framed by Mount Fitzwilliam and Mount Rockingham. It's one of the most beautiful views of the journey.

Mile 24(S): Here you get your first glimpse of the **Fraser River**. It was named after Simon Fraser who in 1808 was the first European to journey the 1368km to the river's mouth.

As you follow the course of the Fraser River, spare a thought for the millions of salmon who don't have such a smooth ride on their way to the Pacific and back again. The headwaters of the river's tributaries are the spawning ground of millions of Pacific Salmon. Around March the newly hatched fry begin their migration down the Fraser River to the Pacific Ocean. Only a quarter will make it. The survivors spend the next two and a half years swimming around the North Pacific where quite a few more will meet their end. Then the ones that are left begin their incredible journey back to the place of their birth, where they will spawn and die. They swim (upstream) at an average speed of 30km per day and literally leap over the obstacles in their path. This amazing cycle takes place once every four years.

Mile 36 (S): Moose Lake The pale green waters of this lake reflect the passing train and surrounding peaks like a mirror image. The lake is full of rainbow trout and is said to be a popular watering spot for moose.

The Travelling Reverend was much taken with the place in 1872 and wrote: 'Moose Lake that we struck last night but only got a tolerable view of today, is a beautiful sheet of water, ten or eleven miles long, by three wide...The survey for the Railway is proceeding along the north side, where the bluffs, though high appear not so sheer as on the south. The hillsides of the country

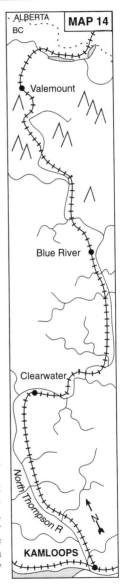

beyond support a growth of splendid spruce, black pine and Douglas fir, some of the spruce the finest any of us had ever seen. So far in our descent from the Pass, the difficulties in the way of the railroad are not formidable nor the grades likely to be heavy. Still, the work that the surveyors are engaged on requires a patience, hardihood, and fore-thought that few who ride in Pullman cars on the road in after years will ever appreciate'.

Mile 50 (S): Look out for a quick glimpse of the roaring waterfall at Glacier Creek.

Mile 52-60(N): Good views of **Mount Robson**, the tallest peak in the Canadian Rockies at 3954m. The native name for this mountain is 'Yuh Hai Has Hun' or 'mountain of spiritual road.'

Mile 66: The tracks veer south and the snow-capped mountains of the **Premier Range** come into view (W). The eleven peaks are named after Canadian and British prime ministers. The dominant peak is Mount Sir Wilfrid Laurier, covered by a huge glacier which also spreads onto Mount Mackenzie King and Mount Arthur Meighen.

Mile 73(S): The mountain you're passing is the **Terry Fox Memorial Mountain**, named in honour of the brave man who attempted to run across Canada to raise money and awareness for cancer research. Fox had already lost one leg to cancer when he set out on his 'marathon of hope' from St John's in April 1980; 5373km further on, in Thunder Bay, it was discovered that the cancer had spread to his lungs and he was forced to abandon the run. He died in June the following year, having raised $24 million.

British Columbia
This is Canada's most westerly province and quite possibly its most beautiful. Just short of a million square km in area, British Columbia embraces gentle ranch land, towering peaks, arid desert land and lush rainforest. About 70% of its land is covered by mountains, with most of this area unpopulated. British Columbians, numbering about three million, tend to live near the south-west coast, the majority of them concentrated in Vancouver. BC's population is the third highest in Canada after Ontario and Quebec. It is also the third largest province in surface area, after Quebec and Ontario. Only one American state, Alaska, is bigger than British Columbia.

   The province is home to an incredibly diverse range of communities, from the great British enclave in Victoria to the young and cosmopolitan crowd of Vancouver; and from the lumberjacks and miners of the interior to the North-West coastal tribes. The latter, which include the Haida, Kwakiutl and Nootka, are among the most culturally distinct native groups in Canada. Their art is currently undergoing a big renaissance, particularly the carving of totem poles.

Mile 74: Valemount* This little lumber town (population 1000) nestles in a wide valley between the Rocky, Cariboo and Monashee mountain ranges, at an elevation of 1100 metres.

Mile 91: Look west for a view of the stunning **Albreda Icefields Glacier** which is over 10,000 feet thick.

Mile 106: The train meets the North Thompson River and follows it for 26 miles to Blue River.

Mile 113 (S): The sparkling **Pyramid Falls** tumble 90 metres from a lake on Mount Cheadle.

Mile 132: Blue River This former railway centre has developed into a thriving outdoor resort, specialising in heli-skiing in the Monashee Mountains. Those mad enough and rich enough to indulge in this activity are whirled along glaciers at the cost of $200-500 a day.

──────── **RAILWAY SUBDIVISION** ────────

Mile 5: As you leave Blue River the landscape begins to change from one of mountains and lakes into a distinctly more rugged terrain.

Mile 8 (E): For the next eight miles the **North Thompson River** narrows into a stretch of turbulent, treacherous rapids known as **Little Hell's Gate** or Porte d'Enfer. The train skirts the river until it joins up with the Fraser River near Lytton, making numerous crossings from one bank to the other, following the path forced by engineers down the canyon.

'The roar of the water, as with increasing impetuosity it rushes past us, is almost deafening. It is, however, a grand sight, this foaming, roaring river forcing its way through a channel much too narrow for it, tearing down immense boulders and washing off portions of the rock in its course. The crash of falling boulders and the rattle of descending stones are frequently heard high above the turmoil of the surging torrent. It is just as if hell's flood were let loose; and the torn character of some of the precipices, with the rugged mass of fallen rocks below, increases the impression that some diabolic agency has been at work'. Cumberland, *The Queen's Highway* (1887)

Mile 20-21: Note the slide detectors along the wall of the mountain. Rock slides are common in this spot.

Mile 42: To the west you can make out the **Mad River Rapids**.

Mile 67: Clearwater* This logging and farming town provides a base for visitors to the Wells Gray Provincial Park, one of the most beautiful wilderness and recreational areas in British Columbia.

Mile 72(W): An osprey nest balances on a telegraph pole. Apparently these things cause so much trouble with the telegraph lines that false lines are erected where the birds can build their nests without disrupting Canada's telecommunications network.

Mile 74: Blackpool Named, apparently, because of the dark waters in this stretch of the river, and not after the great city of lights in the north of England.

'As we drew near Kamloops, characteristics of a different climate could be noted with increasing distinctness. A milder atmosphere, softer skies, easy rolling hills; but the total absence of underbrush and the dry grey grass everywhere covering the ground were the most striking differences to us, accustomed so long to the broad-leaved underbrush and dark green foliage of the humid upper country. We had clearly left the high rainy and entered the lower arid region'. Rev Grant, *Ocean to Ocean* (1873)

Mile 86: Before the highway came, the village of **Little Fort** used to operate a cable ferry across the Thompson River, powered only by the river's waters. You can still see the cables.

Mile 114: Fisherman used to stretch nets across the rapids you can see (W) to catch salmon. They're known as Fishtrap Rapids.

Mile 139: Kamloops [35-minute stop] Kamloops is one of BCs biggest cities with a population of 62,000. It's the province's most important cattle centre. It has also served as a busy centre of the fur trade, with trading bases established by the Pacific Fur Company in 1812 and the Hudson's Bay Company in 1821. The earliest inhabitants of the area were the Shuswap tribe who named their settlement cume-loups, meaning 'meeting of waters'. Kamloops is located at the meeting of the North Thompson and South Thompson Rivers.

───────────── **RAILWAY SUBDIVISION** ─────────────

KAMLOOPS TO VANCOUVER

The portion of the journey between Kamloops and Vancouver takes place mostly overnight on both westbound and eastbound VIA trains. For a detailed description of this route, see the **Rocky Mountaineer** route guide on page 182.

The Skeena:
Jasper to Prince Rupert

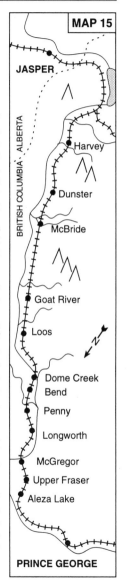

MAP 15

JASPER

Harvey

Dunster

McBride

Goat River

Loos

Dome Creek

Bend

Penny

Longworth

McGregor

Upper Fraser

Aleza Lake

PRINCE GEORGE

BRITISH COLUMBIA, ALBERTA

The Skeena takes you through some of the most beautiful wilderness in British Columbia – through the Rocky Mountains, into BC's Interior Plateau and up the Skeena Valley to Prince Rupert. On the way you'll pass snow-capped peaks, glaciers, fjords and waterfalls, and Indian villages with their famed totem poles. The journey takes just under 21 hours.

Mile 0-43: The train follows the same track as the Canadian between Jasper and Redpass Junction – see page 164.

Mile 0: Redpass Junction Here the Skeena parts company with the route followed by the Canadian.

As you head northwest, look out towards the rear of the train (E) for superb views of **Mount Robson**, the highest peak in the Rockies at 3954 metres (12,972ft). The views are particularly stunning around Mile 10. Look out for bears and moose; it was here that I made my only bear-sighting from any train.

Mile 14.5: The train passes Swiftwater, an old Grand Trunk Pacific stop so named for the racing waters of all the glacial streams nearby.

Mile 17: Here the train crosses the **Fraser River**. To the west are the 10-metre-high Rearguard Falls. In summer you might be able to spot spawning salmon trying to leap over the falls to continue their epic journey up the river.

Mile 20: Taverna This marks the end of an extremely short railway division.

──────────────── RAILWAY SUBDIVISION ────────────────

Mile 4: Tête Jaune This little hamlet is named after Pierre Hatsinaton, an early 19th century trapper who was known by all as Tête Jaune because of his famed golden locks (also celebrated in the name of the Yellowhead Pass).

The village was a stop on the route of the famous **Overlanders**, the name now given to a group of about 150 people who, in 1862, set out from Ontario to make their way to the British Columbian gold fields. The trans-Canada railway had not, of course, been built by then; the Overlanders had to take steamships and American railways to get to Fort Garry (Winnipeg). This marked the end of public transport: from here they continued their arduous journey using horses and carts. They set off from Fort Garry at the beginning of June and arrived in Fort Edmonton 21 July. This is where the going got really tough; they had to trade in their carts for pack horses and hire Indian guides to show them the paths through the Rockies.

The travellers arrived at Tête Jaune in late August. From here some rafted up the Fraser River to Fort George (Prince George); of these only six survived. Others rafted down to Kamloops, including the only woman of the party, Mrs Catherine Shubert who was pregnant at the time! The day following the party's arrival in Kamloops, Mrs Shubert gave birth to her fourth child.

Mile 63: McBride This village stands on a high plateau in the shadow of the Rocky Mountains. It's named after Richard McBride, British Columbia's youngest ever premier (he was 33 when he was elected in 1903). While the Grand Trunk Pacific was being built, this railway divisional point was a busy and booming little town. These days there are only about 500 people left. McBride is the last scheduled stop before Prince George. There are several flag stops dotted along the desolate stretch of track in between, but few people get on or off.

──────────────── RAILWAY SUBDIVISION ────────────────

Mile 69: Penny* This tiny hamlet, with a population of just over thirty people, is typical of the sparsely populated communities along this section of the line.

Mile 79: Longworth* Unlike Penny this settlement doesn't even have a station; just a little shack marking the stop.

Mile 122: Giscome* This is a village come down in the world; it once had the biggest sawmill in northern British Columbia but this was shut down in 1974.

Mile 146: Prince George [30-minute stop]
The train goes over a half-mile-long bridge across the Fraser River on approaching Prince George. The city, with a population of 67,000 is British Columbia's third largest. It's situated at the junction of the Nechako and Fraser Rivers just under 800km north of Vancouver. Simon Fraser established the Fort George fur-trading post here in 1807. The place really took off when the GTP made it an important railway divisional point. Today the main industries are logging and mining. Unless you're getting off here (and to be honest there aren't that many good reasons to) you're not likely to see much of Prince George as the thirty-minute stop takes place in the pitch black of night.

Mile 69: Vanderhoof This little town is named after Herbert Vanderhoof who was hired by the GTP to devise a huge advertising campaign to persuade Americans to move up and settle in the Canadian North West. Apparently his efforts were very successful, though it's hard to believe it travelling through the region today.

Mile 93: This is where the last spike was driven on the Grand Trunk Pacific Railway on 7 April 1914.

Mile 94: Fort Fraser Like Prince George, this was originally a fur-trading post established by Simon Fraser. Today it's a lumbering village of about 400 people.

Mile 115: Endako With a population of just 100, Endako is a tiny railway divisional point. Its economy revolves around the mining of molybdenum (a metallic element with a very high melting point that's used to strengthen iron and steel). This strange substance is Canada's third most valuable metal after copper and gold.

―――――――――――――――― RAILWAY SUBDIVISION ――――――――――――――――

Mile 33: The train skirts Burns Lake (W); note the little island in the middle of the lake. This has been known as **Deadman's Island** ever since an explosion on the track during the construction of the railway caused the death of thirty men, fifteen of whom were standing on this island.

Mile 35: Burns Lake Settlers established a town here in the 1870s when the Overland Telegraph line to Alaska and Siberia was being built (the line was never completed). When the GTP arrived it began to grow quite rapidly and is still flourishing today with four mines (including a molybdenum mine) and two large saw mills.

Mile 51(E): Rose Lake's waters flow in two different directions: east through the Endako and Nechako rivers and west to the Bulkley River. The train now follows the Bulkley westwards.

Mile 85: Houston Originally called Pleasant Valley, the settlement was renamed in 1910 after John Houston who established Prince Rupert's first newspaper. About 4000 people live here today, most of them employed in the town's sawmill or pulp mill.

Mile 105: Look north as the train travels up the Bulkley Valley for your first view of the snow-capped **Skeena Mountains**.

Mile 116: Telkwa Another small settlement established by the Overland Telegraph as it advanced towards Alaska.

Mile 125: Smithers   **[25-minute stop]**
Nestling in the Bulkley Valley and surrounded by four mountain ranges, this busy little town (pop about 5000) has an idyllic setting. The mountains behind the station are part of the Skeena Range, and opposite the station you can see the Hudson Bay Range. This is the first station after your night on the train where you have the opportunity to get off and take a stroll along the platform.

———————————— **RAILWAY SUBDIVISION** ————————————

Mile 3(E): This lake used to be called Chicken Lake but this was deemed inappropriate by the GTP who changed it to the somewhat duller Lake Kathlyn.

Mile 5: For some time the train has been getting closer and closer to Hudson Bay Mountain (W); at this point you get a superb view of the

---

Totem Poles
Everyone knows what a totem pole is, but not everyone knows that they are made almost exclusively in North-West British Columbia by Indian tribes. Contrary to popular belief these carved cedar logs are not used for religious worship. Their functions are as diverse as marking a grave, supporting a roof, celebrating a house-moving, or ridiculing a local individual (whose likeness is painted upside down).

    The tallest, brightest and most elaborately carved totem poles tell of family histories or legends using a complicated series of symbols, often in the form of animals or spirits. Each family has its own symbols, so interpretation of the story on a totem pole usually requires a narrator from the family that constructed it. Unfortunately the poles have a relatively short life span, since the moisture of the climate rots the wood.

Kathlyn Glacier on the mountain – a giant slab of ice more than one hundred metres thick.

Mile 13: The train now takes you through a long tunnel after which it starts to climb high above the Bulkley River.

Mile 28-36: Some wonderful, soaring trestle bridges ahead: one over Boulder Creek at Mile 28, then another over Porphyry Creek at Mile 31. Both bridges sweep round to the north giving excellent views along the train. At Mile 36 you cross a further trestle over Mud Creek – with stunning mountain views on all sides.

Mile 40: The Skeena goes through a 630-metre-long tunnel, the longest of the journey. It's followed by two more tunnels – as the train travels between them look down for a quick glimpse of the Bulkley Gate, a huge 'gate' of rock jutting out into the river.

Mile 45: New Hazleton There are three Hazletons in the area: South Hazleton, New Hazleton and Hazleton. They all have a rich collection of totem poles. It is just after New Hazleton that the train finally joins up with the Skeena River.

Mile 50: Here the train crosses the Sealy Gulch bridge. It's 275 metres long and soars sixty metres above the water. Once over the bridge the train makes its way into the Skeena Valley. The scenery is breath-taking from here to Prince Rupert.

Mile 73: Kitwanga The translation of Kitwanga is 'the people of the place of plenty of rabbits'. No doubt the GTP were unaware of this or they would surely have changed it to something more seemly. This pretty Indian village is famous for its row of enormous, beautifully preserved **totem poles**, some as high as eighteen metres.

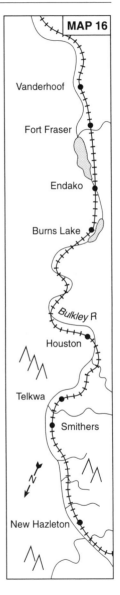

These poles are not visible from the train, but if you look south just after passing the station you can see some other less ornate ones. If you're going to Vancouver be sure to visit the art gallery where you can see some excellent paintings by Emily Carr of the totem poles in this region.

Mile 75: As you leave Kitwanga the view to the south is dominated by the striking **Seven Sisters** mountain. The jagged peaks remain in view for the next 20 miles or so.

Mile 81: Cedarvale Founded in the 1880s by a missionary who successfully converted all of the resident natives and turned the village into a hive of Christianity.

Mile 107: Pacific A former railway divisional point, Pacific was emptied almost overnight when the railway division was transferred to Terrace. For a long while it was an abandoned and derelict ghost town but has recently begun to be repopulated.

Mile 119: Usk Look out for Usk's ferry which uses the force of the waters to power the boat back and forth across the Skeena River.

Mile 121-123: The river banks give way to the solid rock of the Kitselas Canyon which the train cuts through in four tunnels. Just before you enter the first tunnel, look down to the river to see a whirlpool at the canyon's mouth.

Mile 131: Terrace With a population of over 10,000 Terrace is the first community for a long while that can safely be called a town. It was named Terrace because of the flat terraces of land lining the banks of the river.

─────────────── **RAILWAY SUBDIVISION** ───────────────

Mile 45: Travelling through the **Coast Mountains**, the train moves into what is probably the most stunning landscape of the journey. To the south the **Skeena River** is dotted with numerous little islands. Immediately north are the fern-covered mountainsides, just a few

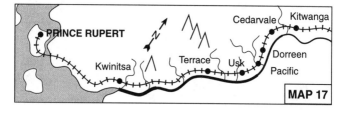

metres from the track. Waterfalls plunge down the rock of the mountains, the most abundant and beautiful occurring between miles 46 and 50.

Look out also for the bald eagles that are very common in this area: about six swooped and circled around our train for almost a mile around this point.

Mile 48: Kwinitsa This very picturesque station is located in a dangerous avalanche spot – note the snowsheds on the side of the mountain.

Miles 65-70: The views across the river (S) are extremely beautiful. The emerald green islands seems to loom out of the swirling mists of the Skeena, an Indian word meaning 'river of mists'. The whole thing looks like a travel brochure for the Norwegian fjords.

Mile 83(S): Smith Island was the location of a remote settlement at the turn of the century, which stands as an abandoned ghost town today.

Mile 87: The train goes over the Zanardi Rapids and onto Kaien Island. Prince Rupert is located a few miles away.

Mile 92: Just before you get to Prince Rupert you pass the ferry terminals (S) from where passengers depart on their journey up to Alaska on the Alaska Marine Highway or down to Vancouver Island with British Columbia Ferries.

Mile 94: Prince Rupert
You'll notice the drop in temperature as soon as you get off the train: Alaska is, after all, just forty miles away. The town (pop. around 16,000) is surrounded by deep-green mountains which seem to rise right out of the sea. The two tallest peaks are over 600 metres. There's not much to do here but it's a beautiful place to do nothing in.

• **Where to stay**: Accommodation isn't too hard to come by in Prince Rupert. If you want to lodge in style and comfort, **The Coast Hotel** (☎ 624-6711) at 118 6th Street has rooms for $99, many of them with stunning harbour views (it's definitely worth checking for discounts here but not in July and August).

You could also try the **Aleeda** (☎ 627-1711) at 900 3rd Ave, where you can get a room from around $50.

Place names

The names of many places or geographic features in Canada are taken from native languages, especially on the West Coast. The translations of these are often highly evocative. Take, for example, Yoho ('awesome'); Kitimat ('people of the snow'); Skeena ('river of mists'); Cowichan ('mountain warming its back'); Squalix ('restful'), Toketic ('beautiful place'); Chaumox ('too hot'); Shawnigan ('great battle') and Nanaimo ('big strong tribe') – all in British Columbia. Manitoba takes its name from the Ojibwan words 'manito waba' which, referring to the rapids of Lake Manitoba, means 'the sound of the great spirit Manitou.' Its capital, Winnipeg, is derived from 'win-nipi', meaning 'murky waters'.

Other interesting Indian place names include Nipigon (ON) meaning 'clear, fast water'; Oakshela (SK), meaning 'child'; Sintaluta (SK) which means 'tail of the red fox; Shubenacadie (NS) meaning 'the place where potatoes grow'; Stewiacke (NS) meaning 'oozing from dead water' and Nappan (NS) which means 'good place for wigwam poles.'

There are also some interesting English and French names. In Quebec there's Rivière-du-Loup (after the wolves that once gathered around the water); Chaudière (describing the rapids as a 'boiling kettle'); Pointe-aux-trembles (after a host of trembling trees) and Grandmère (after a rock in the river looking like a crouching old woman). English names range from the poetic (eg Moonlight in Ontario) to the bizarre, such as Eyebrow in Saskatoon, and Joe Batt's Arm and Come by Chance in Newfoundland. Naturally, you don't get a country with as much water as Canada without a good variety of place names dedicated to the stuff – Swift Current, Clearwater, Floods, Wolf Creek, Moose Lake, Canoe River, Mud Bay, Seal Cove and Ocean Pond, to name but a few.

The Rocky Mountaineer:
Calgary to Vancouver

The privately-owned Rocky Mountaineer travels between Vancouver and Jasper or Vancouver and Banff/Calgary in a two-day journey during daylight hours. Trains for both destinations join together for the journey up to (or back from) Kamloops, where passengers spend the night.

After Kamloops, Jasper-bound trains take the northern route through the Rockies via the Yellowhead Pass, while travellers going to Banff or Calgary take the original, southern route on CPR tracks. This is the only passenger train to travel along part of Canada's first transcontinental line, completed in 1886.

This guide describes the route between Calgary and Kamloops, and then between Kamloops and Vancouver: the latter is also the final portion of VIA Rail's Canadian route between Toronto and Vancouver. The section between Jasper and Kamloops is described in the guide to the Canadian on page 164.

CALGARY/BANFF TO KAMLOOPS

Mile 0: Calgary (MT) Home of cowboys, stampedes and oil-wells, Calgary is Canada's most famous prairie city. It's also the city closest to the Rocky Mountains that has an international airport, with plenty of scheduled and charter flights arriving from all over the world.

Mile 16(S): Look to the front of the train for your first glimpse of the Rocky Mountains, which are about 70km away.

Mile 24: Cochrane Just beyond the station is the Cochrane Landmark, a bronze statue of a cowboy riding his horse.

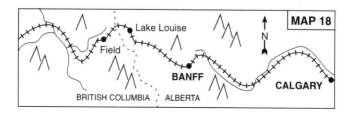

Mile 45: The peaks loom closer and closer as the train advances towards the mountains. To the north you can see Saddle Peak and Orient Peak and to the south you can see Heart Mountain.

Mile 54: Kananaskis The name of this village is Indian for 'man with a tomahawk in his head' and is named after a local native who survived the experience in question.

Mile 66(S): The Three Sisters Mountain was given this name by the brother of Major AB Rogers (the explorer who discovered Rogers Pass) because he thought its peaks looked like three nuns.

Mile 71: Banff National Park At this point the train crosses the eastern boundary of Banff National Park. It was originally known as the Rocky Mountain National Park when it was founded in 1887 (when there were just two other national parks in the world).

It was when the railway was being constructed that Banff's famous hot springs were discovered, prompting immediate claims to the land by men hoping to reap a profit. The Canadian Government decided that the area must be protected from commercial development and established the park. Today it encompasses 6640 square km and is Canada's most heavily visited national park, attracting almost three million visitors each year.

Mile 73(S): For the next eight miles the train skirts the towering **Mount Rundle**.

Mile 81: Banff The station was originally known as 'Siding 29' by the railway men building the line; it was renamed in 1880 by Donald Smith of the CPR.

Today the town (population 4600) is a busy (and some would say overcrowded) base for thousands of tourists, providing them with an impressive quantity of hotels, restaurants and shops.

Its most famous hotel is the exclusive **Banff Springs Hotel**, formally opened by William Cornelius Van Horne for the CPR back in 1888. You can see the green turrets of its copper roof as you pass it on the train at Mile 82 (S).

Mile 99(N): Excellent views of **Castle Mountain**, with its broad, flat top. The mountain was originally named in the 1850s by the explorer, James Hector; but it was officially changed to Mount Eisenhower in 1946. This change of name was strongly resisted by local people who lobbied to have it changed back. In 1979 the government duly gave back the mountain its original name, allotting Eisenhower Peak to the mountain's highest point.

Mile 116(S): Watch out for a quick flash of **Victoria Glacier**. You can't see much of it from the train but fear not; you will see its image rising over Lake Louise thousands of times on thousands of postcards, calendars and tea towels before you get out of Canada.

Mile 116.5(S): Lake Louise station This is no longer used by the railways; the beautifully preserved log building now serves as a restaurant.

Mile 122: Stephen [PT] At 1625 metres above sea level, this is the highest point on the CPR line. It's also the point at which the train crosses the Continental Divide.

Mile 128: Spiral Tunnels Here the train goes through the extraordinary Spiral Tunnels.

When the CPR decided to build the track through the Kicking Horse Pass they hadn't quite reckoned on the steepness of the drop on the western side of Mount Stephen. There was no time or money for building tunnels, so the track plunged straight down for eight miles at a dizzying 4.5 percent gradient – more than twice the grade normally permitted by the government. This hazardous stretch of track was known as the **Big Hill**. Trains made it to the top only with the help of four specially designed locomotives with 154-tonne engines; two pulled at the front, and another two pushed from behind. Most dangerous, though, was the trip down the hill. All passenger trains stopped at the top so that the brakes could be thoroughly checked before the heart-stopping descent began. Safety switches were operated to divert runaway trains onto uphill tracks. Nonetheless, many lives were lost as a result of trains losing control.

The danger was finally eliminated when the **Spiral Tunnels** were built in 1909, reducing the gradient to 2.2%. This was achieved by curving the track 250 degrees through the Upper Spiral, and then 230 degrees through the Lower Spiral. The train loops around in a sort of figure of eight, in such a way that the rear of the train crosses over the front of the train, several feet below.

Mile 136: Field Once a busy railway divisional point, Field's economy now revolves around the tourism industry in Yoho National Park.

──────────────── **RAILWAY SUBDIVISION** ────────────────

Mile 20: The train, following the course of the **Kicking Horse River**, enters the Kicking Horse Canyon. The river takes its name from an incident in which Dr James Hector, a member of the Palliser expedition commissioned to explore western Canada in 1857-60, was thrown off his horse when he rode it into the river's rushing waters. Hector was badly injured by a kick from the frightened horse, but he continued with the expedition.

Mile 35: The Kicking Horse River meets the Columbia River which the train will follow for the next twenty-five miles. To the south you can see the Beaverfoot Range, and to the north the Van Horne Range.

Mile 62: Beavermouth This is the site of the riots by a group of striking railwaymen, desperate for their long-overdue wages in the middle of the CPR's financial crisis of 1884. It's reputed to be a good place for sighting bears.

Mile 70: Photo opportunities abound as the train crosses a series of high bridges. First is the 183-metre-long **Mountain Creek Bridge**. Then, at Mile 74, is a bridge over **Surprise Creek**, over 50 metres below. Finally you reach the climax, the crossing of the highest bridge on the CPR line: **Stoney Creek Bridge** at Mile 76. It's 147 metres long and curves 99 metres over the water. For the next twenty miles you'll be surrounded by breath-taking mountain vistas as you travel through the heart of the Selkirks.

Mile 80: The train enters the five-mile-long **Connaught Tunnel**, built to avoid the dangerous avalanches that plagued the route over Rogers Pass. It was completed in 1916 and until 1988 was the longest tunnel in North America. This record is now held by the **Mount McDonald Tunnel**, nine miles long and built underneath the Connaught Tunnel. It is used by westbound freight trains.

Mile 94: Note the concrete snowsheds above the train (N); there are frequent avalanches in this area.

Mile 125: Revelstoke This small city of around 8000 people was named after Lord Revelstoke, an English banker who helped bail the CPR out of their financial difficulties in 1884.

─────────── **RAILWAY SUBDIVISION** ───────────

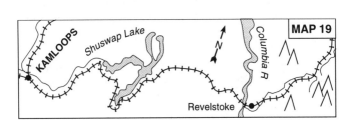

Mile 5: The train is now on its way up the last big climb, this time up the Monashee Mountains which it will cross via Eagle Pass. There are waterfalls at this point on both sides of the train.

Mile 28: Craigellachie On 7 November 1885 when Donald Smith drove in the last spike of the CPR trans-Canada railway here in **Eagle Pass**, no fanfare marked the occasion. The only monument to that triumphant completion is a plaque on a cairn by the side of the track (N).

Mile 44: For the next twenty-five miles the train skirts the Salmon Arm of **Shuswap Lake**, which boasts prodigious quantities of Dolly Varden and kokanee salmon. Note the colourful houseboats moored in the lake.

Mile 82: Look south for a glorious view over Shuswap Lake.

Mile 100: At this point the train starts to move away from the forested mountains into a landscape of gently rolling hills.

Mile 103(N): Look out for the **hoodoos** standing on the hillside. These fantastic pillars of rock have been eroded into strange shapes by wind, rain and running water.

Mile 111(S): If you're wondering what's growing in these fields it is, in fact, ginseng. Once grown only in Korea and Manchuria, this plant is now thriving in British Columbia.

Mile 114: This is the site of Bill Miner's least successful train robbery. Miner, known as the Gentleman Bandit, was a famous Canadian train robber in the early 20th century. In 1904 he had robbed a CPR train near Mission (BC) of $7000, but when he tried to pull off the same stunt at this spot two years later he got the wrong train and ended up with only $15 and a bottle of pills. The robber, getting on for 60 by now, was obviously losing his touch: he was captured by police and sent to jail for 25 years. He did, however, manage to escape a year later and took off to the US where he spent the rest of his days robbing more trains.

Mile 128: Kamloops This is where you get off the Rocky Mountaineer for your overnight stay at a nearby hotel. For a brief description of Kamloops, see page 168. The route description to Vancouver continues overleaf.

RAILWAY SUBDIVISION

KAMLOOPS TO VANCOUVER

Mile 1: The train will follow the South Thompson River (S) as far as Lytton, 97 miles away. The track is carved into the rocky cliffs of the Thompson Canyon and switches back and forth across the river. The colours of the canyon walls are muted reds and browns, and the desert-like landscape contrasts sharply with the lush mountains you passed on your previous day's journey.

Mile 49: Ashcroft This is one of Canada's driest towns, with an average annual rainfall of just 18 centimetres.

Rev Grant was not charmed by the place when he was here in 1872 and wrote: 'The country about Ashcroft is sparsely peopled, and men accustomed to the rich grassy plains on the other side of the mountains might wonder at first sight that it is peopled at all. In appearance, it is little better than a vast sand and gravel pit, bounded by broken hills, bald and arid except on a few summits that support a scanty growth of scrub pines. The cattle had eaten off all the bunch-grass within three or four miles of the road, and a poor substitute for it chiefly in the shape of a bluish weed or shrub, called 'sage grass' or 'sage brush' has taken its place'.

Mile 85-90: The canyon narrows into what is known as **Jaws of Death Gorge**. Look down to the racing waters of **Suicide Rapids** at Mile 87.

Mile 90-95: Rainbow Canyon The walls of the cliffs are suddenly striped with pinks, greens and greys creating a beautiful rainbow effect.

Mile 97: Lytton This is where the Thompson River meets the Fraser River which the train will follow nearly all the way to Vancouver, through the Fraser Canyon. It is said that you can sometimes see a clear line dividing the Thompson's clear waters from the Fraser's murky waters for some distance after they meet.

In *The Queen's Highway* Cumberland described the impressive scene in 1887: 'Six miles below Lytton a gulch, deeper and broader than any of the preceding ones, presents itself. To cross it by an ordinary bridge would be impossible, and a cantilever bridge, 96 feet above low-water mark, has been constructed at a great cost for the purpose.

As one crosses the bridge a magnificent scene presents itself in thus being suspended over the surging, maddening river, increased in force by the waters of the North Thompson River, and with a full view of the gloomy canyon through which we have passed'.

Mile 103: The train crosses the Fraser River on one of the **Cisco Bridges** – a spectacular crossing high above the river's turbulent waters.

There are two bridges side by side – one built by the CPR in the 1880s, the other by the CNR about thirty years later. As you cross the CNR bridge, look behind for a view of the beautiful cantilever CPR bridge.

Mile 125: Boston Bar This village was established by fortune-seekers of the Fraser River gold rush of 1858.

──────── **RAILWAY SUBDIVISION** ────────

Mile 7: Don't miss the dramatic **Hell's Gate** where the river is forced to squeeze through the narrowest point of the gorge at high speed.

The narrowing was caused by a huge landslide triggered off by an explosion during the construction of the CN line. The landslide, blocking the sockeye salmon run that annually ascends the river, had a catastrophic effect on the fishing industry; fishways have since been constructed in an attempt to remedy the problem.

Mile 40: Hope A fur-trading post was established here in 1848 but it was from the 1858 gold rush that the town grew affluent. At Hope the rugged rocks of the Fraser Canyon recede into the fertile Fraser Valley, surrounded by verdant mountains.

Mile 71: Chilliwack This is a busy agriculture-based city of around 42,000 people. Its name is thought to mean 'going back up' (probably from the river) in a local native language.

Mile 87: Matsqui This stop is close to the town of **Mission**, originally settled in 1862 by a Roman Catholic priest who aimed to

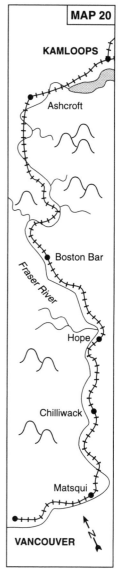

MAP 20

KAMLOOPS

Ashcroft

Boston Bar

Fraser River

Hope

Chilliwack

Matsqui

N

VANCOUVER

convert the Indians. It was also the site of Canada's first train robbery.

Mile 111: Port Coquitlam: The train passes an enormous CP rail yard here (N); it covers 468 acres and can hold 3700 rail cars.

Mile 131: Vancouver The journey ends in Canada's third largest and fastest growing city. For more information on Vancouver, see page 126.

The Hudson Bay: Winnipeg to Churchill

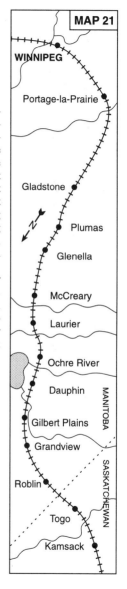

MAP 21

WINNIPEG

Portage-la-Prairie

Gladstone

Plumas

Glenella

McCreary

Laurier

Ochre River

Dauphin

Gilbert Plains

Grandview

Roblin

Togo

Kamsack

MANITOBA

SASKATCHEWAN

What possesses people to travel one thousand miles by train through bleak, monotonous landscape to Canada's freezing subarctic? Especially when they know they've got to get on the same train and make the same long journey back again. There's not much to see (lakes, trees and tundra) but there's something curiously exciting about travelling through such desolation, going somewhere you can't get to by car, reaching the ultimate end-of-the-line. Apart from this, Churchill is a fascinating place to spend some time if you're interested in wildlife.

The railway, built at great expense over many years and completed in 1929, was intended to transport grain up to Hudson Bay where it would be shipped off to Russia. The bay, however, is frozen over for nine months of the year which somewhat restricts ocean going activity.

The line runs at an enormous loss and is probably one of VIA's biggest headaches, but closure would be highly controversial as the train is the only connection with the outside world for the many native communities along the line. Still, it's hard to know how long the service will survive, so take the opportunity to go on this wonderful dinosaur of a journey while you can.

Mile 0: Winnipeg You set out around 10pm from Winnipeg's Union Station. For details on Winnipeg, see page 111.

Mile 55: Portage-la-Prairie At this point the Hudson Bay leaves the tracks used by the Canadian to begin its lonely trek north.

Mile 91: Gladstone Dubbed 'Happy Rock' by the train's mirthful crew, this little town was originally called Palestine when it was settled by Ontario farmers in the 1870s. Today it's famous in the region for its large cattle auction.

Mile 121: Dauphin This prosperous distribution and transportation centre is one of the oldest Ukrainian settlements in Canada (they established an agricultural community here in the 1890s). The Ukrainian influence continues to be strong, and Dauphin hosts Canada's annual National Ukrainian Festival which has been going since the 1960s. Dauphin lies in a fertile valley between Riding Mountain and Duck Lake Provincial Parks.

──────────────── RAILWAY SUBDIVISION ────────────────

Mile 62: Roblin Situated on the banks of Goose Lake near the Manitoba/Saskatchewan border, this small agricultural town was founded by the Canadian Northern Railway after the arrival of the first train from Dauphin in 1903. One of Manitoba's first co-operative grain elevators was built here by local farmers.

Mile 79: Togo Just on the other side of the Manitoba/Saskatchewan border is this little mixed farming village.

Mile 100: Kamsack Named after a prominent local Indian, this village (population about 2500) was on one of the fur-trading routes for many years.

Mile 108: Veregin Founded by the Doukhobors in 1899 and named after the movement's leader, Peter Vasilevish Veregin. The Doukhobors were Russians who dissented radically from the Orthodox Church, believing that God is found not in churches but within each man. They rejected secular governments, advocated pacifism and believed that the Bible should be communicated orally rather than via the written word.

Following periodic persecution in Russia the Doukhobors were permitted to emigrate to Canada in 1898-99, in some part thanks to the efforts of Leo Tolstoy and the Quakers. Over 7000 sailed over, most of these settling in western Canada which the government was doing its best to populate at the time.

Mile 124: Canora Take the first two letters of each word in 'Canadian Northern Railway' and what do you get? Thus the town was established and named by the aforementioned company in 1904 when they located a divisional point here.

Mile 93: Hudson Bay You've still got a long way to go before you get to the bay itself; this town was named by the Canadian Northern Railway in 1908 to commemorate the first phase of the Hudson Bay Railway.

--------- RAILWAY SUBDIVISION ---------

Mile 88: The Pas [75-minute stop]
A welcome chance to get off the train, just after breakfast, to stretch your legs and get some fresh air for a whole hour and a quarter. The Pas lies on the south bank of the Saskatchewan River and has been, in its time, an Indian settlement, a fur-trading centre and a fishing and lumbering town. The town-site was bought in 1906 from the Cree inhabitants, who now live on the northern banks of the river.

Take a look at the attractive **Anglican Church of the Messiah**, dating from 1840. Some of the furniture inside was carved by members of a rescue party searching for **Sir John Franklin** and his fellow explorers who'd disappeared on their search for the North-West Passage. European explorers had been looking for a water route through North America to the Orient ever since it was discovered that this continent blocked the way to Asia. Franklin's expedition was hoping to discover a route through the Arctic when it went missing in 1845; what followed was one of the largest ever rescue operations of its kind. Franklin was never found, and efforts to solve the mystery continued well into the 20th century. The bodies of some crew members were discovered buried on Beechy Island, perfectly preserved by the permafrost. In 1986 these were temporarily exhumed and analysed by scientists: they discovered evidence of scurvy and probably cannibalism among the men.

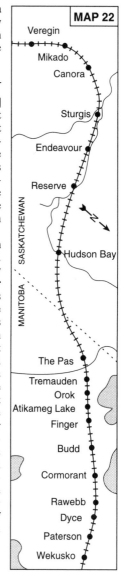

Another famous explorer in search of the elusive North-West Passage was **Henry Hudson** who set out to find it back in 1610. He took his expedition into the huge bay and sailed down the eastern coast, where he was forced to winter his boat.

When the ice broke up Hudson set about continuing the exploration to the dismay of his crew. A mutiny broke out and the rebels packed Hudson, his son and other supporters into a boat and set them adrift on the bay to die. It is in honour of this unfortunate leader that Hudson Bay is named.

As the train pulls out of **The Pas** look north as you cross the river at the Otineka Mall, part of the Indian Reserve and renowned for its finely crafted goods.

──────────────── **RAILWAY SUBDIVISION** ────────────────

Mile 9: This is where the lakes start. The first one you can see is Tremaudan Lake (E). Next, at Mile 13 (W), is Clearwater Lake. Then at Mile 31 you can see **Cormorant Lake** (W). This is an important nesting habitat for waterfowl; keep your eyes open for geese, teal and crow-ducks. You'll pass many more lakes along this stretch.

If you're travelling during spring or summer, look out for the numerous wild flowers growing alongside the track: tiger lilies, brown-eyed Suzies, pink lady's slippers and honeysuckle are particularly abundant. The ground is also punctuated by curious limestone rock formations.

Mile 29: The little village of Budd was named after Henry Budd, the first native in western Canada to be ordained as an Anglican Minister (in 1853).

Mile 37: The train passes two large osprey nests on the top of telegraph poles right by the side of the track (E).

Mile 41: Cormorant This was one of the first settlements to spring up along the line once the railway was completed. There'll probably be quite a few people getting on or off here, mainly Indian or Inuit families. Note that the word 'Eskimo' is not a polite way to refer to an Inuit – it means 'eater of raw flesh' in the Algonquian language. 'Inuit', on the hand, simply means 'people'.

Mile 55: Rawebb You'd be forgiven for thinking Rawebb was an Indian place name – in fact the village was named after a former mayor of Winnipeg, Ralph Webb.

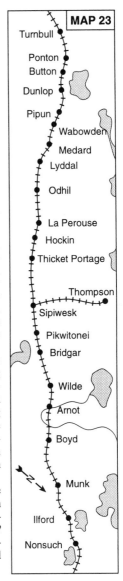

Mile 81: Wekusko This tiny settlement of around fifty people is located on one of the few roads in the region, a thirty-five-mile link to the nearby town of Snow Lake.

Mile 90: The limestone rock gives way to *muskeg* (an Algonquian word meaning 'grassy bog'). Muskeg is organic terrain which produces peat deposits. Where there's muskeg there's often permafrost, which the train will be moving into presently.

Mile 136: Wabowden Situated between the tiny Bowden and Rock Island Lakes, Wabowden serves as a supply centre for the communities in northern Manitoba. Between here and Thicket Portage look out for pelicans and bald eagles.

Mile 177: Hockin This village was named in honour of Corporal CH Hockin of the North West Mounted Police who was killed in 1897 in a shootout with a Cree outlaw known as **Almighty Voice** (or Kah-kee-say-mane-too-wayo). Almighty Voice had been imprisoned for stealing a cow and when he escaped from jail he killed a mountie in the process.

Police hunted him for almost two years before cornering him with a couple of young relatives. The Indians were up against a hundred police and civilians but they put up a fierce fight, killing three men (including Hockin). In the end the fugitives were killed, and the incident has become a symbol of the tragically violent confrontation between the Indians and the whites in North America.

Back in 1872, Butler wrote: 'Terrible deeds have been wrought out in that western land; terrible heart-sickening deeds of cruelty and rapacious infamy – have been I say? no, are to this day and hour, and never perhaps more sickening than now in the full blaze of nineteenth century civilisation. If on the long line of the American frontier, from the Gulf of Mexico to the British boundary, a single life is taken by an Indian, if even horse or ox be stolen from a settler, the fact is chronicled in scores of journals throughout the United States, but the reverse of the story we never know. The countless deeds of perfidious robbery, of ruthless murder done by white savages out in these Western wilds never find the light of day. The poor red man has no telegraph, no newspaper, no type, to tell his sufferings and his woes. My God, what a terrible tale could I not tell of these dark deeds done by the white savage against the far nobler red man!' (*The Great Lone Land*).

Mile 184: Thicket Portage Fur traders used this as a land crossing between the lakes and streams which connect Lake Winnipeg to the Nelson River (which goes up to Hudson Bay).

One of the crew told me that back in the '70s the mayor of Thicket Portage was given a large sum of money to have a road constructed in the area. Instead, he took off to Hawaii with his mates for a holiday. The locals were furious and practically lynched him on his return. For a while he was reduced to trapping and selling furs to earn his crusts, but when it became clear that no one else was willing to do the job, he found himself reinstated as mayor!

Mile 200: At **Sipiwesk** the train leaves the main line to follow a thirty-mile branch line to Thompson and back.

Mile 30: Thompson   [90-minute stop]
This busy industrial city of 15,000 people is something of a surprise after all the remote communities and stretches of wilderness you've been going through. It was created from scratch following the discovery of abundant nickel deposits in 1956, and named after John F Thompson, the chairman of INCO.

Unfortunately the railway station is a few miles from the city, so there's very little to do here in your one and a half hour stop unless you're prepared to take a taxi into town and back. The attractions of Thompson aren't, however, really worth the risk of being left behind by the train.

Mile 200: Four hours later you're back in **Sipiwesk** – a depressing lack of advancement.

Mile 213: Pikwitonei This name is taken from the Cree word meaning 'broken mouth' though no-one seems to be sure why. Perhaps another bust-up between mounties and natives?

Mile 230: Wilde This place name definitely does come from another Indian-NWMP confrontation, this time in 1886. Sergeant WB Wilde was killed in the incident and the village is named to commemorate him.

Mile 238.3 This flag stop is known simply by its mileage. By the time you get here it'll probably be night time again.

Mile 269: Munk Named after Jens Munk, the first European to discover what is now Churchill. The Danish navigator arrived in September 1619 with his two ships carrying forty-eight men. They were forced to spend winter there and suffered an outbreak of scurvy. Only three men survived; Munk was one of them.

Mile 295: Nonsuch This village is named after the famous ship owned by the Hudson's Bay Company.

Mile 326: Gillam With a population of nearly 2000, this is the biggest community since Thompson. The town's economy is based on its three hydroelectric power stations on the Nelson River.

Mile 350: Around here the train leaves the Laurentian Plateau and moves into the Hudson Bay lowlands. From here onwards the muskeg is permanently frozen, a condition known as permafrost. The frost extends about 12 metres down, making engineering

'Beyond a doubt it was cold; I don't mean cold in the ordinary manner, cold such as you can localise to your feet, or your fingers, or your nose, but cold all over, crushing cold. Putting on coat and moccasins as close to the fire as possible, I ran to the tree on which I had hung the thermometer on the previous evening; it stood at 37 below zero'.
Butler, *The Great Lone Land* (1872)

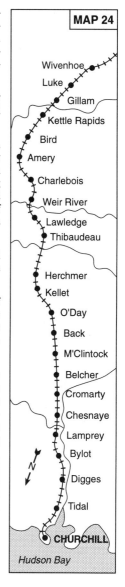

MAP 24

Wivenhoe
Luke
Gillam
Kettle Rapids
Bird
Amery
Charlebois
Weir River
Lawledge
Thibaudeau
Herchmer
Kellet
O'Day
Back
M'Clintock
Belcher
Cromarty
Chesnaye
Lamprey
Bylot
Digges
Tidal
CHURCHILL
Hudson Bay

work extremely difficult. The telegraph wires have to be supported by three poles forming a tripod.

Mile 440-80: When morning breaks you'll probably be travelling through the Barren Lands. Pull up your blinds and prepare to be dazzled by snow (for most of the year, anyway). The trees have nearly all vanished, and the ones that are left are stunted and shrivelled. You've gone beyond the tree line, into the sub-arctic tundra. Keep your eyes peeled for arctic ptarmigan and silver fox.

Mile 509: Churchill At long, long last!

CHURCHILL AT A GLANCE

History
There have been Inuit settlements in this area for thousands of years, though little trace is left of these.

The first Europeans arrived when the Danish navigator Jens Munk led an expedition in search of the North-West Passage 1619-20. He was forced to winter his ship near the mouth of the Churchill River. Of the forty-eight men on board, only he and two others survived the winter; the rest died of scurvy. Later, in 1717, the Hudson's Bay Company established a fur-trading post here which remained active for the next hundred and fifty years. If the journal of Captain James Knight is anything to go by, it was not a popular posting. His entry for 16 July 1717 reads: 'I never did See such a Miserable Place in my Life'.

When the post was no longer used, Churchill was almost forgotten until the grain boom on the prairies at the beginning of this century. Politicians and farmers campaigned for a port on Hudson Bay, and eventually one was established at Churchill, connected to Winnipeg by the new railway line.

Churchill today
The town is as bleak and inhospitable as its sub-arctic surroundings. There's a feeling of dereliction about the place, and unemployment is high among its population of 1000 (especially among the natives). Once you've visited the Eskimo Museum there's very little to do in the town itself; Churchill's principal attraction is its amazing wildlife, especially the polar bears that gather close to the town as they wait for Hudson Bay to freeze over in October.

(Opposite): Views like this are so common in the Rockies you can find yourself taking them for granted...until you're back home. This one's of Lake O'Hara, in Yoho National Park (see p179).

What to see

The main activities for visitors to Churchill are wildlife viewing and dogsled rides. There are many tour operators; only a few can be mentioned here. Some contact numbers and the months when you're most likely to see animals are given below. The Churchill area code is 204.

• **Polar bears**: mid September to November
  (Great White Bear Tours: ☎ 675-2781)
• **Beluga whales**: mid June to August (Sea North Tours: ☎ 675-2195)
• **Birds**: April to June (Churchill Wilderness Encounter: ☎ 675-2248)
• **Iceberg tours**: June (Sea North Tours, as above)
• **Dogsled rides**: November to May (Robert Macdonald: ☎ 675-8878)

Other wildlife you might spot here includes arctic fox, ptarmigan, and caribou. If you visit between January and April you are also likely to see the **Northern Lights**.

Where to stay

Accommodation gets booked up very quickly during the wildlife seasons so you are advised to book ahead. A couple of places to try are the 4-star **Polar Inn** (☎ 675-8878, 15 Franklin Street) where a double is around $77 (and the heating & hot water are wonderfully efficient), or **Vera Gould's B&B** (☎ 675-2544, 87 Hearne Street) where you can get a double for around $40.

(Opposite): Husky teams are still an important means of transportation in the Canadian North. Each dog is capable of hauling up to 180 pounds of weight, and can go for many days with little food. If you go to Churchill between October and May you can try out a sled ride for yourself (see above).

APPENDIX A: TIMETABLES

Ocean: Halifax - Montreal

Station name	km from Halifax	Westbound Day 1 Ex Tue	Eastbound Ex Wed
Halifax	0	14 00	15 30
Truro	103	15 38	14 00
Springhill Jct*	200	16.52	12 42
Amherst	227	17.17	12.21
Sackville	243	17.35	12.03
Moncton	304	ar 18.22	dp 11.10
		dp 18.42	ar 10.50
Rogersville*	397	19.43	09.38
Newcastle	433	20.15	09.09
Bathurst	504	21.11	08.17
Petit Rocher*	521	21.26	07.53
Jacquet River*	549	21.48	07.53
Charlo*	574	22.06	07.15
Campbellton	605	22.50	06.45
Matapédia	624	22.45	04.32
Causapscal	681	23.31	03.47
Amqui	703	23.51	03.28
		Day 2	
Sayabec*	727	00.09	03.08
Mont-Joli	774	00.47	02.33
Rimouski	803	01.11	01.48
Trois-Pistoles	864	01.57	01.06
Rivière-du-Loup	907	02.51	00.34
			Day 2
La Pocatière	975	03.34	23.55
Montmagny	1035	04.08	23.21
Lévis (Quebec)	1093	Ar 04.55	Dp 22.30
		Dp 05.05	Ar 22.20
Charny	1105	05.25	21.53
Drummondville	12.52	06.55	20.25
Saint-Hyacinthe	1298	07.26	19.47
Saint-Lambert	1345	07.58	19.15
Montreal	13.52	08.25	19.00
			Day 1 Ex Tue

Corridor: Montreal - Toronto (westbound)

Station name	km	No 53 Ex Sa Sun	No 653 Sat	No 57 Daily	No 61 Ex Sat	65 Ex Sun	No 67 Ex Sat	No 69 Ex Sun	No 669 Sun
Montreal	0	06.15	07.30	10.00	12.15	15.45	17.00	18.00	18.25
Dorval	19	06.33	07.48	10.21	12.33	16.03	17.18	18.18	18.43
Coteau	63							18.44	19.08
Cornwall	111	07.16	08.31	11.10		16.48		19.12	19.33
Prescott	185							19.49	20.10
Brockville	204			12.00				20.03	20.22
Gananoque	249								
Kingston	285	Ar 08.33 Dp 08.36	Ar 09.48 Dp 09.51	Ar 12.42 Dp 12.45	Ar 14.28 Dp 14.31	Ar 18.04 Dp 18.07		Ar 20.40 Dp 20.43	Ar 20.59 Dp 21.02
Napanee	322								
Belleville	357			13.26	15.03			21.20	21.38
Trenton Jct	377			13.39				21.33	21.50
Cobourg	426			14.06				21.59	22.15
Port Hope	438								
Oshawa	488			14.42				22.32	22.46
Guildwood	518	10.20	11.35	15.00	16.20	19.53		22.48	23.02
Toronto	539	10.42	11.47	15.20	16.39	20.14	20.59	23.05	23.20

Corridor: Toronto - Montreal (eastbound)

Station name	km	No 52 Ex Sun	No 56 Ex Sat	No 60 Daily	No 64 Ex Sun	No 66 Ex Sat	No 68 Daily
Toronto	0	07.10	10.00	12.00	15.45	17.00	18.00
Guildwood	21	07.26	10.15	12.18	16.01		18.21
Oshawa	51	07.43		12.35			
Port Hope	101						
Cobourg	113			13.10			
Trenton Jct	163						19.28
Belleville	182	08.45		13.46			
Napanee	217						
Kingston	254	Ar 09.17 Dp 09.20	Ar 11.57 Dp 12.00	Ar 14.23 Dp 14.28	Ar 17.44 Dp 17.47		Ar 20.10 Dp 20.13
Gananoque	290						20.33
Brockville	335	10.00	12.39	15.12			20.56
Prescott	354						21.10
Cornwall	428	10.44	13.23	16.02	19.05		21.46
Dorval	520	11.28	14.09	16.50	19.51	20.36	22.31
Montreal	539	11.46	14.31	17.13	20.11	20.59	22.51

Canadian: Toronto - Vancouver

Station name	Km	Westbound Day 1 Tu Th Sa	Eastbound Th Su Tu
Toronto	0	12.45	21.00
Newmarket	55	13.34	19.45
Barrie	101	14.06	19.13
Orilla	139	14.36	18.41
Washago	159	14.52	18.25
Parry Sound	257	16.17	16.44
Sudbury Jct	438	19.20	14.01
Capreol	460	Ar 20.00	Dp 13.30
		Dp 20.15	Ar 14.15
Laforest	508	21.02	12.14
McKee's Camp*	518	21.11	12.10
Felix*	536	21.28	11.57
Ruel*	544	21.35	11.50
Westree	565	21.49	11.20
Gogama	600	22.19	10.49
Folyet	700	23.55	09.19
		Day 2 We Fr Su	
Elsas	756	00.42	08.15
Oba	8.75	02.09	06.51
Hornepayne	938	Ar 03.10	Dp 05.55
		Dp 03.40	Ar 05.25
		We Fr Su	
Hillsport	1006	04.46	04.24
Caramat*	1062	05.28	03.39
Longlac	1100	05.53	03.10
Nakina	1149	06.26	02.26
Auden*	1239	07.22	01.22
Ferland*	1281	07.54	00.45
Mud River*	1289	08.06	00.38
Armstrong	1329	08.55	00.10
			Day 4 Th Su Tu
Collins*	1363	08.23	22.28
Allanwater Bridge*	1417	09.02	21.49
Flindt Landing*	1437	09.13	21.36
Savant Lake	1456	09.34	21.22
Sioux Lookout	1553	Ar 10.55	Dp 20.30
		Dp 11.10	Ar 19.48
Amesdale*	1635	12.31	18.38
Red Lake Road	1668	13.00	18.07
Canyon*	1699	13.30	17.31
Farlane*	1736	14.14	16.58
Redditt	1752	14.30	16.41
Minaki	1775	14.52	16.11
Ottermere*	1796	15.09	15.54
Malachi*	1800	15.13	15.44
Copeland's Landing*	1802	15.21	15.40
Rice Lake*	1812	15.28	15.34
Winnitoba*	1817	15.34	15.30
Ophir*	1821	15.35	15.26
Brereton Lake*	1842	16.06	15.01
Elma*	1870	16.28	14.45
Transcona	1945	17.18	13.51
Winnipeg	1958	Ar 17.35	Dp 13.35
		Dp 18.35	Ar 12.35

Canadian: Toronto - Vancouver (cont)

Station name	km	Westbound	Eastbound
Winnipeg	1958	Ar 17.35	Dp 13.35
		Dp 18.35	Ar 12.35
Portage la Prairie	2048	19.33	11.19
Brandon North	2166	20.52	10.13
Rivers	2190	21.09	09.47
Melville	2410	23.47	07.30
		Day 3	
		Th Sa Mo	
Watrous	2618	01.50	05.06
Saskatoon	2718	Ar 02.55	Dp 04.00
		Dp 03.15	Ar 03.40
Biggar	2808	04.34	02.20
Unity	2909	05.33	01.16
			Day 3
			We Sa Mo
Wainwright	3033	05.57	22.57
Viking	3104	06.43	22.11
Edmonton	3236	Ar 08.25	Dp 20.35
		Dp 08.55	Ar 20.05
Evansburg	3345	10.48	18.14
Edson	3445	11.56	17.12
Hinton	3533	12.57	16.04
Jasper	3615	Ar 14.20	Dp 14.55
		DP 15.30	Ar 13.45
Valemount*	3736	16.25	10.47
Blue River	3828	18.19	09.00
Clearwater*	3937	20.25	06.57
Kamloops North	4053	Ar 22.30	Dp 05.06
		Dp 23.05	Ar 04.31
		Day 4	
	4132	Fr Su Tu	
Ashcroft*		00.37	03.00
Boston Bar	4254	03.12	00.28
			Day 2
			Tu Fr Su
Hope*	4319	04.36	23.13
Chilliwack	43.70	05.24	22.30
Matsqui (Mission)	4399	06.00	21.57
Port Coquitlam	4439	07.25	20.55
Vancouver	4467	08.30	20.00
			Day 1
			Mo Th Sa

Skeena: Jasper - Prince Rupert

Station name	km	Westbound	Eastbound
		Day 1	
		We Fr Su	
Jasper	0	20.10	09.00
Harvey*	106	20.54	06.02
Dunster*	142	21.26	05.30
McBride	174	22.05	05.00
Goat River*	217	23.00	03.53
Loos*	232	23.15	03.38
Dome Creek*	262	23.48	03.05
Bend*	265	23.52	03.01
		Day 2	
		Th Sa Mo	
Penny*	285	00.11	02.43
Longworth*	301	00.27	02.27
Hutton*	314	00.41	02.13
Sinclair Mills*	319	00.47	02.07
McGregor*	331	01.01	01.53
Upper Fraser*	341	01.09	01.45
Aleza Lake*	349	01.06	01.38
Willow River*	378	01.51	01.03
Prince George	409	Ar 02.30	Dp 00.35
		Dp 02.45	Ar 00.20
		Day 2	
		We Sa Mo	
Vanderhoof	520	04.35	22.24
Fort Fraser*	560	05.12	21.45
Endako	594	05.57	21.12
Burns Lake	650	06.46	20.13
Houston	734	07.52	19.06
Telkwa*	780	08.36	18.23
Smithers	795	Ar 08.55	Dp 18.10
		Dp 09.20	Ar 17.45
New Hazleton	869	10.36	16.21
Kitwanga*	912	11.22	15.33
Cedarvale*	933	11.43	15.12
Dorreen*	957	12.04	14.51
Pacific*	967	12.13	14.42
Usk*	988	12.30	14.25
Terrace (Kitimat)	1007	13.15	14.05
Kwinitsa*	1084	14.16	12.41
Prince Rupert	1160	15.40	11.30
			Day 1
			Tu Fr Su

Hudson Bay: Winnipeg - Churchill

Station name	km	Northbound Day 1 Su Tu Th	Southbound Th Sa Mo
Winnipeg	0	21.55	08.00
Portage la Prairie	88	23.10	06.50
Gladstone	148	23.55	06.06
		Day 2 Mo We Fr	
Plumas	169	00.12	05.50
Glenella	191	00.28	05.35
McCreary	224	00.53	05.11
Laurier	238	01.03	05.01
Ochre River	262	01.21	04.40
Dauphin	283	01.50	04.20
Gilbert Plains*	315	02.29	03.20
Grandview*	331	02.43	03.06
Roblin	385	03.26	02.20
Togo*	412	03.49	01.59
Kamsack	446	04.28	01.27
Veregin	459	04.38	01.13
Mikado	473	04.47	01.05
Canora	484	05.10	00.55
Sturgis	520	05.49	00.06
		Day 3 Th Sa Mo	
Endeavour	549	06.15	23.40
Reserve*	586	06.51	23.03
Hudson Bay	636	07.40	22.25
The Pas	777	Ar 09.35 Dp 10.50	Dp 20.20 Ar 19.05
Tremaudan*	790	11.07	18.42
Orok*	798	11.16	18.33
Atikameg Lake*	804	11.12	18.27
Finger*	811	11.29	18.20
Budd*	825	11.42	18.07
Halcrow*	837	11.54	17.55
Cormorant	843	12.02	17.48
Dering*	850	12.08	17.41
Rawebb*	864	12.22	17.27
Dyce*	877	12.34	17.15
Paterson*	890	12.47	17.02
Wekusko*	907	13.03	16.45
Turnbull*	927	13.22	16.27
Ponton*	949	13.43	16.06
Button*	961	13.54	15.55
Dunlop*	973	14.06	15.43
Pipun*	985	14.18	15.31
Wabowden	996	14.45	15.29
Medard*	1006	14.52	14.52
Lyddal*	1017	15.01	14.40
Odhill*	1031	15.13	14.27
Earchman*	1041	15.23	14.17
La Perouse*	1052	15.34	14.06
Hockin*	1064	15.44	13.56
Thicket Portage	1073	15.57	13.45
Leven*	1086	16.09	13.11
Thompson	1149	Ar 17.50 Dp 19.20	Dp 11.40 Ar 10.10

Hudson Bay: Winnipeg - Churchill (cont)

Station name	km	Northbouond	Southbound
Thompson	1149	Ar 17.50	Dp 11.40
		Dp 19.20	Ar 10.10
Sipiwesk*	1199	20.32	08.43
Matago*	1218	20.50	08.23
Pikwitonei	1220	20.53	08.20
Bridgar*	1229	21.01	08.08
Wilde*	1249	21.20	07.49
Arnot*	1257	21.29	07.39
Boyd*	1279	21.52	07.16
Pit Siding	1289	22.01	07.06
Munk*	1310	22.23	13.04
Ilford	1337	22.50	06.15
Nonsuch*	1353	23.06	05.57
Wivenhoe*	1366	23.22	05.44
Luke*	1390	23.49	05.21
		Day 3	
		Tu Th Sa	
Gillam	1401	Ar 00.10	Dp 05.10
		Dp 01.25	Ar 03.55
Kettle Rapids*	1414	01.44	03.20
Bird*	1435	02.12	02.50
Amery*	1448	02.32	02.33
Charlebois*	1463	02.51	02.12
Weir River	1477	03.10	01.52
Lawledge*	1492	03.28	01.29
Thibaudeau*	1508	03.47	01.09
Silcox*	1520	04.04	00.51
Herchmer	1540	04.31	00.26
Kellett*	1548	04.42	00.10
			Day 2
			We Fr Su
O'Day*	1562	05.00	23.52
Back*	1575	05.16	23.35
M'Clintock*	1588	05.34	23.19
Belcher*	1603	05.53	23.01
Cromarty*	16.17	06.12	22.42
Chesnaye*	1632	06.30	22.24
Lamprey*	1646	06.47	22.07
Bylot*	1659	07.03	21.51
Digges*	1670	07.19	21.35
Tidal*	1685	07.37	21.17
Churchill	1697	8.20	21.00
			Day 1
			Tu Th Sa

APPENDIX B: FRENCH WORDS AND PHRASES

Many travellers are astonishingly ignorant about the importance of the French language in Canada. A group of backpackers I met in Toronto were flabbergasted when I introduced them to a Quebecker whose English was quite poor – they had assumed that all Canadians speak English as their main language. The fact is that, in theory at least, French has equal status with English; they are the country's two official languages. Over six million Canadians speak French as their first language. These are concentrated in, but not confined to, Quebec. There are also sizeable groups of Francophones in parts of Nova Scotia, New Brunswick, Ontario and Manitoba.

Apart from being a matter of common courtesy, speaking (or attempting to speak) French to a Francophone displays a cultural sensitivity that will be greatly appreciated by your listener, especially in Quebec. Even the clumsiest efforts will be rewarded with smiles and encouragement, and will definitely enhance your experience of French Canada.

MEETING PEOPLE

Hello	Bonjour
Good evening	Bonsoir
How are you?	Ça va? (informal); Comment allez-vous? (polite)
I'm fine, thanks	Ça va bien, merci
Yes	Oui
No	Non
Maybe	Peut-être
Please	S'il vous plaît/s'il te plaît
Thank you	Merci
You're welcome	De rien/bienvenu
Excuse me (in a crowd)	Pardon
Sorry	Je m'excuse
Okay	D'accord
No problem	Pas de problème
I'm called...	Je m'appelle...
What's your name?	Comment vous-appellez vous (polite)
	Comment t'appelles-tu? (informal)
I'm British/American	Je suis Anglais(e)/Américain(e)
I'm Australian/Japanese	Je suis Australien(ne)/Japonais(e)
I'm from New Zealand	Je suis de la Nouvelle-Zélande
I'm French/Belgian	Je suis Français(e)/Belge
I'm Swiss/Swedish	Je suis Suisse/Suédois(e)
I'm Italian/German	Je suis Italien(ne)/Allemand(e)
I'm Dutch/Danish	Je suis Hollondais(e)/Danois(e)

NUMERALS

1	un(e)	21	vingt-et-un
2	deux	22	vingt-deux
3	trois	30	trente
4	quatre	31	trente-et-un
5	cinq	40	quarante
6	six	50	cinquante
7	sept	60	soixante
8	huit	70	soixante-dix
9	neuf	71	soixante-et-onze
10	dix	72	soixante-douze
11	onze	80	quatre-vingt
12	douze	90	quatre-vingt-dix
13	treize	91	quatre-vingt-onze
14	quatorze	100	cent
15	quinze	101	cent-et-un
16	seize	105	cent-cinq
17	dix-sept	200	deux cents
18	dix-huit	500	cinq-cents
19	dix-neuf	1000	mille
20	vingt	1000,000	un million

DIRECTIONS

I'm looking for the tourist office	Je cherche le bureau de tourisme
Where is the ...?	Où est le/la ...?
train station	la gare
town centre	le centre-ville
airport	l'aéroport
bus stop	l'arrêt d'autobus
metro	le métro
museum	le musée
washroom (toilets)	les toilettes
Is it far to walk?	C'est loin à pied?
straight ahead	tout droit
near to	près de
in front of	devant
behind	derrière
to the right	à droite
to the left	à gauche
here	ici
street	la rue
bridge	le pont
square	la place
building	l'immeuble

ACCOMMODATION

hotel	l'hôtel
youth hostel	l'auberge de jeunesse

Do you have a room for one/two people?	Est-ce que vous avez une chambre pour une personne / deux personnes?
for one night / two nights	pour une nuit / deux nuits
with a bathroom	avec salle de bain

Is breakfast included?	Est-ce que le petit-déjeuner est compris?
How much is it?	C'est combien?
Do you have anything cheaper?	Est-ce que vous avez quelque chose moins cher?
May I see the room?	Pourrais-je voir la chambre?
I'll take it.	Je la prends.

MONEY

bank	la banque
money	l'argent
travellers' cheques	chèques de voyages
credit card	une carte de crédit
ATM	distributeur automatique

FOOD AND DRINK

water	de l'eau
orange/pineapple juice	un jus d'orange/ananas
wine	du vin
beer	la bière
(white) coffee	café (au lait)
tea	le thé
menu	le menu
salmon	le saumon
chicken	le poulet
pork	le porc
ham	le jambon
vegetables	les légumes
eggs	des oeufs
salt/pepper	sel/poivre
milk/sugar	lait/sucre

RAILWAY

timetable	l'indicateur / horaire
reservation	une réservation
connection	une correspondance
platform	le quai
ticket	le billet
ticket office	la billètterie
one way	aller simple
return	aller retour
sleeper class	la classe voiture-lits
Silver & Blue class	la classe Bleu d'Argent
economy class	la class économique
conductor	le chef de train
an upgrading	un surclassement
a refund	un remboursement
cancel	annuler
checked luggage	bagages enregistrés
hand luggage	bagages à main
luggage trolley	un chariot à bagages
bedding	la literie
late	en retard
on time	à l'heure

APPENDIX C: BIBLIOGRAPHY

Beattie, Owen and Geiger, John *The Fate of the Franklin Expedition 1845-48*
Berton, Pierre *The National Dream* and *The Last Spike* (1975)
Butler, W F *The Great Lone Land* (1872)
Cumberland, Stuart *The Queen's Highway* (1887)
Dorin, Patrick *Canadian Pacific Railway* (1974)
Dumond, Don *The Eskimos and Aleuts*
Gibbon, J M *Steel of Empire* (1935)
Grant, Rev George M *Ocean to Ocean* (1873)
Hurtig, Mel *The Betrayal of Canada* (1992)
Innes, H A *A History of the Canadian Pacific Railway* (1923)
Lavallée, Omer *Van Horne's Road* (1974)
Lotz, Jim and McKenzie, Keith *Railways of Canada*
MacEwan, G *The Battle for the Bay* (1975)
Macmillan, Alan *Native Peoples and Cultures of Canada*
McKee, Bill and Klassen, G *Trail of Iron*
McNaught, Kenneth *The Penguin History of Canada* (1988)
Mitchell, David *All Aboard* (1995)
Morton, Desmond *A Short History of Canada* (1994)
Pullen-Burry, B *From Halifax to Vancouver* (1912)
Radwanski, George and Luttrell, Julia *Awakening the Canadian Spirit* (1992)
Richler, Mordecai *Oh Canada! Oh Quebec!* (1992)
Roper, Edward *By Track and Trail Through Canada* (1891)
Stephens, D E *Iron Roads* (1972)
Stevens, G R *Canadian National Railways* (1960)
Woodcock, George *A Social History of Canada*

INDEX

Photographs shown by page references in **bold** type

Other guides from Trailblazer Publications

Trekking in the Everest Region (Jamie McGuinness)
The first title in the Nepal Trekking Guides series covers the most famous trekking route in the country. It is, however, through a very fragile environment and this guide shows how to tread lightly and minimise your impact on the trek to Gorak Shep and Everest Base Camp.

Written by an experienced trek leader and climber, the book includes detailed background information on preparing for your trek, getting to Nepal, hotels and restaurants in Kathmandu and protecting your health. There's a fully comprehensive route guide based on 30 detailed maps with inset plans of major villages and information about where to sleep and eat along the way.
ISBN 1-873756-08-9 256pp (+16pp in colour)   Fully revised new edition £8.95

Silk Route by Rail (Dominic Streatfeild-James)
Traversing some of the most inaccessible lands on earth, the Silk Route stretched some 5000 miles west from the ancient Chinese capital, Chang'an (Xi'an), all the way to the Roman Empire. In 1992 a passenger service was inaugurated on the recently-built rail link between Alma Ata (Almati) in Kazakhstan and Urumqi in north-west China. It is, therefore, now possible to travel by rail between Moscow and Beijing on a new route via the cities of the Silk Route. Shortlisted for the Thomas Cook Travel & Guide Book Awards 1994.
ISBN 1-873756-03-8 320pp (+16pp in colour)   £9.95

Trans-Siberian Handbook (Bryn Thomas)
The first edition of this guide to the world's longest rail journey was shortlisted for the Thomas Cook Travel & Guide Book Awards. This comprehensive third edition is packed with practical information on planning your trip and booking tickets from Europe or North America. There's information on major towns, a kilometre-by-kilometre route guide and a full history of Siberia and the railway.
ISBN 1-873756-04-6 320pp (+16pp in colour)   £9.95

Siberian BAM Railway Guide (Athol Yates)
The 2100-mile Baikal Amur Mainline (BAM) Railway traverses north-east Siberia and is sometimes known as the 'Second Trans-Siberian'. This practical guide tells you how to be amongst the first foreign travellers to visit this fascinating new travel destination. Numerous black and white photographs and 30 maps.
ISBN 1-873756-06-2 366pp   £12.95

Trekking in the Annapurna Region (Bryn Thomas)
This second title in the Nepal Trekking Guides series covers the classic treks in the region north of Pokhara, including the Annapurna Circuit, Pokhara to Jomsom and the Annapurna Sanctuary. Fully revised new edition now available.
ISBN 1-873756-07-0 256pp (+16pp in colour)   £8.95

In preparation: **Trekking in Langtang, Helambu and Gosainkund**
Trekking in Ladakh

_____**Route guides for the adventurous traveller**_____

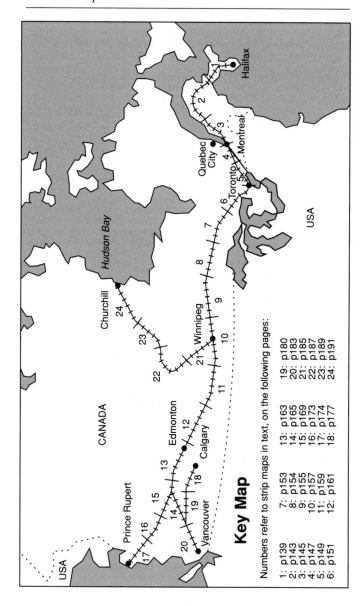

Key Map

Numbers refer to strip maps in text, on the following pages: